Boatbuilding
with
Aluminum

Text and Illustrations by
Stephen F. Pollard

International Marine
Camden, Maine

Published by International Marine®

10 9 8 7 6 5 4 3

Copyright © 1993 International Marine, an imprint
of McGraw-Hill, Inc.

Library of Congress Cataloging-in-Publication Data
Pollard, Stephen F.
    Boatbuilding with aluminum / Stephen F.
    Pollard
    p.   cm.
    Includes index.
    ISBN 0-87742-377-6 (alk. paper)
      1. Aluminum boats—Design and construction—
      Amateurs' manuals.
    I. Title.
    VM321.P56   1993
    623.8'207—dc20   93–26015
                         CIP

Questions regarding the content of this book should
be addressed to:
        International Marine
        P.O. Box 220
        Camden, ME 04843
Questions regarding the ordering of this book
should be addressed to:
        McGraw-Hill, Inc.
        Customer Service Department
        P.O. Box 547
        Blacklick, OH 43004
        1-800-822-8158
This book is printed on acid-free paper.
Printed by Arcata Graphics, Fairfield, PA
Design by Patrice M. Rossi
Production and page layout by Janet Robbins
Edited by J. R. Babb, Don Casey, Tom McCarthy

Dedication

To my loving wife, Linda, for her
constant support, tireless assistance,
and endless patience.

Contents

Acknowledgments

I wish to thank Raymond H. Richards of Newport Beach, California—naval architect, marine engineer, longtime business associate, brilliant designer, and very good friend—for his assistance with my continual technical questioning.

A special thanks to Tom Hukle of Yacht Riggers of Seattle for his generous contribution of time pointing out various aspects of spar manufacturing, and his willingness to show me some tricks of the trade.

Thanks also to Mr. Henry H. Wheeler of Downey, California, for his ongoing interest in boats, their design, construction, and coating systems, and his willingness to share technical data. As the skipper of *Aoranji*, Mr. Wheeler holds the corrected time record for the Tahiti race.

Many thanks to Tim Hill and Al Jaques of J & H Boat Works, Astoria, Oregon; Bob Fievez and Mike Sandeman of Almar, Tacoma, Washington; Mike Lorenzen, North River Boats, Roseburg, Oregon; Bruce Reagan, Sovereign Yachts, Seattle, Washington; Michael Bouton, Jetcraft, Medford, Oregon; Willie Illingsworth, Willie Boats, Central Point, Oregon; and others that I may have unintentionally omitted, who have assisted in putting together this book.

Introduction

The characteristics of the material used to construct a boat hull are of primary interest to any boat owner. There has long been a lack of readily available data on aluminum hull construction, a dilemma for potential aluminum-boat owners. Questions as to aluminum's resistance to corrosion and its compatibility with other boatbuilding materials are common. The lack of knowledge about aluminum hull characteristics and fabrication techniques can result in reluctance to either buy or attempt to construct an aluminum boat. I believe that if a person becomes knowledgeable about aluminum-boat building, that person will give serious consideration to building a boat of welded-aluminum in preference to building with other materials. This is simply because aluminum boats have so many positive aspects that it's difficult not to make aluminum the material of choice.

This book takes a hands-on approach to the construction of a welded-aluminum boat from the perspective of the boatbuilder—from basic conceptual needs through sea trials. This is a *how-to* book, and it includes information on the characteristics of aluminum, fabrication techniques, boat propulsion, fuel and electrical systems, insulation, woodwork, and fairing and painting. Each topic discusses procedures on dealing with other materials that aren't compatible with aluminum but ones you will nevertheless be required to use. You will also find a chapter devoted to laying out, or lofting, for aluminum-boat building, with emphasis on taking full advantage of aluminum's capacity to be formed.

This book provides guidance in the selection of the method of construction for a welded-aluminum boat and details the steps needed to actually build your boat. A number of appendixes are included that contain information necessary to fully cover the scope of aluminum-boat building, but which did not fit neatly into the body of the manuscript. I have also sprinkled helpful tips throughout the narrative that can be used to both evaluate quality and speed production.

I realize that potential boat owners and builders have a wide variety of interests, including powerboats and sailboats, and for both pleasure and commercial use. I have not segregated this book into sections devoted exclusively to each boat type since the fabricating techniques and installation procedures covered are common to most all aluminum boats. Since most welded-aluminum boats currently being produced are small planing boats, this has been my primary emphasis, but you will also find, for example, a chapter devoted to sailboat construction that includes such topics as aluminum spars and lead-ballasted keels limited to this particular type of boat.

I have also include a brief history of how small welded-aluminum boats have evolved, including the development of special extrusions and of design features that are currently employed. Since this evolution in design and techniques has resulted in the present style of the small welded-aluminum boat, I believe this information will be useful.

Limited-production boatbuilding with aluminum can be faster, simpler, and least costly when compared with other hull materials. The manufacturing technology has been simplified to such an extent that a high-quality welded-aluminum hull can be constructed rapidly, even by a novice home builder. I have worked this lightweight metal for over 25 years and am often pleasantly reminded of just how easily it can be fabricated. The peculiar workability of aluminum, specifically the ability to cut it with woodworking tools, reduces the need for special metal-working skills.

The proliferation of boatbuilders capable of producing welded-aluminum boats and marketing them successfully is quite obvious in the Pacific Northwest of the United States. Every weekend it appears that about half the trailer boats heading toward the Oregon coast—or inland to white-water rivers—are welded aluminum and have been constructed locally.

The Pacific Northwest coast, including the infamous Columbia River bar, has some of the most treacherous waters in the world. Locally constructed boats routinely operate in these waters, including Alaska. Pacific Northwest aluminum-boat builders, including builders of commercial fishing boats, utilize the techniques found in this book.

Stephen F. Pollard
Scappoose, Oregon
July 1993

Evolution Of The Aluminum
Hull Form

A boat's hull form depends upon a number of factors: the type of boat, its intended operating environment, styling preferences, the economics of manufacture, and the material of construction all contribute to the boat's final lines. The flowing curves endemic to wood-plank construction are both utilitarian and attractive and have evolved over the years to suit all of these factors, but the sweeping curves so important to sound hull construction in planked wood are often impractical for other materials.

Plywood, for example, can be easily wrapped around a structure in large sheets, providing the hull's design consists of *developable surfaces*. A developable surface can consist of flat areas, sections of cylinders, sections of cones, or a combination of flats, cylinders, and cones. Each of these surfaces individually can be *developed* from a flat sheet of material. When these surface areas abut each other on a hull surface, the transition from one form to another still allows the composite surface to be formed from a single flat sheet.

After World War II there was an explosion of plywood boats, which are most economically constructed utilizing developable hull surfaces. Unfortunately, most small-boat designs of that era were for wood-plank construction, and the hull surfaces were generally *nondevelopable* (i.e., exhibiting concurrent curvature in more than one direction). This resulted in designs evolving to take advantage of the plywood material and started the trend to change the traditional hull

FIGURE 1-1. Multi-chine aluminum 23-foot *Tar Bucket* designed by naval architect Raymond H. Richards, Newport Beach, California.

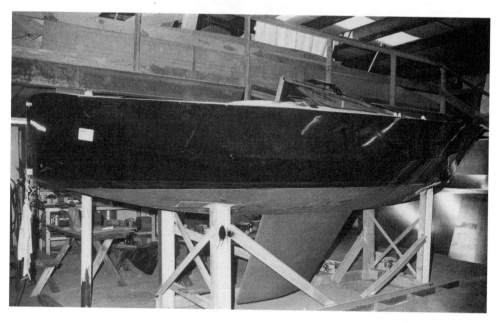

form from nondevelopable surfaces to a shape that could be developed by bending flat sheets.

Boats made of fiberglass followed, imitating wooden boats initially, but as fiberglass construction became established, designs evolved to suit the material and the method of manufacture, particularly with smaller production boats. Fiberglass construction does not restrict hull form to conical developable surfaces; compound curvature has become the norm.

Initially, welded-aluminum boats were built to planked-wood or fiberglass boat designs, attempting to copy their graceful curves and hull forms. But what is easily constructed of wood or in a fiberglass mold can be much more difficult to construct in metal. The nondevelopable surfaces of a wood-planked or molded-fiberglass hull are difficult to imitate in metal and very labor intensive. Because of the higher labor costs associated with nondevelopable hull surfaces, aluminum hulls have evolved to utilize developable surfaces, resembling hull designs for plywood.

An artistic boat designer can produce a very attractive hull and outboard profile for a welded-aluminum boat using fully developable surfaces. Carefully

FIGURE 1-2. Aluminum Sportfisher 23 designed by Raymond H. Richards.

fairing together developable plates (see *Tar Bucket*, Figure 1-1) gives the illusion of compound curvature. Or designs intended specifically for aluminum construction with developable surfaces, such as the Sportfisher 23 (Figure 1-2), can yield attractive and functional boats in their own right.

Driven primarily by economics, aluminum-hull-form evolution is likely to continue, resulting in a more and more distinctive look.

Factors Contributing to Hull Design

Welded-aluminum boats fall into two distinct groups: smaller production boats constructed right side up using special extrusions at the plate joints, and conventional welded large boats (and limited-production small ones) with both transverse and longitudinal framing—often constructed inverted. The differences between the two in manufacturing methods and hull design are significant.

Small production boats are usually planing powerboats constructed in the upright position on some type of a jig. The developable shell plate is formed from a single large sheet of aluminum and joined at the corners by the use of special extrusions. An example of this type of construction is the very rugged North River boat shown in Figure 1-3.

Larger boats and custom small boats are usually constructed over an inverted aluminum framework of transverse and longitudinal members. Joint extrusions are not used; plates are welded edge to edge. The limited-production Almar search-and-rescue craft in Figure 1-4 is fabricated in this manner. To achieve the compound curvature of the hull required in many large designs (Figure 1-5), the shell plating consists of a number of pieces that must be butt-welded.

FIGURE 1-3. **North River aluminum jet boats (Roseburg, Oregon) use extrusions at the chine to join plates.**

FIGURE 1-4. **Limited-production aluminum search-and-rescue boat by Almar (Tacoma, Washington).**

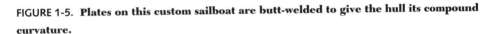

FIGURE 1-5. Plates on this custom sailboat are butt-welded to give the hull its compound curvature.

Small Boats

The hull form of small production boats built in aluminum has evolved to suit the material. Specialized extrusions and the availability of aluminum sheets in large sizes have contributed to the present-day look of welded-aluminum boats. Almost exclusively powerboats, their hulls typically exhibit hard chines, straight sheerlines, flat sloping transoms, and fully developable surfaces. Designs for small welded-aluminum sailboats have not yet evolved suitably for economical production, although a few, such as the *Tar Bucket* (Figure 1-1), have been constructed in limited quantities.

Smaller boats are constructed without butt-welding the shell plating, so their width, length, and depth are primarily determined by the size of available aluminum sheet. It's not uncommon for a small-boat manufacturer to advertise a "5-foot bottom" or a "6-foot bottom," indicating the width of the original aluminum sheet used to construct the bottom shell plate.

The high cost of marine-grade aluminum has encouraged builders to maximize the size boats that can be built from readily available and more economically priced 5-foot and 6-foot (width) material. And waste is held to an absolute minimum, approaching five percent in most small-boat production operations.

Aluminum extrusions at the chine, keel, and gunnel greatly speed production and improve exterior appearance. This method of framing is almost all longitudinal, with most transverse members intentionally *not* in contact with the shell plates. Small boats are usually built upright in a construction fixture, allowing the assembly of precut bottom and side panels with special extrusions at the seams before the interior framing is installed. In effect the shell is constructed first, then the boat is framed to fit the shell—directly opposite to conventional construction practices. Best suited to production operations turning out large quantities of a similar design, this method allows small aluminum hulls to be built very quickly once the templates and tooling are in place.

Because it is so functional, the oft cited "boxy" look of small welded-aluminum boats constructed in this manner is becoming less objectionable to the boating public as time passes. And the shape has become familiar, having evolved over the past 20 years.

The upper size limit of boats currently constructed with corner extrusions is about 26 feet. Small-boat manufacturers have been reluctant to try larger sizes, believing that the big-boat market will require customization to the extent that small-boat building techniques can no longer be used and production costs will soar. Once again the method of construction and consequently boat style are determined by economics.

Larger Boats

Larger aluminum boats—generally over 26 feet—are constructed in the more traditional method—over a rigid framework of transverse frames, bulkheads, and longitudinal members. Transverse framing is often spaced at large intervals, with heavy longitudinal members (such as T-bar) used to fully develop the form and give structural strength (see Figure 1-6). This method of framing allows a greater latitude in hull form and is commonly used to construct hulls with compound curvature. A large number of butt-welded seams are usually required.

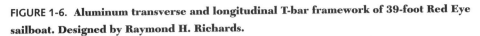

FIGURE 1-6. Aluminum transverse and longitudinal T-bar framework of 39-foot Red Eye sailboat. Designed by Raymond H. Richards.

The availability of large sheets of aluminum has encouraged fully developable hull surfaces—free of compound curvature—on the larger boats. Traditional bow flair, for example, is eliminated from large powerboats. Or large sailboats with traditionally round bilges are redesigned to allow use of large, flat sheets of material on large sections of the hull, limiting nondevelopable areas. If carefully designed, changes in hull appearance resulting from developable surfaces can be subtle.

Impact of Extrusions

Of the common boatbuilding materials, only aluminum can be extruded. Extruding is a manufacturing process that forces the material through a die to form it into the desired shape. Modern production-built small welded-

FIGURE 1-7. Aluminum chine and gunnel extrusions.

aluminum boats are using more and more aluminum extrusion to expedite production and improve appearance. The widespread use of special extrusions at the chine and gunnel (examples are pictured in Figure 1-7) has been a major contributor to design evolution and allowed manufacturers to greatly speed production. Extrusions allow a loose tolerance for plate cutting and expedite the welding process by providing a consistently tight and uniform fit-up.

Often the extrusions used at the chine and gunnel are very sturdy, resulting in an exceptionally strong hull. Many boat manufacturers weld the extrusions to the plates 100 percent on the inside of the hull, with either no welding or very light intermittent welding on the outside. This technique avoids weld spatter on the outside surface of the shell plate, maintaining the original high-quality finish of the aluminum sheet, and it makes the extrusions at the chine and gunnel areas appear to be trim strips.

Aluminum-boat Owners

Early purchasers of small welded-aluminum boats were serious commercial boat operators or, to a more limited extent, experienced sportsmen on their third or fourth boat. These buyers wanted a robust boat capable of high speeds and of carrying heavy loads, and providing superior maneuverability even when fully loaded. That small one-off aluminum boats could be built without large set-up costs made aluminum the logical choice for custom commercial boats. These boats were intended to be functional and their finish was a secondary consideration.

These early owners pioneered the development of welded-aluminum boats and introduced them to the general public. The superior performance, rugged construction, and simplicity of aluminum boats resulted in a rapid acceptance by the boating public.

Impact of the Water-jet

In the Pacific Northwest, the explosion in welded-aluminum boatbuilding can be directly linked to the introduction of the water-jet unit. Aluminum's high strength-to-weight ratio and its ability to withstand impact made its marriage with the water-jet drive ideal for river *white-water* boating and resulted in a whole new concept in boatbuilding technology.

FIGURE 1-8. White-water jet boat by Almar (Tacoma, Washington).

The small aluminum "jet sled" has proved to be the single most popular boat for river running in the Pacific Northwest over the past 20 years. The remarkable maneuverability and shallow-draft capability of the water-jet, combined with an extremely tough and lightweight aluminum hull, provide a thrilling white-water ride. Welded-aluminum jet boats have become a standard off-the-shelf item, as exemplified by the well-built stock boats from Almar (Figure 1-8).

McKenzie River Drift Boat

Aluminum has also become a popular choice for double-ended drift boats (Figure 1-9) used for fishing the fast flowing rivers of the western United States. These boats exploit aluminum's dual advantages of toughness and light weight. In light of a drift boat's high incidence of grounding on rocks, the damage resistance of aluminum makes it a superior hull material to the traditional plywood, and the light weight of an aluminum boat eases launch and recovery.

The Boatbuilders

Early builders of small welded-aluminum boats were almost all small, informal operations employing fewer than half a dozen workers. Each boatshop developed

FIGURE 1-9. A typical aluminum drift boat used on Western rivers.

its own techniques as well as blatantly "borrowing" design and construction methods from each other. With little professional design work involved, approaches to boat design were often quite innovative—some successful, some not. Design innovations that worked were exchanged among builders, often by movement of key personnel from one shop to another through normal layoff and hiring.

This natural evolution of the welded-aluminum boat has resulted in current designs all looking similar; only minor variations in design are apparent among major manufacturers.

Trends

The trend is toward larger and better-finished boats, including the application of paints for cosmetic purposes. As welded-aluminum boats have moved from the purely functional to the pleasure category, improved paint systems (such as the polyurethanes) have found wide acceptance with aluminum-boat buyers. Decorative paint schemes, including stripes and contrasting patterns, are becoming much more popular. The sanded, swirled pattern on the hull side is a thing of the past; buyers now demand a high degree of surface luster in bare metal or a paint scheme applied in good taste.

As the small aluminum boat continues to evolve, more attention is being paid to the methods of propulsion. The once-reigning water-jet unit, though still immensely popular, is slowly losing its river dominance because of more and more restrictions on its operation. Wake, noise, damage to gravel spawning beds, and general nuisance level are all contributing factors to the gradual demise of the free reign of the water-jet.

The increase in popularity of offshore sportfishing along the Pacific Coast has resulted in a creeping growth in boat size. Welded-aluminum boats larger than those used for white-water work have evolved for sportfishing in the open ocean and in semi-protected bays and sounds. These larger, beamier boats offer more security, fuel capacity, and accommodation.

Boat owners may still want to trailer boats in the 26- to 30-foot range and not be required to obtain special oversize-load permits. On the West Coast, including Washington, Oregon, and California, the maximum legal width is 8 feet 6 inches. Other states may have different size restrictions. Boats over the size limits may require a special permit that usually restricts their movement to daylight hours. And towing weight becomes a significant factor for these larger vessels, pointing out another advantage of the lightweight aluminum boat.

The dual requirements of reliability and ease of maintenance suggest that aluminum will continue to gain popularity for serious fishing machines. And higher freeboard, deeper-V hull form, and fully enclosed cabins are the wave of the future for aluminum boats. So let's take a closer look at this remarkable material.

Advantages of Aluminum Boat Construction

Boatbuilding with aluminum can be faster, simpler, and the least costly when compared with other hull materials. The manufacturing technology has been refined and simplified to such an extent as to allow rapid and efficient construction of an aluminum hull, even by the novice home boatbuilder. In fact, the virtues of aluminum are so numerous that it's difficult not to make it the material of choice for a new boat.

Light weight heads the list of factors in favor of aluminum hull construction. Appreciation of this attribute begins with the ease of handling the material during construction and continues through to the operational efficiency demonstrated by the finished boat. Movement of mass requires energy; the less the mass, the less energy is required. The economic advantage of energy savings is readily apparent when considering the high cost of fuel.

Aluminum doesn't need painting. It's nearly impervious to seawater corrosion; it isn't affected by ultra-violet light; it doesn't rot or attract worms; and it doesn't rust. The time and cost savings realized with a boat that doesn't require routine hull maintenance to protect it from the environment are significant.

Strength-to-Weight Ratio

One primary advantage of aluminum is its high strength-to-weight ratio, a comparison of the dead weight of the material to its mechanical properties. In simplest terms, the higher the strength-to-weight ratio of the hull material, the lighter the boat can be constructed while maintaining a given level of strength. An equivalent hull constructed from a material with a lower strength-to-weight ratio will be heavier.

This favorable ratio allows aluminum sailboats to have a higher percentage of ballast in the keel, making them *stiffer* and enabling them to carry more sail than sailboats constructed of a heavier hull material. This single factor caused a great surge in aluminum construction of large racing sailboats in the 1960s and 1970s (see Figure 2-1).

Aluminum's high strength-to-weight ratio has also made it an excellent material for planing hulls. The simplest method of increasing boat speed in a planing hull is to reduce the weight of the boat. When speed is increased without increasing horsepower, obviously the boat's operational efficiency has been improved. This results in lower fuel cost for the same distance traveled, longer engine life (fewer engine revolutions) for equivalent speed, and so forth.

FIGURE 2-1. **The William Lapworth–designed aluminum racing sailboat** *Aoranji II.*

FIGURE 2-2. Speed/displacement monogram for planing hulls.

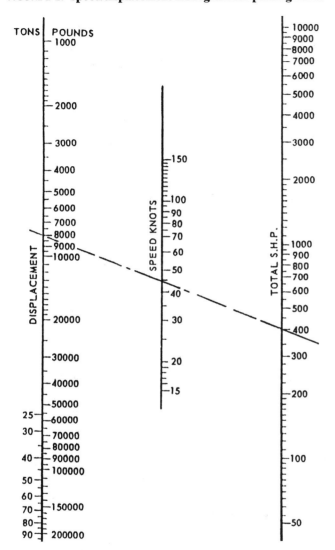

The monogram shown in Figure 2-2 is a good method of estimating planing hull speed. This monogram uses displacement (boat dead weight) and shaft horsepower to estimate speed in knots. From this monogram, a sample boat of 8,000 pounds displacement and 400 SHP (shaft horsepower) will reach 45 knots, as shown by the dashed line. If the same boat's displacement is reduced to 6,000 pounds by switching to a hull material with a high strength-to-weight ratio, such as aluminum, projected speed increases to 50 knots.

The high strength-to-weight ratio of aluminum is beneficial to all boat types. Weight savings result in reduced draft, lower power requirements to drive the boat, lower fuel consumption, bigger payload capacity, and reduced engine operating hours—meaning less frequent overhauls.

Ease of Building Aluminum Hulls

Few special skills are required for working with aluminum. While it is similar to working with steel, aluminum is much lighter and can be cut and fabricated faster; builders experienced with steel fabrication will need to rethink fabricating techniques. Aluminum can be sawed, planed, and drilled with standard power woodworking tools. Special blades for aluminum will improve efficiency, but less expensive carbide-tipped woodworking blades will almost always suffice.

The fastest and most practical method of welding aluminum (described in detail in Chapter 6) is the semi-automatic MIG process, which uses a consumable aluminum electrode and an inert shielding gas. Experience has shown that a learning welder can become proficient with aluminum welding quicker than with steel. And weld metal can be deposited at a far faster rate than equivalent steel welding simply because aluminum fusion requires considerably less heat than steel.

Durability of Aluminum Hulls

In addition to light weight and high strength, aluminum is also much more impact-resistant than steel or fiberglass. Aluminum is very ductile; even in the tempered condition it will stretch up to 12 percent before rupturing—about three times the elasticity of ship steel—in the working-stress range (tensile yield).

The inherent ductility of aluminum allows it to absorb more energy than other hull materials before rupture, making it one of the toughest boatbuilding materials. This impact resistance was clearly demonstrated by the boat in Figure 2-3.

As a hull material, aluminum will last indefinitely with just a little care. Low maintenance is a major benefit of aluminum hulls. Marine alloys in the 5000 series and structural alloys in the 6000 series are almost impervious to atmospheric and seawater corrosion. A clear, ceramic-like oxide that forms almost immediately on the metal's surface serves as a tough surface protectant. Since the

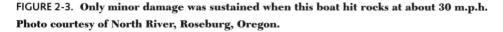

FIGURE 2-3. **Only minor damage was sustained when this boat hit rocks at about 30 m.p.h. Photo courtesy of North River, Roseburg, Oregon.**

aluminum oxide protects the surface from further corrosion, painting isn't necessary. Aluminum hulls are generally painted for reasons other than control of saltwater corrosion.

Often overlooked as a major cost savings is the complete lack of a requirement to prepare for, apply, or maintain *interior* hull paints for corrosion protection. This factor alone often makes an aluminum hull *less* expensive than a comparable steel hull.

Repair of Aluminum Hull Damage

Repair to an aluminum hull is very simple compared with fiberglass or steel. The reduction in man-hours represents a considerable cost savings. Almost any sheet-metal shop should be able to handle minor repairs since most have aluminum welding capability. Normally the damaged area is cut out and a new section is installed. Once the repair is completed, no painting is required except for cosmetic purposes.

Economics of the Welded-Aluminum Hull

The advantages of a welded-aluminum boat may be partially offset by the higher initial cost, compared with steel or fiberglass, of the bare hull.

An aluminum hull can cost more than a comparable steel hull, but in most cases they will be about equal when the sand-blasting and painting processes steel requires are considered. The aluminum hull will weigh about half as much and take about 20 percent less labor to construct. And by completely eliminating the need to sand-blast, considerable clean-up time is saved.

A welded-aluminum hull is still labor intensive compared with a boat constructed in a mold. The skilled labor required for welded hull construction, aluminum or steel, results in a higher unit hull cost than fiberglass. However, when the longevity of aluminum, the increased performance, and the resulting economy of operation of an aluminum boat verses one of fiberglass (or steel) are considered, the long-term cost savings makes aluminum more attractive than other boatbuilding materials. This is particularly evident with unpainted commercial aluminum boats.

Long-term Savings

So while the initial out-of-pocket cost of an aluminum hull is often higher than one of fiberglass or steel, a net savings can accrue in the long term. Low maintenance and high operational efficiency make long-term savings significant. Such savings are realized faster if the boat is used frequently. Commercial operators, for example, have for a number of years selected aluminum boats both for their ruggedness and their economy of operation.

If the boat will be used a high percentage of the time, operational cost savings alone can justify a higher initial cost for aluminum. But in some cases, aluminum is simply the only hull material that will provide the desired performance characteristics.

Resale Value

Aluminum boats manufactured by known professional builders generally have an extremely high resale value. A properly maintained three-year-old boat can return nearly 90 percent of the original purchase price. Jet boats and outboards command the best resale, with values somewhat regionalized; i.e., a boat constructed in southern Oregon will have a higher resale value in southern Oregon than in Seattle. This is because buyers of aluminum boats often shop for a particular brand in a certain geographic area since the boats seem to evolve to suit local conditions.

In some cases, particularly with jet sleds, 10-year-old boats have sold for more than their original cost. Such potential appreciation can make a well-designed aluminum boat a good investment.

Another interesting aspect is the salvage value of the basic aluminum. Aluminum in a clean condition will scrap for a significant amount of money. Few aluminum boats will be abandoned and left to deteriorate on some sandbar. They will be cut up for scrap value, contributing their bit to recycling.

Economics of Trailer-Boating

For a boat that will be trailered, the overall light weight of an aluminum boat reduces the tow vehicle requirements and allows the use of a smaller and lighter boat trailer. It also provides for more economical operation of the tow vehicle which, for a boat often towed long distances, can be a significant savings.

Characteristics of Marine Aluminum

In its pure state, aluminum is much too soft to be of any practical commercial use. To obtain the high welded strength and resistance to the marine environment necessary for boat construction, alloying elements—manganese, magnesium, silicon, and others—are introduced into the aluminum during its manufacture. The relative compositions of four alloys used in boat construction are shown in Table 3-1.

The mechanical strength of aluminum alloys can be greatly improved by tempering the material after the alloying is complete. Aluminum in the non-tempered condition is classified as fully annealed and is identified by a -0 following the alloy identification number. This is the softest material available in the designated alloy.

Mechanical strength is improved by both heat-treatment processes and strain-hardening. Heat-treatable alloys, such as 6061 and 6063, show considerable increase in strength after heat-treatment-and-aging process. To heat treat the alloy, the temperature of the material is elevated, then rapidly cooled by immersing it in water. This is followed by aging at room temperature. After the initial tempering, artificial aging, involving slightly elevated temperatures, can be used to increase strength.

Non-heat-treatable alloys, such as 5086 and 5052, are tempered by cold working, such as rolling and stretching, to improve mechanical properties. After cold working, alloys having a high percentage of magnesium are often

TABLE 3-1. **Alloying element upper limits for four aluminum alloys.**

Alloy	Si	Fe	Cu	Mn	Mg	Cr	Zn	Ti	Other	Aluminum
5052	0.25	0.40	0.10	0.10	2.80	0.35	0.10	——	0.15	Remainder
5086	0.40	0.50	0.10	0.70	4.50	0.25	0.25	0.15	0.15	Remainder
6061	0.80	0.70	0.40	0.15	1.20	0.35	0.25	0.15	0.15	Remainder
6063	0.60	0.35	0.10	0.10	0.90	0.10	0.10	0.10	0.15	Remainder

given a final low-temperature heating—called stabilizing—to ensure stability of properties. This treatment slightly reduces strength, but increases ductility.

Heat-treatment is designated by a -T following the alloy designation; strain-hardening is identified by a -H. Numbers that follow the "-T" or "-H" designations indicate the degree of hardness and other properties of the material.

The various aluminum alloys and tempers provide a wide range of strengths and ductility, as shown in Table 3-2. Corrosion resistance, weldability, forming

TABLE 3-2. **Mechanical properties of various unwelded aluminum alloys.**

Alloy & Temperature	Tensile (PSI)	Yield (PSI)	Elong. (% in 2")
5052-0	28,000	13,000	25
5052-H32	33,000	28,000	12
5086-0	38,000	17,000	22
5086-H116	40,000	28,000	10
5086-H32	40,000	28,000	12
6061-0	13,000	8,000	25
6061-T6	45,000	40,000	12
6063-0	13,000	7,000	25
6063-T4	25,000	13,000	22
6063-T5	27,000	21,000	12
6063-T6	35,000	31,000	12

TABLE 3-3. **Characteristics of various aluminum alloys.**

Alloy	Resistance to Corrosion		Workablilty		
	Atmospheric	Marine	Welding	Forming	Machining
5052-0	A	A	A	A	D
5052-H32	A	A	A	B	D
5086-0	A	A	A	A	D
5086-H116	A	A	A	B	D
5086-H32	A	A	A	B	D
6061-0	A	B	A	A	D
6061-T4	A	B	A	C	C
6061-T6	A	B	A	C	C
6063-0	A	B	A	A	D
6063-T4	A	B	A	B	C
6063-T5	A	B	A	B	C

ability and machining ability are shown in Table 3-3. Selection of the proper aluminum alloy for boat construction must take into consideration ductility for forming, weldability, strength in the welded condition, resistance to atmospheric and saltwater corrosion, availability, and price. After careful review of alloy and temper characteristics and the data shown in the tables, it becomes obvious that the 5000 series aluminum alloys best suit the requirements for welded-boat construction.

Use of the 5000 Series Alloys

The most commonly used aluminum alloys for marine applications are indeed the 5000 series, which have magnesium as their primary alloying element. Their resistance to saltwater corrosion is excellent, they have high welded strength, and they're fairly ductile. As indicated by the -H temper designation, the 5000 series alloys are strain-hardened for strength. Because they are strain-hardened instead of heat-treated, they will retain their high strength and not fully anneal when heated by welding. The heat-affected zone is generally considered to be within one inch of the weld bead, as shown in Figure 3-1. The material can become partially annealed within this zone by the heat of welding, but in

FIGURE 3-1. The heat-affected zone in welded aluminum.

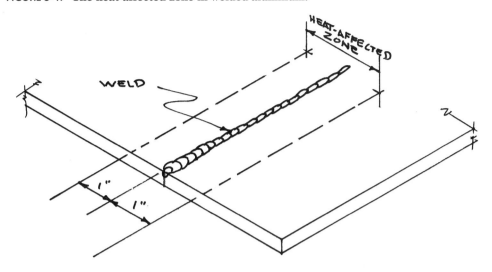

strain-hardened alloys, such as 5086-H116, the resulting strength loss is usually no more than 10 percent.

For boatbuilding, it is almost always safe to select aluminum alloy 5086-H116. This alloy is available in a large assortment of thickness and plate sizes, has good weld strength, and is fairly ductile. Its only negative is that it is usually comparatively expensive.

Alloys 5086-H116 or 5086-H32 should be used for critical high-strength areas requiring welding. All bottom plating and fabricated structural framing should be 5086-H116. Where less than maximum strength is required, consider 5086-H32 for the sides. Alloy 5086 can be extruded into special shapes and, after tempering, is usually designated 5086-H112. The high cost of a 5086 extrusion, when compared with a 6061 extrusion, usually rules 5086 out unless there is a very specific requirement for its use, such as for maximum strength in the welded condition. The U. S. Navy usually specifies that all hull material, including extrusions, must be alloy 5086.

One of the most popular alloys for building small boats is 5052-H32. This is the common aluminum sheet for forming. It's very ductile and has good strength in the welded condition. Available in a large number of sizes, 5052 costs considerably less than 5086. Use this material for fuel tanks, formed hatch covers, and applications not requiring high strength. Many builders of small welded-aluminum boats use this alloy for sides and decks to reduce cost, even though it deforms easily.

Use of 6000 Series Aluminum Alloys

A wide selection of standard structural shapes—angle, T-bar, pipe, etc.—as well as numerous special extrusions are available in 6061-T6 aluminum alloy. Essentially a structural alloy, 6061 has magnesium and silicon as the primary alloying elements. It exhibits very good resistance to saltwater corrosion and can be used effectively in boat construction for such things as cabin sole framing and longitudinal T members—almost any application not requiring high weld

FIGURE 3-2. Careful design (lower right) will allow the use of 6061-T6 in welded applications.

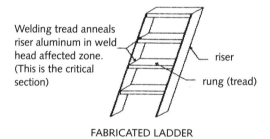

Welding tread anneals riser aluminum in weld head affected zone. (This is the critical section)

riser

rung (tread)

FABRICATED LADDER

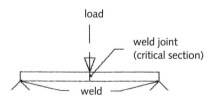

load

weld joint (critical section)

weld

Poor design for aluminum alloy 6061-T6, since weld heat will anneal the aluminum in the weld zone, reducing strength up to 80% in the critical area at the center of the span.

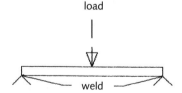

load

weld

This design is O.K. for aluminum alloy 6061-T, since there is no welding in the critical area of the beam. Weld heat at each end is acceptable, since the ends of the beam are not the critical section.

strength. Don't use 6061-T6 in critical welded areas, because welding heat can reduce strength up to 80 percent in the heat-affected zone. Careful design, with welds located outside critical sections, will allow wide use of 6061-T6 in welded applications (see Figure 3-2).

Alloy 6061 and 6063 chine extrusions are widely used in small welded-aluminum powerboats and drift boats. Since the chine of a boat is often submerged, it requires 100 percent welding on at least one side of each seam to ensure a watertight hull. The heating of the extrusion during welding causes annealing of the metal, resulting in loss of strength.

This loss of strength is not a problem in a typical chine extrusion. Chine extrusions are usually designed with a rather massive cross section compared with the cross-sectional area of the abutting alloy 5086 boat bottom and sides. It follows that if a loss of strength occurs becuase of the weld heat, the cross-section area in the heat-affected zone should be increased by at least 80 percent to compensate.

The 6061-T6 alloy is one of the least expensive boatbuilding aluminums for structural shapes, but don't try to do much cold bending with this material because it fractures very easily. Most boatyards will not attempt to make formed handrail from 6061-T6 for this reason. Check in Appendix II (Table II-1) for the minimum bend radii before attempting to form it.

In contrast, alloy 6063-T4 forms quite easily. Commonly, small-boat manufacturers will select this material for pipe that requires bending—such as handrail. It's about 50 percent as strong as 6061-T6, and the strength in the welded zone is not good, making its use for handrail questionable.

Stock Sizes of Marine Aluminum

Aluminum plate and sheet in the 5000 series can be readily obtained from most aluminum suppliers in lengths up to 20 feet. If the material is available in coil stock, it can be cut to any length that is practical to handle. (Coil cutting also incorporates flattening since the coiled material does have a memory.) Stock widths up to 8 feet are available; wider material can be special ordered. Upon request, suppliers can give the surface of the aluminum a thin plastic protective covering.

Most standard structural shapes, including angle, channel, I-beam, pipe, and others, are available in 6061 and, to a much more limited extent, in 5086. In addition to standard structural shapes, a number of sharp-corner shapes are available, including square and rectangular tubing, angle, and channel. Lengths vary from 12 feet to 25 feet, depending on the shape and the manufacturer.

Special Aluminum Extrusions

Special proprietary extrusions are commonly found on the chine, gunnel, and along the keel of most small planing aluminum boats. Extrusions are usually manufactured in special mill runs for a specific customer and are not economical to produce for orders of less than 500 pounds. For this reason, large boat manufacturers have a considerable advantage over small boatshops simply with purchase power. However, a few suppliers do carry a limited stock of common small-boat extrusions. Call aluminum suppliers to determine what's available. The extrusion in Figure 3-3 is used to join the plates at the chine of a McKenzie River drift boat and is currently available from Pacific Metals Company in Portland, Oregon. Some other special extrusions designed for boat manufacturers are shown in Figure 1-7.

FIGURE 3-3. **Drift-boat chine extrusion, die number 285954, available from Pacific Metals, Portland, Oregon.**

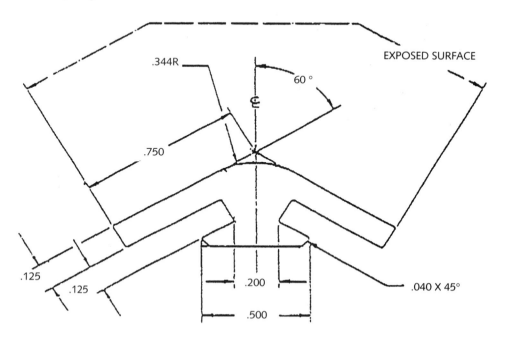

Purchasing Aluminum

Suppliers' price books will have numerous price breaks based upon the quantity of material purchased. Price may be quoted based upon total poundage for the order, or separated into each different material size and alloy. It's very important to shop around when purchasing aluminum until you find a supplier who can provide all of the sizes needed, and who will give appropriate price breaks for the quantity purchased.

The cost of the different aluminum alloys can vary considerably, particularly between aluminum extrusions. This may require a compromise as to the quality of the final product.

Filler wire for welding the 5000 series marine alloys is usually alloy 5356. This material also works well with 6061-T6 and is what boatyards most commonly use.

Aluminum alloys with high copper content, such as aircraft alloys, are not recommended for saltwater usage.

References

Welding Kaiser Aluminum. Oakland, CA: Kaiser Aluminum and Chemical Sales, Inc., 1978.

Aluminum Boats. 2nd ed. Oakland, CA: Kaiser Aluminum and Chemical Sales, Inc., 1978.

4

Designing for Aluminum

What follows is an overview of the design reasoning today's aluminum boat-builders commonly employ—in concert with established boat design criteria—to develop functional and economical boats. Although certain design principles are discussed, this chapter is not a comprehensive examination of all aspects of aluminum hull design. Nor should it be construed as a design guide; it is rather a discussion of design options currently favored by boatbuilders. Anyone contemplating the construction of a new boat should become familiar with these design options and discuss them with the designer.

The need to use a professional naval architect to design an aluminum boat cannot be overemphasized. For reasonable assurance of achieving the desired design criteria, check the credentials of the architect to make sure he (or she) is familiar with aluminum hull construction and experienced in the type of boat you want. Using a naval architect is particularly important to the professional boat-builder, who will then be protected, to some extent, from the legal liability related directly to the boat design.

Good hull design takes numerous criteria into consideration, including appearance, intended use, performance, seaworthiness, structural integrity, safety standards, and compliance with state and federal regulations. But usually the single biggest factor in the design of a welded-aluminum boat is economic feasibility. It's nice to dream about the ideal boat, but no matter how wonderful the design, if the boat can't be built within the required budget, the design is of little value. To hold construction cost down, the design of every detail must take both labor and material costs into consideration.

Often a choice must be made between quality and cost savings. A gray area divides the need to hold down cost and that of maintaining an acceptable standard of quality. In boatbuilding vernacular, the term *good boatbuilding practice* is used to characterize an acceptable quality standard for the type of product being produced. While this term has no clear definition, it generally means a standard of quality commonly accepted by boatbuilders and boatowners, based on experience and tradition.

Some techniques and materials that are used, even by professional builders, are highly suspect as to the resulting quality. Others, although not up to the purists' standards, may certainly be adequate for a trailer boat that will spend 99 percent of its life out of the water. Techniques and materials recommended in

FIGURE 4-1. ABYC publications list. Courtesy of the American Boat and Yacht Council, Inc.

Title	Date	Price
HULL DIVISION		
Visibility From the Helm	1988	$10.00
Ventilation of Boats - Gasoline	1989	$10.00
Hatches and Doors	1988	$10.00
Cockpits and Scuppers	1972	$10.00
Boat Load Capacity	1988	$10.00
Buoyancy in the Event of Swamping	1987	$16.00
Glazing Materials	1987	$10.00
Bilge Pumps	1986	$10.00
Potable Water Systems	1983	$10.00
Fuel Systems - Gasoline	1989	$14.00
Portable Fuel Systems	1986	$10.00
Powering of Boats	1989	$10.00
Seacocks, Thru-Hull Connections, etc.	1988	$10.00
Inflatable Boats	1983	$10.00
Canoes and Kayaks	1986	$10.00
Hydraulic Systems	1983	$10.00
Ventilation of Boats - Diesel	1987	$10.00
Fuel Systems - Diesel	1989	$10.00
Powering and Capacity of Pontoon Boats	1989	$10.00
EQUIPMENT DIVISION		
Liquified Petroleum Gas		
(LPG) Systems	1990	$10.00
Galley Stoves	1965	$10.00
Fire Fighting Equipment	1985	$10.00
Ground Tackle	1983	$10.00
Refrigeration & Air Conditioning		
Equipment	1966	$10.00
Boat Heating Systems	1970	$10.00
Flammable (Combustible) Gas		
Indicators	1973	$10.00
Navigation Lights	1989	$10.00
Boarding Means, Ladders,		
Handholds, Rails and Lifelines	1988	$10.00
Battery Chargers	1973	$10.00
Compressed Natural Gas (CNG) Systems	1978	$10.00
Sound Signal Appliances	1985	$10.00

Title	Date	Price
MACHINERY DIVISION		
Exhaust Systems	1986	$10.00
Liquid Cooled Marine Engines	1989	$10.00
Propeller Shafting	1980	$12.00
Control Systems	1981	$10.00
Steering Systems - Outboard Boats	1989	$10.00
Cable Over Pulley Steering Systems		
for Outboard Motors	1983	$10.00
ELECTRICAL DIVISION		
Bonding of Direct Current Systems	1972	$10.00
Cathodic Protection	1981	$10.00
Wiring Identification	1973	$10.00
Lightning Protection	1985	$10.00
AC Electrical Systems	1985	$40.00
DC Electrical Systems Under 50 Volts	1990	$20.00
Batteries	1989	$10.00
TECHNICAL INFORMATION DIVISION		
Technical Information Reports		
Aluminum Applications	1971	$10.00
Owner's Manual - Inboard Engines	1970	$10.00
Safety Signs and Labels	1990	$10.00
Instrument Panel/Speedometer Instal.	1970	$10.00
Hull Identification Number (HIN)	1989	$10.00
Fabrication Equipment, Procedures and		
Materials Quality Control	1990	$10.00
Industry Conformity Standards		
Boat Capacity Labels	1987	$10.00
Boat Measurements and Weight	1989	$10.00
Outboard Motorboat Transom		
and Motor Well Dimensions	1983	$10.00

this book reflect reasonable compromises between quality and cost. If serious questions arise, discuss them with the architect of the design.

One of the best publications available to assist the boatbuilder, both novice and professional, with the design and quality standards for a small boat is *Standards and Recommended Practices for Small Craft* by the American Boat and Yacht Council (ABYC). The ABYC's *Standards and Practices* is actually made up of individual standards for more than fifty areas of boat design and construction, and if the novice follows the ABYC recommendations, quality in those areas covered will result. This publication can be purchased as a complete set or by individual sections, as shown in Figure 4-1.

Design Parameters

Boat design usually starts with the intended use of the boat. Other considerations are the desired size, performance, style, and cost of the boat. As each of these is broken down into specific parameters, a design begins to evolve.

The intended use might be sportfishing, water skiing, white-water running, drifting, cruising, commercial fishing, hauling, or some combination of these or other uses. There is no ideal, all-purpose boat design; the features that suit a boat for one application are often the very features that make it less suitable for a different use.

Size is usually dictated by intended usage—and by the budget of the buyer. A boat that is to be trailered, for instance, usually has its beam limited to the maximum width allowed without a special permit on the highways—8 feet 6 inches on the Pacific Coast. A larger boat with higher freeboard is likely when the intended use is offshore.

Performance criteria include speed, quality of ride, fuel economy, pulling power, and reliability. Speed is determined by the combination of horsepower and boat design. One method of estimating the performance of a planing boat is to measure the angle at the stern between a horizontal plane and the bottom of the hull, as shown in Figure 4-2. This angle is called the *deadrise* and is a good indicator of boat speed, quality of ride, and fuel consumption. Since a boat rises up out of the water to plane, the flatter the bottom, the easier it will be for the boat to get on the plane—which translates into higher speed (with given horsepower) and lower fuel consumption. Unfortunately, the flatter the bottom, the harder the on-plane ride will be.

The view from the transom shows only the deadrise at the extreme stern of the boat. In most cases, the deadrise will remain constant over the aft third of the bottom, then gradually increase as it approaches the bow.

FIGURE 4-2. Deadrise of 15 degrees as viewed at the stern.

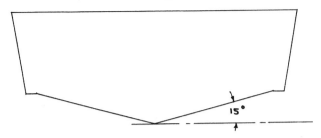

15°

For the smoothest ride at planing speed in a choppy seaway, the true deep-V hull form—25 degrees or more deadrise at the stern—is hard to beat. But the advantages of the deep-V hull are likely to be offset by higher power requirements and greater fuel consumption. Another objection to the deep-V hull is that it tends to "flop over" excessively, both at rest and during a turn reversal. The semi-deep-V hull form, with about a 15-degree deadrise at the transom, offers a good compromise. A typical semi-deep-V hull form is as shown in figure 4-2. Although it isn't as smooth in rough water as the true deep-V, the higher speed, better fuel economy, and level ride the semi-V hull provides makes it a good compromise.

The cost of a boat is generally a function of its size, but the relationship between length and cost is closer to exponential than direct. As a boat increases in length, the width, depth, and thickness also increase, resulting in a rapid increase in the mass of the boat and an equally dramatic rise in the cost. Occasionally a small-boat design can be stretched somewhat without a large increase in cost if the propulsion system is unaffected.

Style is strictly a matter of taste, but some styles can be built rapidly and efficiently in aluminum and some can't. It's very important to understand early that if the design isn't compatible with aluminum, costs can skyrocket. Designs requiring the aluminum to be formed into nondevelopable surfaces are always more expensive to construct than those with shell surfaces developable from flat plate.

The simplest developable surface to lay out is the flat panel with no twist. When the panel requires some curvature, then the panel becomes a section of either a cylinder or a cone. The technique used to develop a surface from a cylinder is termed *cylindrical development*, and the development of surfaces from cones is called *conical development*. Since most developable hull surfaces are developed from a number of conical sections, they are often termed conically developed, even though they may contain flats or cylinders. (Interestingly enough, an absolutely flat surface is more expensive to construct than one with a slight curvature because additional panel stiffeners are needed to prevent the flat surface from "oil canning.") Compound curvature is sometimes essential to make the selected design acceptable, forcing a compromise between price and style.

Considering the vast array of design possibilities, determining specific design criteria requires a logical approach. Begin by making two lists, one of the mandatory design requirements and the second of the desired additional features. "Shop" the second list for features that provide the greatest utility or the best compromise in value or performance. These combined with the mandatory requirements will establish the design parameters. Additional features from the second list may now be incorporated if they aren't in conflict with these parameters.

Cost of Materials

Often the price of materials can influence the basic boat design. Consider first the availability and price of aluminum sheets in the sizes needed. Economical sizes for marine alloy plates are used frequently and commonly stocked by suppliers. This typically includes 4- and 5-foot widths, and 8-, 12-, and 20-foot lengths. Other sizes, particularly large sheets, will usually cost more per pound, but this doesn't necessarily rule out very long or wide plates since their use may provide a net cost saving by eliminating butt welding and its associated problems. Some suppliers stock aluminum sheet in coil form, allowing custom cutting a standard width to any practical length, but there is usually a set-up cost to run coil, so large orders are normally needed to justify the cutting cost.

The choice of alloys is also an economic consideration. Appropriate selections generally include 5052 and 5086 marine alloys and 6061-T6 and 6063-T4 structural alloys. The per-pound price of each alloy will vary.

Design Drawings

Although this chapter deals with design, novice boatbuilders are strongly urged to obtain professionally developed boat drawings, particularly for their first boat.

The scope of the drawings needed to construct a boat is in direct relationship to the boat's size and complexity. Small outboard-powered boats require only a few drawings while the construction of a yacht, power or sail, requires drawings that provide considerably more detail.

Construction drawings from a plan service are usually a bare minimum. They typically are accompanied by a set of construction guidelines, or specifications, that describe specific details that may not be shown on the drawings. The amount of detail on the drawings is in direct relationship to the plan costs: highly detailed plans for a late model design generally are considerably more expensive than an off-the-shelf set of plans intended for the novice builder.

Before starting any layout or construction work, carefully review the drawings and all the pertinent data supplied with the set of plans. The drawing review process starts with the *contract drawings*, the set of drawings provided by the designer to the boatbuilder. They include the *lines drawing*, with its table of offsets, and construction drawings. Contract drawings usually fall short of being the complete detail drawings needed to construct all parts of the boat, so the basic boat structure often needs further development.

Planned production methods or the boatowner's requirements may necessitate actual design changes. Such alterations can be made (at an additional cost) by the original designer or, if minor, by the builder. Keep in mind that seemingly minor alterations to a design can have serious consequences, so be cautious when revising plans. It's always best to consult a naval architect prior to finalizing any design changes.

Contract drawings may also include detailed construction specifications to specify materials, machinery, and other items needing clarification and not shown on the drawings. A careful examination of both the drawings and the specifications will reveal the exact shape, style, machinery, construction details, and accommodations of the subject boat.

Lines Drawing and Table of Offsets

The lines drawing shows only the outline of the boat and includes very little construction information. Its primary use to the builder is to determine the shape and size of a boat and its parts. Drawn full size on a loft floor, the lines can be used to make templates for fabricating parts. Or their coordinates are used in computerized lofting to generate cutting tapes for automatic cutting equipment.

For those unfamiliar with lines drawings, the first view can be confusing. The meaning of the lines will be easier to visualize if the lines drawing (Figure 4-3) is compared with the construction drawing (Figure 4-4) of the same boat. The construction drawing shows the boat in sufficient detail to allow fabrication—except for the absence of critical dimensions defining the shape of the hull. Those essential dimensions are found on the lines drawing.

The lines drawing shows only a boat's geometry. The designer draws the *profile* (side elevation) and *plan view* (looking down from above) of the lines drawing first, then divides them into conveniently spaced equal longitudinal

FIGURE 4-3. Preliminary lines drawing for a McKenzie River drift boat.

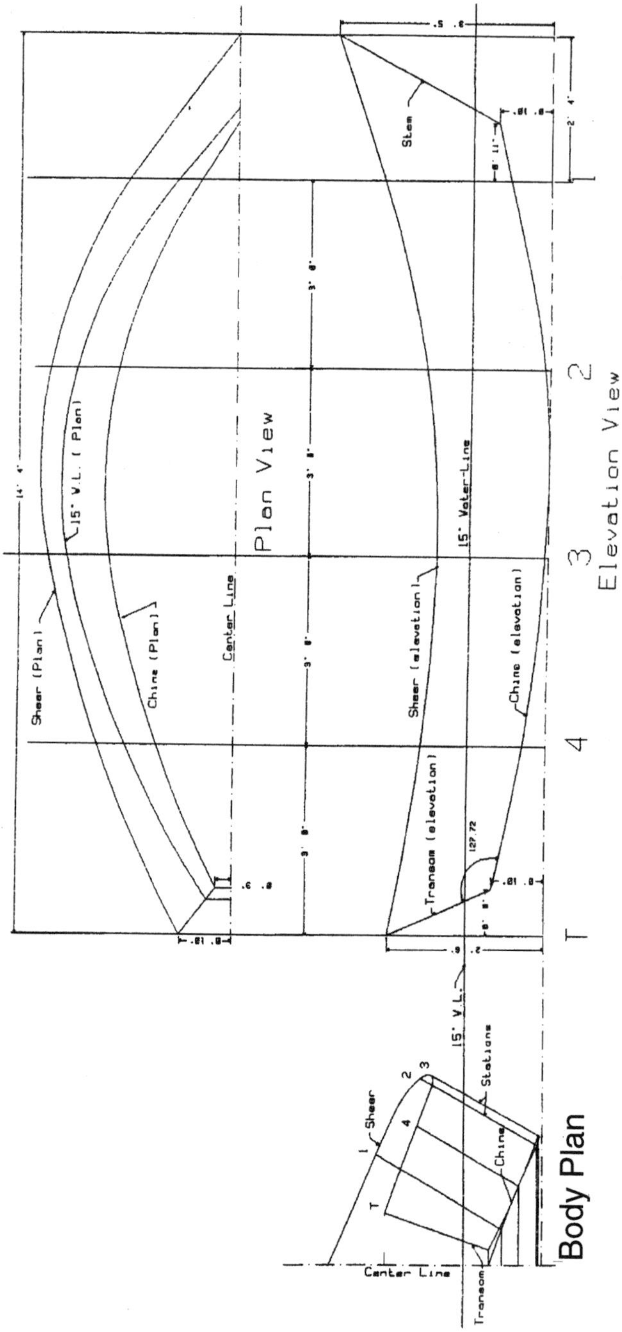

FIGURE 4-4. Typical construction drawing for a McKenzie River drift boat.

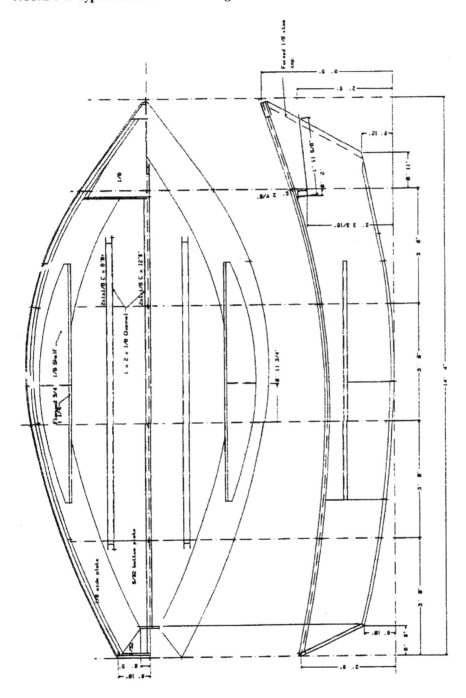

intervals along the boat's design waterline. Each *station* is a "cut" through the boat in the transverse axis and is represented by a *station line* drawn at 90 degrees to the baseline in the profile view and 90 degrees to the centerline in the plan view. Station lines are numbered from the forward end of the boat. The relatively simple boat in Figure 4-3 has only four stations—numbered 1 through 4—on the lines drawing.

Taking the dimensions from the profile and plan views, the designer projects the station lines into a *body plan view*, positioning them from the centerline of the boat and connecting them by the sheer and chine lines. Providing an aft view of the hull, this will become the primary view to develop the actual outline shape of transverse frames.

The designer can further define the hull shape by the use of waterlines, buttock lines, and diagonals. Waterlines are drawn parallel to the smooth surface of the water on which the boat floats. (This flotation plane is called the *design waterline*, or DWL.) Waterlines depict level planes that cut the boat at various vertical intervals. The 15-inch waterline shown in Figure 4-3 represents a horizontal plane 15 inches above the design waterline. Waterlines appear as straight lines in the profile and body plan views.

Buttock lines are drawn parallel to the boat's centerline plane and represent vertical cuts through the boat. Buttock lines appear in the plan and body plan views as straight lines parallel to the centerline.

Diagonals also appear as straight lines in the body plan view, but they are not parallel to the DWL or the centerline since they represent planes cut through the boat that are not level or vertical. Diagonals are often used to better define round-bilge hulls. (Figure 4-3 shows neither buttock lines nor diagonals.)

Assuming a clear understanding thus far, now look at Figure 4-5. Lines drawings will normally be presented in this manner. Note that the plan view is superimposed over the profile view with the same line serving as the profile baseline and the plan centerline. The body plan has been moved to midships and uses station 3 in the profile view as its centerline. This arrangement not only reduces the size of the drawing (and/or the loft floor), but the shared baseline/centerline reduces the chance of error.

The lines drawing usually includes a table of offsets that gives dimensions at critical points. The dimensions are divided into *heights*, which are measured vertically above the baseline, and *half-breadths*, which are measured transversely from the centerline. The columns give the dimensions in feet, inches, and eighths of an inch. A notation of a + or - following an offset adds or subtracts a sixteenth of an inch. (For example, 1-10-6+ represents 1 foot 10^{13}⁄$_{16}$ inches.) The dimensions found in the table of offsets are scaled very carefully from the com-

FIGURE 4-5. Finished lines drawing for a McKenzie River drift boat.

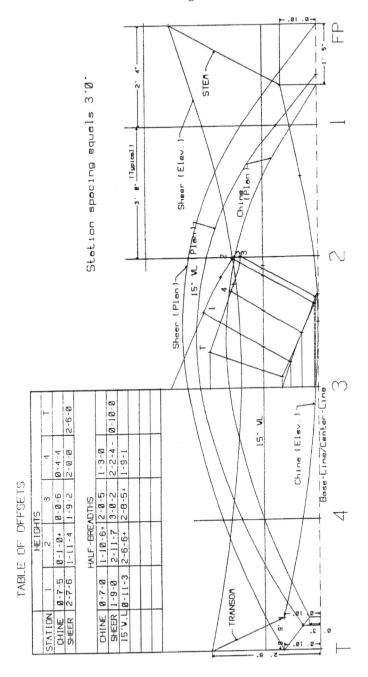

pleted lines drawing by the boat designer and are used to layout a full size drawing of the boat on the loft floor.

Construction Drawings

A basic construction drawing (Figure 4-4) includes an inboard profile, a deck
plan, and a midships section. An inboard profile is an elevation (side) view of
the boat shown as if it had been cut at the centerline to reveal the interior structure. A deck plan is a view from above looking down at the deck or, in the case
of an open boat, at the interior. A midships section is a transverse view of the boat
at about midships showing structural details.

The construction drawings of a more complex boat will also include an interior layout—a view from above the boat with the main deck removed to show
the interior details—and usually an outboard profile as well. Additional drawings
may be required to show details.

For larger boats, each drawing will probably be on an individual sheet; for
small boats they are likely to be combined on a single sheet or two. It's common to show split views in plan, such as a deck plan from centerline to starboard and the interior layout from centerline to port. It's also common to show
only a half of a view through a bulkhead or frame location since they are usually
symmetrical.

Superstructure

Small boats, say under 20 feet, don't normally have any structure above the
gunnel except a windshield and perhaps a convertible soft top. Larger boats, such
as sportfishing boats or cruising yachts, will have some type of enclosure for the
operator and often a cabin of some kind. It's not unusual for the boat designer
to leave the design of the deckhouse structure incomplete, requiring the builder
to fill in the structural details.

Design Modifications

After review of the contract drawings, and prior to lofting, required modifications are incorporated into the design. Modifications might be alterations to
the interior layout, different construction details, or any other change the boatowner desires. In small boatshops, modifications often are simply red-pencil
marks on the contract drawings, requiring the loftsman to incorporate the
changes on the loft floor. It is preferable to develop *construction* or *working
drawings* before the lofting process that reflect the desired changes.

The builder should also conduct a review of the drawings to identify areas of the design needing revision to minimize production costs. This is particularly important when bending (with a press brake) can be substituted for welding. Modifications to the original contract drawings are customarily reviewed with the naval architect prior to construction start.

Modifying the Lines for a Developable Surface

A hull with an abrupt transition from the bottom plate to the side plate at the chine, defined as a hard-chine hull, often can be designed with developable hull surfaces. This can be a major cost savings. By careful design, the shell plate can be curved in only one direction and still be in 100 percent contact with structural members. In order to design the boat with developable surfaces, certain parameters must be met.

In descriptive geometry this type of hull surface is called a *ruled surface*. A straightedge can be placed on a ruled surface and oriented—in only one direction—so that it contacts the surface over the entire length of the straightedge. A line drawn along this straight edge is properly called an *element of the generatrix*, but in the marine industry, it's usually referred to as a *ruling*.

To better visualize a ruled surface and a ruling, hold a pencil horizontally by one end and drape a piece of paper gently over it. The natural curve the paper assumes is a ruled surface, and it should be easy enough to see that a line drawn on the paper where it's in contact with the pencil would be straight and would run from edge to edge of the paper normal to the direction of curvature. This line would be a ruling.

The design challenge for a hull that is to be constructed using flat-plate development is ensuring that the hull surfaces are all ruled surfaces, not compound-curved ones. Straight-line rulings must be located on the surfaces. When a number of rulings have been located, the station lines, buttock lines, and waterlines on the lines drawing are corrected to these rulings, ensuring a surface that can be formed from flat plate. (See Appendix III for a method of finding rulings and fairing the lines to these rulings.) The interior framing of the boat is then designed to conform with the corrected lines drawing and the natural development of the hull surface.

The way small aluminum hulls are constructed, including the use of large sheets of material, typically eliminates the need to confirm that the hull is a ruled surface. By precutting the bottom and side plates and joining them together until the edges are either in contact or within a special extrusion, the plates curve naturally into a ruled surface. After the plates are joined at the keel and chine to form the shell, the framing is fitted into the interior. This ensures that the framing conforms to the developed surfaces. In a sense, the small-boat builder designs developable surfaces by working backward.

Small-Boat Versus Large-Boat Design

As noted in Chapter 1, aluminum hulls may be plated and framed in two distinctly different ways, the method selected usually depending on the size of the boat. Boats that have a conventional framing system, where transverse and longitudinal framing is constructed first, followed by the installation of shell plate, are referred to in this book as "large" boats. Conversely, "small" boats have the shell assembled first and the interior framing added afterward.

The working drawings and specifications for a large boat are prepared by a naval architect. As provided to the builder, these drawings will include sufficient structural details to allow construction of the boat. Design details not covered by the drawings—engine beds, fuel tanks, etc.—are developed by the boatbuilder to conform to the specifications.

The design of a small boat to be built in aluminum will have to be modified to conform with small-boat, welded-aluminum construction techniques, requiring the designer to make numerous decisions about the boat's structure. The remainder of this chapter deals primarily with designing the small welded-aluminum hull, but potential builders of large boats should find that similarities between small and large aluminum boats make much of what follows useful for them as well.

Engineering for Small Welded-Aluminum Boats

A common method of selecting a small welded-aluminum boat is to start with a stock design. Stock plans for small boats can be obtained from Ken Hankinson Associates, P. O. Box 2251, La Habra, CA 90631, and from Glen-L Marine Designs, 9152 Rosecrans, Bellflower, CA 90706. Both firms have catalogs containing a number of stock designs for aluminum boats, and they can provide—for a fee—study plans for some of the larger boat designs. But since few stock designs meet all of a potential owner's requirements, they are often modified.

The various engineering considerations and calculations required to properly evaluate a design modification for aluminum construction are often beyond the capability of the potential owner or builder, so a boat designer, preferably a naval architect with experience in small aluminum boats, should be retained. However, small-boat engineering is frequently accomplished without professional help by trial and error. As an example, a prototype boat may be constructed based solely on the boatbuilder's experience with specific geometric shapes, framing styles, plate thicknesses, and propulsion systems. The prototype is operated throughout its entire performance envelope to determine problem areas, and remedies are developed and tried until the boat operates without apparent problems.

The trial-and-error approach to small-boat design has many advocates, but to be effective it can involve a great deal of time. So in the final analysis, you usually get what you pay for, and a professionally prepared design often turns out to be the less-expensive route to a satisfactory small boat.

Structural Considerations

Structural considerations include plate thicknesses and framing sizes (scantlings) and their arrangement for adequate strength to meet the required loads. The location of welds, the deflection of structural members under load, the effects of vibration, and the potential for buckling or fatigue should all be analyzed. An explanation of the engineering required for each of these is available in Kaiser Aluminum's book *Aluminum Boats*.

When a planing boat rises up on a plane, a large portion of the forward hull is actually out of the water. This overhang causes considerable hull stress as the bow impacts with waves. These impacts place high positive *g-loads* on the bow (acceleration is measured in g units, one g being equal to the force of gravity), resulting in high compressive stresses that tend to buckle the bottom plates of the hull.

If a planing boat has longitudinal framing, buckling of the bottom plates is not usually a problem since slamming-induced g-loads are absorbed by the longitudinal members. But designs with little or no longitudinal framing can experience buckling of the bottom and the sides under severe loading conditions. Stress damage from slamming also occurs in the gunnel area. Thicker plates will improve the bottom's resistance to buckling, and giving adequate cross-section to the gunnel will avoid failure there.

Potential Structural Problem Areas

Welded-aluminum boats have historically exhibited structural failures in a number of specific areas. These problem areas require special design accommodations.

Center-mounted consoles. Center-mounted consoles frequently tear loose during a rough ride, causing significant damage and often injuring the boat operator. Center consoles must be securely anchored to the boat's structural framing, preferably by through-bolting.

Motor wells. Weld cracks often occur between the members forming the well for the outboard motor. They are the result of metal fatigue due primarily to engine vibrations. Long, continuous members through the motor support area reduce the likelihood of this kind of failure.

Hull seams welded from only one side. Aluminum welds break more easily if welded from only one side. This is caused in part by defects on the nonaccessible side of the weld that allow cracks to start. Unless there is a compelling reason not to, weld both sides of all plate seams. (However, most small-boat manufacturers that use chine extrusion weld the plates to the extrusion on the inside surface only. While this appears contrary to recommended practice, there are a large number of boats in service that have been welded in this manner and have had no apparent problems—probably because the extrusion itself actually develops the strength at the chine, reducing the stress on the weld.)

Stitch-welded longitudinal members. Longitudinal members that are stitch-welded to the bottom will often break loose from the shell plate in the forward half of the boat. All bottom longitudinal members in the forward half of the boat should have a continuous weld on at least one side; they may have a continuous or an intermittent weld on the other.

Bottom plating. The forward third to half of the bottom of a planing boat is subject to slamming impact. If the bottom plates are undersized or not sufficiently longitudinally framed, they may fracture.

Entrapped water. The alloys commonly used in boat construction are nearly impervious to corrosion from either fresh or salt water in a free flowing state. However, entrapped water, such as that found between two overlapping layers of aluminum, loses its oxygen and becomes corrosive. This makes aluminum hull doublers a bad idea.

Hard spots. Hull stiffeners and other structural members lying against the shell must not end abruptly or a *hard spot* is created that will eventually result in a fracture of the shell plate. Taper the ends of the stiffeners gradually to reduce the cross-sectional area to a minimum at the end; this usually means trimming stiffeners to about ½ inch high at the terminal end.

Hull Design

Every hull design must meet a combination of engineering principles. The ultimate configuration of a hull depends to a great deal upon the desired performance criteria and the propulsion system to be used. A boat can have a displacement or planing hull. It can be hard-chined or have rounded bilges. It can be designed for speed or for comfort. But note that in each case, the choice is between one form *or* another: no single hull can excel in all areas of performance.

Hull Bottom

A planing boat is designed with the keel line sloping upward at about 1½ to 2 degrees in relation to the design waterline. This ensures that the boat will ride rather flat when on the plane, yet not so flat to cause *bow-keeling*—the tendency for the forward part of the keel to submerge and act as a rudder, causing erratic directional control. For optimum performance, the after portion of the bottom plate, each side of the centerline, will be in a flat plane, free of twist. This requires the keel line and the chine to be parallel in the aft portion of the hull.

The chine line rises fairly high as it approaches the bow. Moving forward on the hull bottom, the hull plate will take a twist to allow the chine line to rise and also increase the bottom deadrise. For a developable bottom surface, this twist is usually gradual, not so severe that the bottom plate cannot be placed without undue force. The shape of the bottom and side plate transverse sections of small aluminum boats are greatly influenced by the highly desirable characteristic of having the plating developable (see Appendix III).

The plate thickness on a small hull often seems to be excessive because it is selected for ease of workability rather than minimum structural requirements. The thicker material allows greater spacing between frames, reducing the number of parts and the labor cost to make and install them. As a compromise between cost of material, required hull strength, and labor savings, $\frac{3}{16}$ inch is about the minimum bottom thickness on small welded-aluminum boats.

The additional strength of a thicker bottom plate allows the elimination of some longitudinal stiffeners. Given that economics are the primary driving force behind small-boat design, the slightly heavier boat that results from the thicker bottom plate is acceptable.

Similar logic applies to the side panels, which are normally ⅛ inch. This thickness is selected because it's about the minimum thickness that can be efficiently welded using the MIG production welding process. Transverse framing that was once common between the chine and the gunnel is now mostly missing in newer designs. An aluminum angle with the flange turned up (see Figure 4-13) is typically used on the inside face of the side plate as longitudinal framing from the stern to a point about ⅔ of the distance to the bow. (This also serves as a stowage shelf for small tools and fishing tackle.) Side panels on some boats over 20 feet are $\frac{5}{32}$-inch material, allowing for higher freeboard without additional stiffeners.

Static pressure, a major consideration for displacement hulls, is usually not a serious consideration for planing boats since the bottom and side plates are usually out of the water during operation. Besides, the bottom and side plates are over-thickness to start with for the reasons mentioned earlier. The thicker plates also tend to minimize hull deflection.

A high percentage of aluminum planing boats have a flat area, sometimes called the *shoe* or *ski*, along the keel on the aft portion of the hull. A shoe on the bottom provides additional lift for rapid acceleration, allows the boat to plane at a lower speed, reduces draft, and provides a base to mount a water-jet intake. This flat is typically about 20 inches wide at the transom, on the centerline of the hull, and extends forward ⅓ to ⅔ the length of the boat, terminating in a point at the keel.

Strakes

Contrary to common belief, the angle shapes usually found running in the longitudinal axis on the bottom of a hull are not primarily for additional lift. Such *strakes* add stiffness to the bottom, and they're also effective at breaking down spray to reduce airborne water when the boat is on plane.

Strakes on an aluminum hull are often cut down angle shapes, or they may be special extrusions. They should be 100 percent welded to minimize the potential of coming off. Strakes are often left open at the aft end to allow water to freely exit.

Chine

The intersection of the bottom of the hull and the side is called the chine—typically characterized as either hard or soft. A hard-chine hull has its bottom and side plates meeting at a relatively sharp angle, a hull shape commonly associated with planing powerboats. Soft chine suggests a more gradual, rounded transition between the bottom of the hull and the side.

To minimize the wetness often associated with a high-speed boat, a narrow *chine flat* (see Figure 4-6) may be used. In addition to knocking down the spray considerably, the chine flat provides a production expedient and reinforces the chine area. Special chine extrusions have replaced the chine flat in many small production hard-chine boats.

The widespread use of chine extrusions on small production-built welded-aluminum boats has increased production efficiency by eliminating the imperative of a precise fit when simply fitting two plates together. One such extrusion

FIGURE 4-6. Chine design.

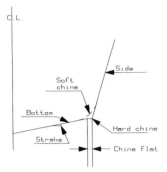

is shown in Figure 4-7. This particular extrusion is designed for the constant angle (120 degrees) between the bottom and the sides of a McKenzie River drift boat (Figure 1-9) and provides little allowance for any twist to develop in the plates. But most hard-chine boats do have some bottom shape, and the angle between bottom and hull side isn't constant. This requires an extrusion with an entry approximating the hull material thickness and a wider chamber inside the opening that will allow some twist of the bottom or side plate (see Figure 4-8).

FIGURE 4-7. Chine extrusion for a McKenzie River drift boat.

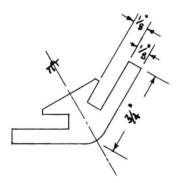

6063-T5 CHINE EXTRUSION

FIGURE 4-8. Chine extrusion designed to allow for some change in the chine angle. Photo courtesy of North River Boats, Roseburg, Oregon.

FIGURE 4-9. **Formed gunnel piece.**

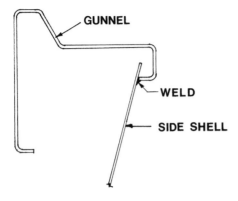

FIGURE 4-10. **Formed channel used in the forward gunnel area.**

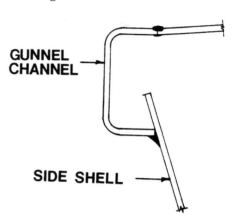

Chine extrusions diminish the need for a precise fit between adjacent plates because of the adjustments that can be made in the extrusion slots. And it provides the option of welding only on the inside of the hull, eliminating unsightly weld spatter from exterior surfaces of the boat. If chine extrusions are kept small, they can be bent by hand around a jig or over a precut side or bottom plate, greatly simplifying their installation.

Transom

On small-planing-boat designs, the transom usually rakes aft at about 12 degrees since this is a fairly standard slope for inboard/outboard and water-jet units. This is primarily a production expedient.

Gunnel

Formed gunnels, like the one illustrated in Figure 4-9, have evolved for welded-aluminum boat construction. Aside from providing sufficient strength to handle anticipated forces in this area of the hull, formed gunnel members also serve as a conduit for control cables and wiring, a cavity for upright flotation material, and a rain flashing surface to which a canvas top can be attached.

FIGURE 4-11. **Aluminum gunnel extrusion.**
Courtesy of North River Boats.

FIGURE 4-12. **Typical plate edge-to-edge**
joint at the gunnel.

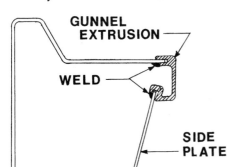

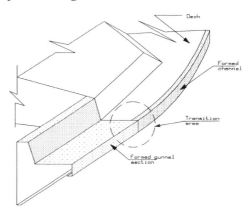

The gunnel from the transom to the foredeck is composed of sheet aluminum press-brake-formed into a shape similar to Figure 4-9. A formed channel (Figure 4-10) from the forward end of the formed gunnel to the bow completes the gunnel, providing a smooth transition piece and a simple method of attaching the deck to the hull side and maintaining a fair line.

Note that the top of the side plate in Figure 4-9 extends beyond the bottom flange of the formed gunnel section. This allows a loose tolerance for cutting and fitting the side plate, thus expediting production. The disadvantage of this expedient is that the side-to-gunnel joint is inaccessible on the inside for welding. As a practical matter, this weld is ignored with no apparent ill effects. Figure 4-11 illustrates an alternative configuration employing a special gunnel extrusion that North River Boats (Roseburg, Oregon) presently uses to complete and attach the formed gunnel section. A typical gunnel and deck edge arrangement is shown in Figure 4-12.

Framing

Framing in small welded-aluminum boats has evolved into bottom longitudinal frames and some transverse framing under the floorboards, which are not in contact with the bottom plate, as illustrated in Figure 4-13. Additional transverse framing may be located in the area of a bow deck, and the sides of the

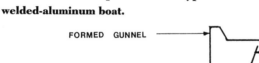

FIGURE 4-13. **Midships section of a typical small welded-aluminum boat.**

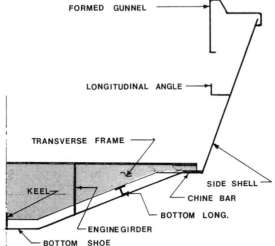

hull normally have one large structural angle longitudinal located about mid-span, which also serves as a storage shelf.

The elimination of transverse framing in direct contact with the bottom plate means less impact damage when grounding on rocks. The bottom plate may crease, but shearing of the bottom plate over a transverse frame during grounding has been mostly eliminated. This kind of framing also does away with the need to notch the frames for through-passing longitudinal members and reduces the material required, providing both labor and cost savings.

Decks

Small boats (under 20 feet) normally have ¾-inch plywood walking decks over aluminum angle subframing. Such decks are not watertight. They are secured with self-tapping oval-head screws, and stainless steel finish washers. The wood decking is usually well-painted and often covered with some type of nonskid material.

For boats over 20 feet, wood weather decks, when used, are usually bolted to aluminum *margin plates* welded to the sides of the shell. Although wood has been used with success for decks on steel hulls, aluminum expands and contracts and "works" much more than steel, so the attachment bolts are sure to egg-out their holes and leak. For a watertight deck, use aluminum.

Welded-aluminum decks can be as light as ⅛-inch plate on small boats, but under-deck stiffeners on about 12-inch centers will be needed to prevent deflection under foot. Even with closely spaced stiffeners, the deck may still be springy. Sprayed-in-place polyurethane foam under the deck will greatly reduce the tendency of the deck to move under the weight of walking. A good camber will also help stiffen the deck plate. On larger boats, the minimum deck plate thickness is 3/16 inch.

Aluminum decks are usually welded 100 percent to the shell on the outside to be watertight but intermittent welded on the underside to minimize the weld shrink mark—a slight ridge on the side plate. Careful placement of rubrails and decorative paint schemes can help hide the deck-weld ridge.

Engine Bed

The general layout of the engine bed is usually called out by the naval architect, but engine bed details are often developed by the boatbuilder. As a general rule, an engine bed consists of longitudinal girders within the engine compartment, welded to the bottom shell plate and adjacent framing. The ends of girders can extend into adjacent areas, and on boats with an aft-mounted engine, the aft ends of the engine-bed girders usually terminate at the transom. The forward end of the girders should taper uniformly into the shell plate so that an abrupt change of cross-sectional area does not occur.

The web of the longitudinal girder is often constructed from the same thickness of aluminum material as the hull plate. An upper flange, often of heavier material than the web, is welded to the top of the girder into an L shape, with the toe of the flange toed outboard.

Engine-bed girders for aluminum boats are often spaced apart slightly less than the distance between the engine mounts. Most standard V-8 marine engines have their forward engine mount bolts located at 11¼ inches off centerline—port and starboard. Engine-bed girder spacing will often be 10¼ inches from centerline to the inboard faces of the girders—port and starboard—with the engine girder flange turned outboard for ease of access to the mount bolts. Large diameter holes, called *lightening holes*, are cut through the girder web to both reduce weight and to allow access to the underside of the engine. Large limber holes should be cut through the aft end of the engine-bed girders at the transom and bottom plate intersection to facilitate drainage to the bilge. Since the engine girders are subject to high stresses, they are usually double continuous welded to the shell plate and adjoining boat hull structure.

Design considerations for engine-bed location and geometry must consider access to the underside of the engine for oil change and service, at least 2 inches of clearance between the shell plate and the engine, and access to the mounting bolts and nuts used to mount the engine.

When using flexible *isolation* mounts, set the top flange of the engine girder at the anticipated height of the base of the isolation mounts so that when the engine and gear are set in position on the engine bed, the shaft angle will be correct and the engine's output-gear flange will align with the propeller-shaft flange. If isolation mounts are not to be used, set the engine-bed top flanges slightly lower than the anticipated location of the engine mounts to allow for some vertical adjustment during engine and shaft alignment.

Superstructure

The superstructure on an aluminum hull should be aluminum—⅛-inch material on small boats and ⁵⁄₃₂- or ³⁄₁₆-inch plate on larger ones.

Superstructure styles vary widely, depending on the owner's preference. On larger boats, the windshield may slope forward or aft. In northern, wet climates, a forward-sloping windshield fitted with a visor is popular because rain doesn't run down the glass, which translates into a clearer view when at anchor. The forward-sloping windshield also gives more headroom in the cabin.

The sides of any superstructure must tilt inward at the top or an optical illusion makes them appear to be sloping outboard. This looks terrible! The proper term for this tilting inboard of side panels is *tumblehome*. The superstructure sides on commercial boats tilt inboard about 2½ degrees to appear to be plumb; on yachts, the tumblehome is about 8 degrees.

Construction Details

The wise utilization of various construction practices saves a lot of shop time and man-hours and improves quality. As a general rule, use the largest piece of material that is practical. Try to minimize the amount of welding. Preform members with a press brake to save welding time and improve quality. Design to allow for loose fit-up tolerance. Think out each joint and use a lap instead of a butt, if possible. Allow access for welding.

A number of proven time-saving practices merit consideration:

- Use offsets where practical to act as a built-in backing bar on ⅛ inch or thinner material (Figure 4-14A).

- Lap joints (Figure 4-14B) allow very loose tolerances compared to butt joints and are much quicker.
- Figure 4-14C illustrates a typical large-boat chine using a separate cut member for the chine bar. This joint requires a good fit-up, but a chine using a standard angle for the chine flat (Figure 4-14D) can often be substituted. This allows for a loose tolerance between the bottom and side plates since this joint is covered by the chine angle. And because the angle is fillet-welded (Figure 4-15), it's usually faster and simpler than the butt welds required with a

Figure 4-14. **Hull-construction details.**

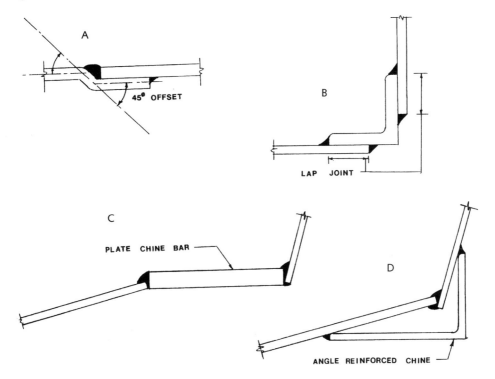

FIGURE 4-15. **Butt weld and fillet weld.**

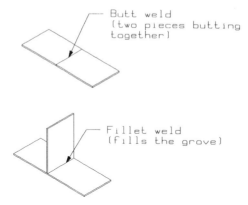

Butt weld
(two pieces butting
together)

Fillet weld
(fills the grove)

FIGURE 4-16. **Round bar as chine rein-forcement.**

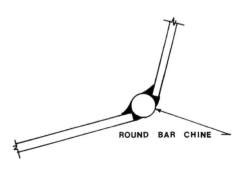

ROUND BAR CHINE

Figure 4-17. **Typical plate edge-to-edge joint at the gunnel.**

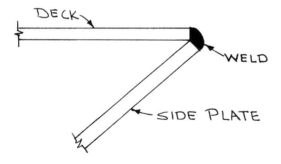

DECK

WELD

SIDE PLATE

conventional chine bar. A round-bar chine (Figure 4-16) isn't a good selection, because it's very difficult to maintain a fair line to the round bar.

- The gunnel configuration illustrated in Figure 4-17 is much more difficult to fit up than the various formed gunnels detailed earlier

FIGURE 4-18. **Extending one plate for a simpler fit and weld.**

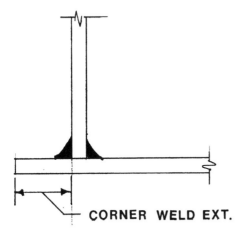

CORNER WELD EXT.

(see Figures 4-9, 4-10, and 4-11). A formed gunnel or channel allows the side plate to be cut to a much looser tolerance than the edge-to-edge fit-up and weld (shown in Figure 4-12) requires.

• Letting one member run slightly past another transforms a corner weld into fillet weld (Figure 4-18). This is commonly done where the transom attaches to the bottom and sides of the hull.

Preforming Material

A press brake is a powerful machine that bends metal into straight and uniform creases. The use of various dies allows different bend radii to be formed. (See Chapter 5 for detailed information on the press brake.) Most boatbuilders won't have a press brake, sub-contracting forming work to sheet-metal shops.

Complex shapes can be developed from parts formed from flat patterns. Simple formed parts are designed to interconnect by welding to develop complex shapes and still stay within the parameters of flat-plate development. Well-thought-out use of the press brake will both speed production and greatly improve quality.

Preforming is not limited just to the press brake. Other methods of bending or rolling aluminum into the desired shape are available. To take full advantage of preforming, the boat designer must be familiar with forming equipment procedures and limitations.

Sea Trials

A sea trial is the actual operation of a boat on the type of waters it was designed for. An experienced aluminum-boat builder will recognize potential operational problems with a boat's design during the sea trial. Performance problems identified are often remedied by minor modifications, easily accomplished on an aluminum boat by cutting, fitting, and rewelding. Once an acceptable level of performance is achieved, structural problems that may have shown up are isolated and solved.

Boatbuilder's sea trials should involve tests of the boat's maximum performance under various sea conditions. ABYC Section H-26, *Powering of Boats*, considered the industry standard, includes sea-trial tests for small boats. These tests are conducted using the maximum allowable horsepower for the boat, as determined by United States Coast Guard (USCG) regulations, and as further defined by ABYC H-26.

ABYC test guidelines recommend quick-turn tests under specified conditions, but they don't include slamming tests. Slamming tests are necessary to test hull structural integrity and can best be accomplished by actually running fast in rough water. A reasonable structural test under slamming conditions for a pleasure boat would be 4 g's at the bow, and 2 g's at the center of gravity. This is generally lower than the likely design criteria for military or racing boats, which can be subject to extreme slamming conditions. (Tests conducted on the U. S. Navy YP-110 recorded 11.3 g's at the bow, 4.8 g's at the center of gravity, and –2 g's at the stern.)

After sea trials, thoroughly inspect the entire boat. If broken welds are discovered, a change in the welding design, sequence, or location will usually solve the problem.

Aluminum is subject to fatigue failure, but whether this will become a problem in a particular design can't be adequately determined until the boat has had extensive running time. Most fatigue problems will be associated with vibrations originating from the propulsion system, so the area around an outboard-motor mount should be carefully watched for cracks caused by fatigue. Fatigue-related structural problems can only be corrected—usually by the subsequent incorporation of compensating design revisions—as the areas are determined.

Panel vibrations can result in a buzzing or zinging sound. Locate such vibrations by touching the buzzing member with your hand. Relocating panel stiffeners, or simply altering the affected panel by placement of pads, insulation, or other means to disturb the frequency, will often eliminate such vibrations.

Regulations

The only mandatory regulations for small boats are the USCG safety requirements, essentially limited to flotation, gasoline fuel systems, horsepower rating, and people-carrying capacity. There are *no* mandatory regulations pertaining to small-boat structural integrity. The boat's ability to withstand structural loads that may be imposed during operation is entirely in the hands of the boat designer and builder.

USCG regulations require positive flotation in boats under 20 feet long and level flotation if they are outboard-powered. In addition, boats under 20 feet must display a plaque that shows safe loading and capacity and, if the boat is outboard-powered, the maximum horsepower rating. All boats, both under and over 20 feet, must meet USCG safety standards for ventilation of gasoline fumes and must have a hull identification number.

The USCG regulations apply to boats both professionally built and home built, and they are readily available from any USCG office. A simple explanation of these regulations, *Safety Standards for Backyard Boatbuilders*, publication COMDTPUB P16761.3A, is also available.

If the boat is to be used for other than pleasure, such as carrying passengers, other regulations may apply. Contact the nearest USCG office for *Subchapter T—Small Passenger Vessels (Under 100 Gross Tons)*. Subchapter T is a part of the *Code of Federal Regulation (CFR), Title 46, Parts 166-199*, and is available from the U. S. Government Printing Office, Washington, D. C.

Passenger-carrying vessels require plan approval prior to the start of construction and in-process inspections during boat construction. Welding procedures and welding-machine operators must be certified for the welding process and the type of material welded. This certification can be obtained by following the guidelines specified in the U. S. Navy standard for qualification of welders (MIL-STD-248) or other USCG approved guidelines. To meet the criteria of MIL-STD-248, each individual welder must demonstrate skill in welding in various positions. A welder is certified for the welding process, material, and welding position for which he was successfully tested.

References

Lord, Lindsay. *Naval Architecture of Planing Hulls*. New York: Cornell Maritime Press, 1946.

Standards and Recommended Practices for Small Craft. Millersville, MD: American Boat and Yacht Council, Inc., 1991.

Aluminum Boats. 2d ed. Oakland, CA: Kaiser Aluminum & Chemical Sales, Inc., 1978.

U. S. Coast Guard. *Safety Standards for Backyard Boatbuilders*. COMDT-PUB P16761.3A. Washington, DC: U. S. Department of Transportation, 1985.

46 CFR, Parts 166-199. Washington, DC: U. S. Department of Transportation (U. S. Coast Guard), 1988.

5

Fabricating Techniques

Working with aluminum is similar to working with wood. Most standard power woodworking tools can saw, plane, and drill aluminum. Special blades designed for aluminum improve efficiency, but in most cases, less-expensive woodworking blades will suffice. An inexpensive hardware-store carbide-tipped woodcutting blade in a 7¼-inch hand-held power saw (almost universally known as a Skilsaw, the most well-known trademark) is adequate for cutting aluminum. A heavy-duty power hand plane—the Porter Cable Versa-Plane, for example—that comes with a spiral carbide-tipped cutter, can easily plane aluminum to obtain a professional looking finish.

Larger professional boatbuilding shops will have hand-held *plasma-arc* cutters, which are both fast and safe, but all the parts needed to construct a 40-foot aluminum powerboat hull can be cut out with a Skilsaw and a bandsaw. The Skilsaw is one of the most versatile aluminum-cutting tools. It can make straight and large-radius cuts in flat plate; almost all plate cuts for framing and shell plate can be Skilsaw cut. A vertical bandsaw is safer and quieter than a Skilsaw, but the throat depth (the distance from the blade to the frame) restricts the size of the piece that may be cut.

The fastest and most accurate method of cutting straight strips is with a power shear. Routers, nibblers, hand grinders, reciprocating saws, and jig saws will also cut aluminum.

Fabrication Facility Required

The size of the boat to be constructed determines the size of the shop required. A two-car garage is easily big enough for the construction of a small boat—about 14 feet or under—provided there's access to 230-volt single-phase electrical power (normally available in most modern homes) for welding. For larger boats, consider overhead room, working space around the hull, and adequate space to turn the inverted hull over once it's nearly complete. It's also nice to be able to get the boat out the door without tearing down the shop.

Aluminum doesn't like temperatures colder than 55 degrees Fahrenheit when welding, so in a cold climate, a facility providing at least a partially controlled environment is needed.

Boats with shell plate thickness of ¼ inch and greater should be welded with 230-volt or 460-volt three-phase welding machines, which usually means construction at a location that can provide industrial three-phase power. Aluminum plate 3⁄16 inch thick or less can be welded on household single-phase power.

Cutting aluminum with a hand power saw is noisy, but since the bulk of the saw-cutting is done early on in the project, exposure to high noise levels is shortened. If you're working in a residential neighborhood, take noise control into account. (Sharp saw blades cut much quieter than dull ones.)

Tools Required

Any well-equipped home workshop will contain almost all the tools required to construct a small welded-aluminum boat. A few additional tools (if not already found in the workshop) are required:

- A right-angle drive, 7¼-inch hand-held power saw (Skilsaw #77 or similar): $130; equipped with a carbide-tipped blade for saw: $18. (A straight-drive saw can be used but will not stand up to the heavy demand of aluminum sawing.)
- A right-angle grinder, preferably a 4½-inch (Black & Decker #4247 or equivalent): $80; fitted with an aluminum grinding disc (4½-inch x ⅛-inch Brilliant T27): $2.40; and a stainless-steel cup brush (Weiler M10 1.24 S.S.): $11.
- A 230-volt single-phase welding power supply compatible with MIG 1-pound spool welding gun, an argon bottle, flow meter, and adequate power and ground welding leads: $2,000. (Note: An aluminum MIG welding outfit can be rented for about $60 daily, $125 weekly, or $300 monthly.)

FIGURE 5-1. Electric die grinder with cone-shaped cutter.

- A vertical bandsaw (Rockwell-Delta or equivalent): $500; with a ½-inch-wide, 8-tooth blade: $8.
- Six 4-inch forged steel C-clamps: $22 each.

A few additional tools will make the job a lot easier:

- A high-speed die grinder (Makita GEO600 or equivalent): $65; fitted with a cone-shaped carbide cutter (Brilliant 7D13956; similar to the one shown in Figure 5-1): $34.
- A 7-inch angle grinder (Black & Decker or equivalent): $155; with aluminum grinding disc (Brilliant T27) $6.50; and a rubber backing pad and abrasive discs for sanding: $15.
- A hand-held power plane (Porter Cable Versa-Plane): $250; with a spiral carbide cutter: $80.
- A reciprocating saw (Makita JR3000V or equivalent): $150; with extra blades: $1.50 each.

Marking Aluminum for Cutting

The shiny surface of aluminum can be very reflective, making layout lines difficult to see. Combined with poor lighting, this can make layout marks almost impossible to follow with a cutting tool. The importance of clear and distinct layout lines requires an appropriate marking method and a location with good lighting.

Lay out the cutting lines on aluminum with an ink pencil or felt-tip marker. Black, blue, and red are good colors for the markers. Felt-tip markers don't last long when used to mark aluminum; a thin coat of oil on the surface of the aluminum collects dirt, and this dirty oil film damages the tips of the markers. The ink pencil (sometimes called an indelible pencil) will last considerably longer than a felt-tip marker and makes a very distinct line that can be seen even in poor light.

Most felt-tip markers wash off aluminum easily with a little water, but some don't wash off at all, not even with standard industrial solvents such as acetone. While a permanent mark can be desirable in some instances, improperly removed felt-tip markings have been known to show through finish paint. On the hull exterior and anywhere the mark will show, a water-soluble marker is needed. A little experimenting with markers will determine which one to use.

Aluminum should not be scribed by making a deliberate scratch in the work surface; it's too easy to mistake a nonintentional scratch on the surface for the scribed line. For example, a metal burr between the Skilsaw and work being cut can put a scratch in the surface that, in poor light, might be taken for a scribed line. And if a scribed line ends up in a bent or high-stress area, it can cause a *notch effect* that will encourage the start of a crack.

Cutting Aluminum

Aluminum is quite easily sawed with power woodworking tools using carbide-tipped blades. Because aluminum tends to adhere to the saw blade and plug the gap between the teeth, select a blade with large, widely-spaced teeth and a wide set, similar to a rough-cut blade for wood. The past practice of using wax to stop aluminum build-up on saw blades isn't necessary, and it's a bad practice when welding is anticipated: the wax is difficult to remove thoroughly and will cause welding problems.

Hand Power Saw

On the West Coast, most small boatshops use the 7 ¼-inch worm-drive hand power saw, the Skilsaw, as their *primary* method of cutting aluminum. This saw is one of the most versatile aluminum-cutting tools, capable of almost all framing and shell plate cuts.

But first, a few words of caution about cutting aluminum with a Skilsaw are in order. *Always* wear a face shield; safety glasses alone are not sufficient. Both safety glasses and a full-face shield are recommended when sawing any metal because the chips thrown off by the blade sometimes stick to the skin, and they're hot enough to cause a mild burn. Wear a long-sleeved shirt or coveralls to protect your arms. Snug-fitting leather work gloves are a nice plus, both as hot metal protection and protection from the razor-sharp fresh-cut edge. Wearing nonmarking knee pads will help prevent the sharp saw chips from penetrating your knees, and they'll add to your kneeling comfort.

The noise level associated with cutting aluminum with a Skilsaw is loud enough to cause ear damage. Always wear ear protectors or plugs, both for protection from noise and to prevent cutting chips from entering the ear. A dull saw blade—the aluminum oxide present in aluminum welds is highly-abrasive— slows the cutting rate and increases the noise level substantially; both problems are solved by changing blades.

When Skilsaw-cutting aluminum plate thinner than $3/16$ inch, the initial entry cut direction is important. The thin metal sliver that will be on one side of an entry cut when entering the material at a shallow angle to the edge can catch and bend into the rotating saw blade. This is usually accompanied with a loud

FIGURE 5-2. A safe entry cut.

FIGURE 5-3. Sawing out to the edge for a shallow entry cut.

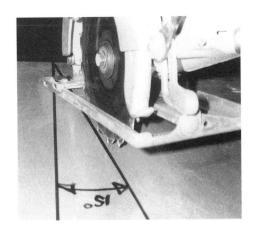

bang as the blade leaps out of the cut. To avoid this problem, always enter a piece of aluminum under $\frac{3}{16}$ inch thick at no more than 15 degrees off of a square (perpendicular) entry to the edge (see Figure 5-2). When a shallower entry cut is required, avoid the potential kick-back and resulting damage to the aluminum by simply turning the saw around (180 degrees). Holding back the blade guard, start the saw and lower the blade against the aluminum, letting the saw plunge-cut an entry into the plate inside the plate edges, then saw out to the edge (Figure 5-3).

Don't let these safety precautions eliminate or reduce your use of the Skilsaw; it's fast and safe when used properly. Psychological resistance to cut-

FIGURE 5-4. Skilsaw cutting procedures for thin plate.

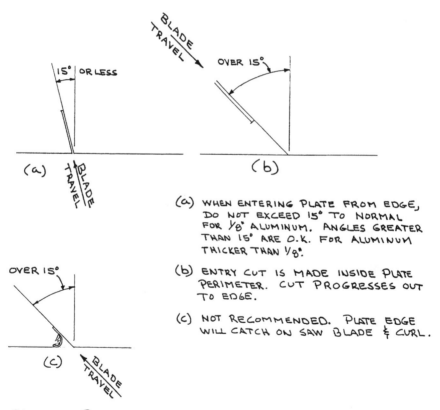

(a) WHEN ENTERING PLATE FROM EDGE, DO NOT EXCEED 15° TO NORMAL FOR $\frac{1}{8}$" ALUMINUM. ANGLES GREATER THAN 15° ARE O.K. FOR ALUMINUM THICKER THAN $\frac{1}{8}$".

(b) ENTRY CUT IS MADE INSIDE PLATE PERIMETER. CUT PROGRESSES OUT TO EDGE.

(c) NOT RECOMMENDED. PLATE EDGE WILL CATCH ON SAW BLADE & CURL.

SKILSAW BLADE ENTRY ANGLE, $\frac{1}{8}$" ALUMINUM

FIGURE 5-5. Aluminum-cutting blade with zero-degree tooth rake angle.

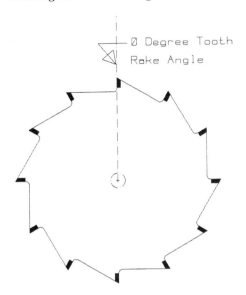

0 Degree Tooth
Rake Angle

ting metal with a Skilsaw is only overcome by actually trying it. With a little practice, your cuts will be straight and accurate. Use a ⅛-inch kerf allowance (the width of the saw blade cut) when laying out material. If you anticipate a lot of cutting, then get a blade designed for aluminum cutting, one with a zero-degree tooth-face rake angle (Figure 5-5). This blade will produce a smoother and quieter cut but costs more and isn't as readily available as a wood-cutting blade.

Large-radius cuts (1 foot and larger) on flat plate can be outside cut with a Skilsaw by a series of short, straight cuts, as shown in Figure 5-6. Inside radius cuts can also be made with a Skilsaw, but ample room for the start and reentry cuts for the blade must be allowed. Cut an inside curve by setting the Skilsaw blade depth very shallow—not much deeper than the thickness of the material. By cutting with the blade barely breaking through the material, you can easily cut an inside radius as tight as 12 inches. The start and reentry technique for circle cutting involves a kind of pumping motion, but a proficient Skilsaw operator can make a rapid circular cut in aluminum plate with barely perceptible vertical movement of the saw.

FIGURE 5-6. Circle cutting with a Skilsaw.

When cutting flat material with the Skilsaw, always consider what's under the material being cut. To ensure adequate blade-tip clearance, position the material on a cutting grid (Figure 5-7) or on 2 x 4s about 18 inches apart laid flat between the floor and the work. There must be adequate support and clearance under the aluminum to keep the saw blade from contacting the floor when you kneel on the material during cutting.

Keep in mind that sawing metal generates a considerable amount of heat. A little WD-40 squirted periodically on the saw blade will reduce the heat and also speed cutting and hold down the noise level.

Carbide-tipped blades can still be used with one or two missing tips, but when a blade loses a carbide tip that sticks in the metal, all of the tips will probably be knocked out with the next rotation. More than two missing tips requires blade replacement. A few spare blades should be available.

FIGURE 5-7. Cutting grid.

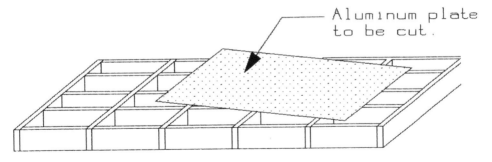

Aluminum plate to be cut.

Wood cutting grid constructed of 2x6 lumber

The chips generated from sawing aluminum will collect in trouser cuffs and other areas of clothing. These small, sharp chips are very difficult to remove from carpet. Thoroughly empty your cuffs and pockets of aluminum chips before leaving the work place.

Vertical Bandsaw

A vertical bandsaw is safer and quieter than a Skilsaw, but its throat depth limits the size of the piece that it can cut. It is the preferred cutting tool for small parts. A 14-inch (throat depth) woodworker's bandsaw commonly has a ½-h.p. motor, but a bandsaw equipped with a ¾-h.p. motor will have a substantially faster cutting rate in aluminum.

Use a ½-inch-wide 8-tooth-per-inch blade for general cutting. This blade will cut alloys 5052, 5086, or 6061 without loading up between the teeth, and it will last for many hours of cutting. For cutting softer alloys, such as 6063, the 8-tooth blade may load up; switch to a 4-tooth-per-inch skip-tooth plywood-cutting blade for soft alloys. Allow approximately ⅟₁₆ inch for a bandsaw kerf.

The single most-common problem with a bandsaw is that it may not track true. This is usually the result of loose blade guides. Keep the guides properly adjusted.

Blade width determines the minimum radius that can be cut. For most purposes, the ½-inch-wide blade works well, but ⅜- and ¼-inch blades may be

FIGURE 5-8. Preventing round pipe from rotating a bandsaw.

needed for special applications. It can be difficult to adjust the guides so that these narrower blades track true.

Use a constant pressure to hand-feed a bandsaw. To ensure a true cut, watch both the blade and the mark on the material. If the cut doesn't appear to be in line with the centerline of the table, check the guides for proper adjustment. A little WD-40 on the blade will ease cutting, reduce heat, and lengthen blade life.

A cross-cut guide is provided with a wood-cutting bandsaw, but it has little application for aluminum since experience has shown that the cut in aluminum will be little influenced by the guide.

A word of caution when cutting round pipe on a bandsaw: the saw will tend to "grab" the pipe and rotate it. When this happens, the blade usually jams and either breaks or kinks. So clamp round pipe to another piece of material (see Figure 5-8) so it can't rotate during the cut.

Power Shear

The fastest and most accurate method of making straight cuts is with a power shear (Figure 5-9). A local sheet-metal shop should be able to provide this service. Shear cuts are true and uniform, and in addition to the excellent appearance, there's no wastage and no need for a kerf allowance. Shearing is economical if the sheet-metal shop doesn't have to do the layout; layout consumes man-hours, and man-hours consume dollars. Limit the sheet-metal shop's time to shearing, and it can be a very cost-effective way to cut out parts.

Other Cutting Methods

A number of other power woodworking tools can perform their functions equally well on aluminum, and in most cases, the wood-cutting blade will be adequate.

FIGURE 5-9. Power shear.

FIGURE 5-10. Router circle-cutting-guide extensions.

Router. For cutting uniform holes, such as lightening holes and circular access holes, a hand-held electric router fitted with a single-flute carbide-tipped cutter works well. Circle-cutting guides—a slide-mounted center pin that attaches to the router with a pair of threaded ¼-inch rods—are commercially available. Longer guide arms will be needed on a number of boatbuilding applications; simply thread longer rods (usually NF thread), as pictured in Figure 5-10.

A hand-held router can also be used freehand, but it must be held very securely. Cutting notches in frames for through-passing longitudinal T-bar is a good application for the hand-held router. Typically, ¼-inch holes are drilled at the corners of the notch first and the sides of the notch are saw-cut to the holes. Then the notch is completed by using the router to plunge cut between the two saw cuts, forming the bottom of the notch (Figure 5-11).

Aluminum will tend to load up in the cutter if it's allowed to get too hot. For sustained cutting, use WD-40 on the cutter to help keep it cool.

FIGURE 5-11. Notching a frame member.

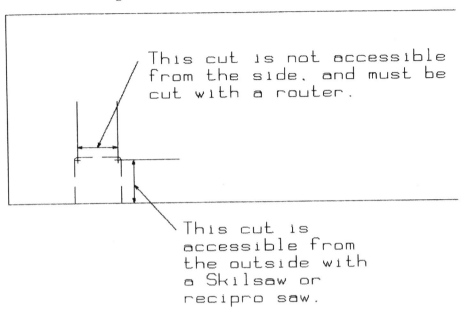

This cut is not accessible from the side, and must be cut with a router.

This cut is accessible from the outside with a Skilsaw or recipro saw.

TYPICAL CUTOUT FOR A THROUGH PASSING "T"

Die grinder. A small electric or air router, called a die grinder, is a must. This handy tool can reach into areas not accessible with other tools. Fitted with a conical cutter, a die grinder can be used to de-burr, enlarge holes, chamfer sides of cut members, and gouge out hard-to-reach welds for repair. Grinder bits intended for aluminum have large, open flukes that resist loading up (Figure 5-12).

Aluminum welds often require the removal of contamination or poor weld deposit metal from the weld zone prior to completing the weld joint. This process is called *gouging* or *back-chipping*, terms usually associated with pneumatic air tools. For aluminum back-chipping, it's often much faster and more convenient to saw out the contaminated weld rather than chip it out with an air chisel. The high-speed saw shown in Figure 5-13 is a very fast and easy-to-use tool for back-chipping.

FIGURE 5-12. Die-grinder bit used for aluminum.

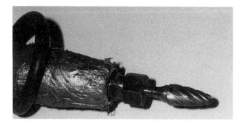

FIGURE 5-13. Right-angle attachment and saw blade.

Reciprocating saw. The reciprocating saw (recipro-saw) is useful where a narrow kerf is needed or where accessibility to the part being cut is limited. It cuts rapidly, making cuts comparable to those made by a bandsaw. The recipro-saw is often used to cut shell plate already fitted to the boat structure to mate it with adjoining plate.

Angle grinder. An angle grinder—or sander—fitted with an aluminum-grinding disc can be used to cut items like temporary lifting eyes and strongbacks flush with a surface, and the perimeter of the grinding disc can be used as a cutting wheel (making a wide kerf). The grinding disc will wear very rapidly, and in some cases, pieces will slough off during the cutting process, making a full face shield a must.

Some boatshops use a 4½-inch angle grinder fitted with a saw blade for weld-bead removal. The bead-removal rate is very high, and in some shops, this blade-fitted grinder is a primary back-chipping tool. This is obviously a very dangerous tool, and in one large Northwest boatyard it has acquired the nickname of "meat axe."

Hand nibbler. The electric nibbler is used primarily for light gauge (⅛ inch and less) material requiring neat cuts, such as electrical panels. The nibbler is a common sheet-metal-shop tool.

FIGURE 5-14. **Power hand plane with a spiral cutter.**

FIGURE 5-15. **Planing aluminum with a power plane.**

Planing Aluminum

The electric hand plane with a spiral carbide-tipped cutter (Figure 5-14), such as the Versa-Plane manufactured by Porter Cable, works very well on aluminum. This tool easily planes aluminum in a similar manner to wood, as shown in Figure 5-15. Cuts of $\frac{1}{32}$ inch per pass on the edge of a ¼-inch plate are rapid and don't overwork the plane.

Any sawed edge that will show in the finished boat should be planed to enhance the appearance. The power plane can prepare an edge very nicely, including beveling for welding. The plane will tend to grab as the cutter passes off of the material being planed. To counteract this, maintain firm downward pressure on the heel of the plane when ending a cut at the end of the material. Keep in mind that the chips the plane generates are hot and can cause a mild burn; use the same safety equipment when power-planing you use with the Skilsaw.

Forming Aluminum

A number of forming techniques can be employed on aluminum, including the press brake, the bending roll, and the pipe bender. A large number of sheet-metal and fabrication shops have adequate tooling readily available to do a nice job of preforming aluminum.

One concern is the cleanliness of the forming tools. Most sheet-metal shops are likely to have clean tooling that will form or roll aluminum with minimum marking. Structural-steel shops, on the other hand, can be very rough with aluminum and don't usually consider the surface finish. Be aware of this and address the surface finish during preliminary discussions with your forming shop. Plate-forming rolls in steel fabrication shops are often oily and have numerous "dings" on the roll surfaces that will damage the aluminum finish. Determine how much surface damage you can accept prior to starting the forming operation.

Press Brake

A press brake is a powerful forming machine used to crease or bend metal (Figure 5-16). It can be mechanically or hydraulically powered and comes in a large assortment of sizes and capacities. Those typically found in modern sheet-metal shops can accommodate most bending requirements for small aluminum-boat construction. For heavier bending needs, larger brakes are available at metal fabrication shops.

FIGURE 5-16. **Press brake.**

Wherever practical, use press-brake forming to reduce welding and improve fairness. A brake-formed plate crease is a straight line, free of weld distortion, and smooth and pleasing to the eye. There are many areas of the boat where wise use of the press brake can make a definite difference in the quality of the finished product.

Press brakes require bending dies. These are used in pairs, with the female, or lower, die fixed and the male die attached to the movable upper portion of the brake (Figure 5-17). Various bend diameters can be obtained by varying the die geometry. Angle bends, from small bend radii approaching zero to large radius bends, can be accomplished on the press brake. All developable surfaces can be either formed or very closely approximated.

Press brake dies can be constructed to form circular bends. However, when large radius bends or conical forming is required, it is more common to form a series of small angle bends spaced closely together, resulting in a series of adjoining flats that approximate a curved surface (like that shown in Figure 5-18). This type of forming is called *air bending* in that the male die of the press brake usually does not bottom out in the female die. The quality of a bend is directly related to the condition of the equipment and the skill of the press-brake operator.

One area that almost always requires forming is cabin-window mullions (Figure 5-19). Welding this narrow strip will result in distortion that may not be

FIGURE 5-17. Press-brake dies, male and female.

FIGURE 5-18. Air bend.

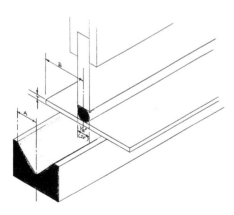

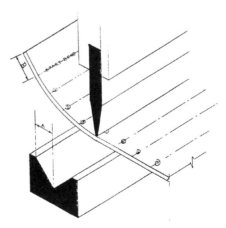

FIGURE 5-19. Cabin-window mullions.

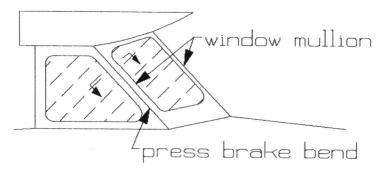

acceptable. If the mullion is creased with the press brake where it changes direction (knuckles), a lot of problems are solved. There are many other areas on a superstructure where a smooth, distortion-free bend from a press brake can be used to advantage.

In place of welded-on flanges, brake-form flanges on frames and engine girders to save both weld time and weld distortion. Form steps, cockpits, and superstructure items. Visors, metal doors, fuel tanks, rudder parts, and the leading edge of hollow keels are all ideal for press brake work. The whole trick is to lay them out accurately.

The prevailing opinion in some small-boat shops is that press-brake work is too expensive. Any work that is highly labor-intensive is expensive, but placing the material in the brake and operating the controls isn't time consuming at all; in fact, it's very fast. It's the layout that consumes the man-hours. To save dollars, don't leave this function up to the press-brake shop. Lay out all the bends prior to delivering the material to the press-brake shop. This requires some time but is well worth the effort when the end cost is considered. (See Appendix II for press brake layout specifics.)

When a batch of material is laid out and ready for forming, load it onto a trailer and take it to the press-brake shop. Explain your markings to the shop foreman so there won't be any misunderstanding. Provide angle-of-bend templates if bends other than 30, 45, 60, or 90 degrees are required. Be sure to note on the material whether each bend is up or down, and mark each piece with the appropriate identification. Provide sketches of the "as formed" pieces if you can. If possible, have someone present during the forming to answer any questions; it will save a lot of shop time if they can be answered on the spot.

Bending Rolls

A bending roll is used to put permanent curvature into flat plate. It can also be used, to a limited extent, to put a gentle curve in pipe (such as handrail) and T-bar. Sheet-metal shops usually have small bending rolls for light-gauge metal. Larger rolls suitable for rolling ¼-inch plate or heavier are commonly available at steel fabricators.

FIGURE 5-20. A pyramid bending roll.

A typical plate roll (Figure 5-20) consists of two lower power-driven rolls and one adjustable upper idler roll. This configuration is called a pyramid roll. In operation, the end of a plate to be formed is placed between the upper and lower rolls, and the idler-roll adjustment screws are tightened to clamp down on the material and engage the power-roll drive. The plate is drawn into the machine between the top and bottom rolls, forcing curvature into the plate in proportion to the pressure exerted by the upper roll. The rolled plate curves upward as it travels through the roll. A very small vertical adjustment to the idler roll makes a large difference in the curvature diameter of the rolled plate.

One drawback of the pyramid roll is a flat spot at the start and stop of each piece that is rolled. The width of this flat is equal to half the distance between the drive rolls. To compensate for this, material can be intentionally left long, rolled, and then trimmed to remove the flat areas. Another option is to put curvature in the start and end of the bend with a press brake. As a practical matter, trimming the flat from the plate after it is rolled is the usual choice.

The pyramid roll turns slowly and its safety is sometimes taken for granted, but it can easily pull a person into the roll. Never wear loose clothing around a roll, and stay constantly alert to danger. Never work alone on this machine; an operator should be at the controls at all times in the event of mishap. This is one piece of equipment where rapid reaction to danger could save a life.

Pipe Bending

For handrail and structural trim, bent pipe is often specified. Specialty fabricators can bend pipe to almost any radius, but by far the easiest and least expensive way to bend aluminum tubing is to rent or borrow an electrician's hydraulic conduit bender, like the one manufactured by Enerpac. A standard heavy-wall-conduit bender has bending shoes of a fixed radii for standard pipe sizes from ½ to 4 inches. For accurate layout of pipe bends, radii at the center of the bends can be obtained from manufacturers' data or from experiment.

Forming Compound Curvature in Shell Plate

For round-bilge hulls, as associated with sailboats, the shell plate must be given compound curvature. This requires actually stretching or shrinking the metal. The usual technique for introducing compound curvature into flat plate requires large presses and special forming dies so that the material can be pressed into the desired shape. Another method, used by the aircraft industry to form relatively thin aluminum, is the stretch forming process. This process also requires large dies. A third alternative is explosive forming, using explosives in place of powerful presses to develop the substantial force necessary to force the aluminum into a die.

Small hulls have been successfully produced using presses and stretch forming. Larger boats, however, require presses and stretch-forming equipment too large to be economical, so the common practice is to construct the hull from a number of pieces. These are first preformed using rolls or a brake, then welded together over a rigid framework to approximate a compound curvature surface. Weld beads are ground flush, and judicious use of mallets on the weld seams bring the surface closer to the shape desired. An inert filler is finally used to fair any imperfections.

Because this method of forming a true round-bilge boat in aluminum is so extremely labor-intensive, let's examine explosive forming as a possible solution to this problem.

Explosive Forming

Explosive forming (also called high-energy-rate forming, or *HERF*) is a field of effort that was worked in the U. S. during the 1960s and early 1970s. The process is simply an explosive force used as a source of pressure to force a piece of metal into a die cavity. The operation is usually carried out under water, with the water transmitting the explosive force to the material. The ability to develop extremely large forces with explosives allows compound curvature formation. The apparent limitation to this technique is die size.

Conventional explosive forming is conducted in a water tank or pond sufficiently large to hold the die. The water becomes the medium that actually forces the material into the die immediately following detonation of the explosive charge. The water also tends to muffle the noise.

A blank—the piece of material to be formed—is placed over the die cavity and clamped down very securely. This normally involves a stout clamping ring with either a large number of C-clamps or special bolt-down clamps. The material to be formed must be held with sufficient pressure to prevent wrinkles when it is drawn out from under the clamping ring to fill the die cavity during the actual forming process. (The compound curvature is formed by the metal "flowing" out from under the clamping ring rather than stretching over the surface of the die.)

The die cavity is evacuated to a near-vacuum prior to the detonation of the charge. This prevents air trapped in the die cavity from becoming super-heated and damaging the blank during the rapid compression that occurs during the forming process.

An explosive charge is placed at some distance from the blank piece of material. This is called the *stand-off distance* and is calculated to form a shock wave in the water transfer medium that will provide optimum results.

Although the principle is quite simple, the practical matters of actually constructing and handling the die are not. Dies can become massive, requiring cranes to place them in the water. A pond or large tank must be suitably designed to withstand explosive impact. The charge must be carefully placed at an appropriate distance from the work, often by trial and error. The blank must be very securely clamped to the die to prevent wrinkling, and the die must be capable of sustaining a near vacuum. Qualified personnel are required to handle the explosives. When all the variables are considered, explosive forming becomes less attractive as a production method except under very special circumstances, which must include a very generous budget and the availability of highly skilled personnel.

These very special circumstances were in place in the 1960s during the race to the moon. Explosive forming was used to form large dished sections of the Saturn 5 rocket fuel tanks and other limited-production rocket parts. Since the

FIGURE 5-21. Die used in explosive-forming experiments.

slowdown in the space program (and resulting tighter funds), the process of explosive forming has been largely abandoned in the United States. This is most likely due to the unpredictability of the process as an established manufacturing method. Although there are mathematical formulas, graphs, and charts available, the actual sizing and placement of charges seems to be more of an art than a science, with trial and error the norm.

I tried some explosive forming in 1990 in an effort to evaluate the possibility of forming a hard-chine hull in one piece, to include a chine bar. I first constructed the die shown in Figure 5-22 by welding an aluminum form of a 5-foot sample planing-boat hull bottom, installing in it a vacuum connection for evacuation of the die cavity. A 3/16-inch-wide x 1/8-inch-deep groove to accommodate a 3/16-inch-diameter O-ring was milled with a router around the top of the die. Concrete and re-bar were poured into the hollow cavity to give the die strength and allowed to cure for about two weeks.

With the O-ring in place, I cut a blank of .060-inch 5052-H32 alloy and

FIGURE 5-22. Explosive-formed hull bottom.

clamped it to the die face with a steel retaining ring and about twenty 4-inch forged C-clamps. The O-ring acted as a gasket, allowing the cavity between the die and the blank to be pumped down with a small vacuum pump.

Figure 5-22 shows one of the hull bottoms that was explosively formed. The die flange turned out to be too narrow to adequately hold the clamping ring in place, which resulted in wrinkles developing during the process of pumping down the die cavity to a near vacuum. Note also the tear at the deep part of the bow; this was caused by attempting to draw the metal more than 12 percent in one shot, and by a blowout caused by some entrapped air. The experiment was abandoned after two shots.

I used 1-inch x 8-inch sticks of 40-percent extra gel with no-delay electric caps. This slow-burning powder is known in the trade as *heaving powder* and pushes rather than shatters the metal. The die cavity was evacuated to a desired minimum of 28 inches of mercury with a small vacuum pump connected to the die with a rubber air hose. The explosive charge was attached to a wire suspended between three supports on the die, allowing accurate placement of the charge. A 10-ton mobile crane lowered the evacuated die, with blank and charge in place, into a water tank 9 feet in diameter and 10 feet deep, constructed of ⅝-inch steel and buried flush with the ground. The explosive was detonated when the charge was approximately 3 feet under water.

The forming shown in Figure 5-23 was the result of a number of tests, none of which used more than one piece of stick explosive, cut to no more than 1¼ inches long. Notes on the formed blanks indicate date, shot number (for record keeping), stand-off distance of the charge from the blank, and the estimated vacuum at the time of the shot. (Considerable vacuum loss was experienced during the shots, resulting in less than the desired 28 inches Hg.) Materials tested ranged from .090-inch 5052-H32 aluminum to ⅛-inch mild steel.

Some Titan rocket parts are currently being explosive-formed in Port Angeles, Washington, and there are reports from Australia of efforts there to form sailboat hulls. If and when this process is better defined for boat hulls, it could hold a lot of promise.

Explosive forming can be a fascinating undertaking but must not be approached casually. This can be a very hazardous undertaking that can kill; I include my experiments with explosive forming for information only. They are *not* intended as procedures for actually accomplishing explosive forming. Licensed professional explosive experts are required to determine that a procedure is safe and in compliance with local laws. An explosive expert must also determine the charge size and type and must set and detonate the charge. An amateur should *never* attempt this process.

FIGURE 5-23. Explosive-formed parts.

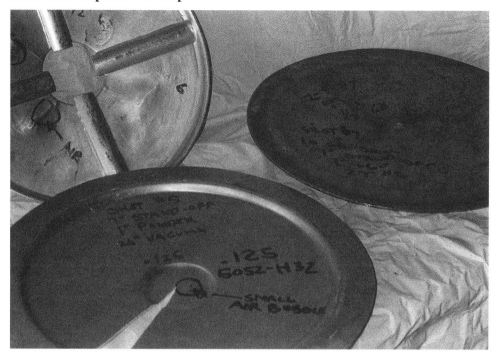

References

Dallas, Daniel B. *Tool and Manufacturing Engineers Handbook*. 4th ed. Dearborn, MI: McGraw-Hill, 1984.

Bruno, E. J. *High-velocity Forming of Metals*. Dearborn, MI: American Society of Tool and Manufacturing Engineers, 1968.

Forming Alcoa Aluminum. Pittsburgh, PA: Aluminum Company of America, 1962.

6

Welding Aluminum

A commercial welding shop with 440-volt three-phase electrical power has a number of aluminum arc welding processes available, but few of these processes will operate on the 220-volt single-phase power commonly available in a home workshop. Constant-potential aluminum-welding power sources that will provide a professional quality weld are usually heavy and awkward to handle. Fortunately, a recent development in arc welding equipment is the *DC inverter*, a lightweight, powerful welding power source operating on 208/230-volt single-phase 50-hertz electrical power—standard *220 single-phase* household power. With this equipment, a novice boatbuilder can do professional-quality aluminum welding in a home workshop.

MIG, *TIG*, and *pulse-arc* are three typical electric-arc aluminum-welding processes. All three use an inert shielding gas, usually 100 percent argon, to cover the weld zone. The gas flows over the weld area to create a gas envelope that protects the molten weld puddle from contamination by the atmosphere.

Each welding process has a particular application. The TIG (Tungsten Inert Gas) process is similar to an electric brazing operation, where the filler metal is hand-fed into the weld puddle. TIG is very slow compared with other aluminum-welding processes and allows high heat build-up, but because it is slow, it gives the machine operator more time to carefully deposit the weld metal, resulting in very high-quality welds. TIG welding is often used for items that require a weld bead that will be the finished product without further dressing—handrails and fuel tanks, for example.

MIG (Metal Inert Gas) welding is a semi-automatic welding process that utilizes a welding-wire feeder unit and a welding gun, in addition to the welding power source. It is very fast and is the primary production welding process for aluminum boatbuilding. The MIG process works well on aluminum ⅛ inch and thicker, but on lighter-gauge metals it requires such a high rate of speed to keep weld heat under control that few welding-machine operators can keep up, and poor quality welds result.

Pulse-arc is a refinement of the MIG process. Pulse-arc welding equipment pulses rapidly on and off, allowing the welder to better control the weld heat. It's used to weld very thin metal—from .060 inch to .160 inch—and an average-skilled operator can produce consistent, high-quality, spatter-free welds with it. Pulse-arc equipment is expensive and usually requires industrial three-phase power.

The best welding process for small aluminum boats is the MIG process using 100 percent argon shielding gas and a push/pull wire feeder. The MIG process is the most versatile, the fastest, the most economical, and the easiest to learn of the commercial aluminum-welding processes. The appropriate power source for home workshop use is the DC inverter wired for 208/230-volt single-phase 50-Hz input power. This power source is not a toy but a sturdy commercial welding machine used in many metal-fabricating firms.

To operate this equipment in your home workshop, first check your circuit-breaker panel for the amperage available to the 220-volt outlet you plan to use. A 200- or 300-amp DC inverter operating on 220-volt single-phase input power can draw up to 55 amps under full load. A typical 220 circuit for a clothes dryer or a kitchen range that is rated at 50 amps will usually be of adequate capacity since the maximum draw of 55 amps is rarely required. If in doubt, check with your local welding-equipment supplier and a licensed electrician.

Aluminum-welding equipment can be rented, a course worth considering if you don't already have the required welding equipment. Not all rental outfits will be able to provide a DC inverter power source, but they can offer a constant-potential power source as an alternative, although such units are usually quite heavy. Your local welding-supply house should also be able to provide rental equipment compatible with your needs. A MIG welding outfit that utilizes a one-pound spool of welding wire is often a good choice for a small boat.

Direct Current MIG Welding Equipment

MIG welding uses a consumable aluminum wire (electrode) to transfer metal to the joint and an inert gas to shield the weld area from the atmosphere. The process uses direct current (positive electrode), and the ground clamp is negative. MIG equipment is designed to automatically feed filler wire and shielding gas through the gun and into the weld area. With the tip of the filler wire from the gun in near proximity to the work, pull the trigger on the welding gun to start the wire feed and activate the welding current and the inert gas flow. When the wire makes contact with the item to be welded, the arc is established.

MIG welding equipment consists of three basic parts—the DC power source, the wire feeder, and the welding gun. A separate bottle of compressed gas, usually argon, is connected to the feeder. The gas flows from the bottle to the wire feeder and then to the welding gun, with the rate of gas flow established by a separate regulator/flow meter attached to the bottle.

A *power cord* is the heavy electrical cable that connects the welding power source to the electrical outlet. Contrast that with a *stretch*, the bundle of electrical wire that provides welding current and welding-machine electronic information from the power source to the feeder; sometimes the argon tube is included in the stretch. A *whip* is a bundle of conduit, tubes, and electrical cables that provides filler wire, shielding gas, electrical power, and electronic information to the welding gun from the wire feeder. A *ground* lead with a *ground clamp* provides a current path from the work back to the welding power source. Often the ground clamp can be attached to a convenient position on the boat hull close to the welding power source, effectively using the new hull as a portion of the ground circuit. This eliminates the need for a long ground lead.

Welding Power Source

As mentioned previously, a DC power source that operates on normal 220-volt single-phase household power is the DC inverter. Appropriate inverters, such as those manufactured by PowCon or Miller, will be rated at either 200 or 300 amps. The Miller XMT 200 CC/CV inverter is factory-set at 208/230-volt single-phase input power and can weld aluminum up to ³⁄₁₆ inch thick. The Miller XMT 300 CC/CV offers 230- or 460-volt and single- or three-phase settings, and it can weld the thicker aluminum when used on three-phase power. Single-phase power reduces the maximum welding amperage of a 300-amp power source to approximately the same as 200-amp units, so the home builder should stick to the 200-amp inverter to save cost.

A 200-amp DC inverter is ready to go on household single-phase power as soon as a compatible male plug is attached to the power cord. If you prefer the added potential of a 300-amp power source, your welding-supply house can

FIGURE 6-1. A PowCon DC inverter.

provide a 300-amp inverter preset for 230-volt single-phase input. My supplier delivered the PowCon 300 SM shown in Figure 6-1 with a plug to fit a dryer outlet.

Controls on a DC inverter are the on/off power switch, a control for type of welding process (Stick or MIG—*stick* meaning conventional powdered electrode for manual welding), amperage- and voltage-setting rheostats, and a low and high range switch. An LCD digital meter shows the voltage or amperage being used while the machine is in operation. The predetermined machine settings for specific welding circumstances are listed in Table 6-1, but as you gain experience with your welding system, you can fine-tune these settings through trial and error.

There are other MIG welding power sources besides DC inverters, such as the constant-potential rectifier. These are available from welding-equipment suppliers and will work with MIG welding on 220-volt single-phase power. Whatever your DC power source, it should have a power cord and ground lead long enough to locate it anywhere in your workshop area and be capable of producing consistent, high-quality aluminum welds.

TABLE 6-1. Welding machine settings for ⅛-inch and ³⁄₁₆-inch aluminum.

	Stock Thickness, Inches	Position	Welding — Passes/Weld	Welding — Speed Inches/Min/Pass	Arc — Current Amps. D.C.	Arc — Voltage, Volts	Argon — Flow Rate Cubic FT/HR	Argon — Used/100 FT Cubic FT	Electrode — Diameter, Inches	Electrode — Speed/Inch/Minute	Electrode — Used Per 100 Feet Weld
Butt Welding	⅛	Flat	1	24	110	20	30	34	³⁄₆₄	175	2
		H & V			100		30	35		170	2
		OVHD			105		40	58		170	2.5
	³⁄₁₆	Flat	1	24	170	20	30	57	³⁄₆₄	235	4.5
		H & V		20	150		35	75		215	4.5
		OVHD		18	160		40	90		225	5
Fillet Welding	⅛	Flat	1	30	125	20	30	55	³⁄₆₄	190	2
		H & V		24	115		30	70		180	
		OVHD		24	110		40	75		175	
	³⁄₁₆	Flat	1	24	190	20	30	55	³⁄₆₄	255	4.5
		H & V		20	165		35	70		230	
		OVHD		20	180		40	75		245	
Corner Welds	⅛	Flat	1	30	110	20	30		³⁄₆₄	175	2
		H & V		24	100		30			170	
		OVHD		24	100		40			170	
	³⁄₁₆	Flat	1	30	170	20	30		³⁄₆₄	235	4.5
		H & V		24	150		35			215	
		OVHD		24	160		35			225	

For welding material over ³⁄₁₆ inch consult the Aluminum Association's "Aluminum Welder's Training Manual." (Washington, D.C., 1986).

Weld Feeder

Two types of welding feeders are commonly used by small boatshops: the one-pound-spool gun (such as the one manufactured by Miller) and the production feeder with the wire canister separate from the gun (available from a number of sources).

The one-pound-spool gun (Figure 6-2) has a small (one pound) spool of aluminum welding (filler) wire mounted on the gun itself. The elimination of a separate welding-wire canister makes the spool-gun feeder the least expensive of the two. The spool gun is very mobile and is popular for tack-welding. It's often found in shops that do occasional aluminum welding. The price per pound for one-pound spools of welding wire is considerably more than for the larger welding-wire spools, but despite this, some professional aluminum-boat builders use the one-pound-spool gun exclusively.

The most popular production aluminum-welding feeder uses a 10-pound spool of welding wire mounted in a separate canister unit that feeds the wire

FIGURE 6-2. A one-pound-spool welding gun.

FIGURE 6-3. **Cobramatic welder with push/pull feeder and gooseneck-type gun.**

through a conduit to the gun. Similar systems for welding steel have a push-only feeder, but aluminum, because of its high coefficient of friction, requires a push/pull type of wire feeder. This requires feed rollers in both the feeder unit and at the welding gun. Although a push-only wire feeder can be used with aluminum, the length of the whip, the cable connecting the feeder to the gun, is often too short to be of practical use for boatbuilding.

There are a number of styles and manufacturers of push/pull feeders and guns. A Cobramatic push/pull feeder is shown in Figure 6-3. MIG guns can be either air- or water-cooled, but for small-boat building, an air-cooled welding gun is preferred because of its simplicity and lower maintenance. Your local welding-equipment supplier can show you the various systems available.

The whip between the wire feeder and the welding gun should be at least 15 feet long. A conduit inside the whip delivers the welding wire from the feeder to the gun. The whip also contains the electric power lead, the shielding-gas tube, and for guns that are water-cooled, the tubing for the water.

The welding gun itself can be either the pistol-grip or the gooseneck (Figure 6-3) type. The gooseneck gun provides better access to tight areas; access to tight spots when using a pistol-grip welding gun is gained through the use of special readily installed and removable tip attachments. Despite this inconvenience, many welders still prefer the pistol-grip gun.

The welding gun incorporates a set of rollers, preferably electrically powered, that pull the weld wire through the whip. (Some older welding guns have air-driven feed rollers that have been known to allow small amounts of lubricating oil on the filler wire, resulting in weld porosity.) The rollers are sized for the welding wire being used, and proper tension on them is important. A feed control on the gun adjusts the speed of the wire feed.

MIG welding guns have a removable contact tip (Figure 6-4) that provides the electrical contact between the power source and the welding wire. Tips usually are copper and are sized for the welding wire being used. Have a few spare contact tips available while you're learning because they're easily destroyed by improper welding technique.

FIGURE 6-4. Cobramatic gun with the gas cup removed to show the contact tip in place.

Stretch

The stretch is the electrical cable connecting the DC power source to the wire feeder. For building a small boat, the stretch should be at least 20 feet. Adequate stretch length allows the feeder to be located at most any location around the boat so that the gun can be used to weld all parts of the boat without moving the power source. The combined lengths of the power cord, whip, and stretch set the maximum reach for the welding gun from the electrical outlet supplying the DC power source.

On a one-pound-spool gun, because the feeder is attached to the gun, the stretch connects the gun directly to the power source and to the gas bottle; there isn't a whip. For the spool gun, at least 30 feet of stretch is recommended. This allows the gun to reach all parts of a 20-foot boat without moving the power source. It's not uncommon for boatbuilding shops to outfit their spool gun with 100 feet of stretch.

Inert Shielding Gas

Integral with the MIG welding process is the use of an inert shielding gas, normally argon (although helium is sometimes used, and mixtures of gases may be recommended for special applications). The shielding gas provides a better path for current transfer than air, and it provides a gas envelope at the weld zone that protects the molten weld puddle from contamination from the atmosphere. In addition, argon partially removes aluminum oxide from the weld area, although the reason for this oxide removal is not well understood.

The shielding gas envelope must be protected from wind that can blow the gas away from the weld zone, which will result in contamination of the weld puddle. This is one of the primary reasons why MIG welding of aluminum should be done indoors, free from drafts. If working outside, avoid windy days, and shield the work area from the wind with tarps or other means.

Argon (100%) is preferred by most boatbuilders for MIG-welding aluminum since it provides additional cleaning action, a more stable arc, and less weld spatter then helium. Helium is preferred when using fully automatic welding, for heavy weldments, and in some overhead applications because of the gas density. Mixtures of helium and argon are available from welding suppliers for improved characteristics for certain applications.

Shielding-gas flow is started and stopped by the MIG welding-gun trigger-switch. Some welding machines have a post-flow timer, allowing shielding gas to continue to flow for a brief period after the release of the trigger-switch to provide shielding gas to the weld until it solidifies.

Shielding-gas rate-of-flow must be adequate to protect the weld puddle. Since shielding gases are expensive, excessive flow rates are not recommended. Some recommended flow rates are shown in Table 6-1. Common practice is to experiment by turning down the flow rate until weld contamination is evident, then turning the flow rate back up slightly for a safety margin.

Welding Filler Wire

MIG welding filler wire is available in either one-pound spools or in spools of about 10 pounds. Most aluminum-wire feeders use the 10-pound spool; the special one-pound-spool gun uses the smaller spool. The cost of the welding wire is considerably more if purchased in one-pound spools.

Welding-wire sizes vary, depending upon the application. For most aluminum boatbuilding applications, a wire diameter of .045 inch is a good choice and about the maximum size that can be used with 220 single-phase MIG welding systems.

The most common welding filler wire is alloy 5356, which is compatible with a wide range of aluminum alloys commonly used in boatbuilding. It can be used to join alloys 5052, 5086, 6061, or 6063 to themselves or to dissimilar alloys.

Welding wire should be clean and of high quality. The best method of insuring quality wire is to use it as soon as possible after removal from the package. Keep the wire clean and dry, free from dirt, water, oils, or other surface contaminants. Weld-wire feeders, conduits, and drive rollers must be kept clean to prevent contamination of the welding wire. Oils, which can often be present on drive rollers in feeders and welding guns that have been used to weld steel, must be removed prior to loading aluminum filler wire. Keep the welding spool covered during welding to prevent dirt build-up. If the wire appears dirty, remove and discard about two full wraps from the spool prior to attempting any welding. A good visual inspection of welding wire is usually adequate to ensure cleanliness.

Welding Equipment Required

The cost of welding equipment varies from under $2,000 to more than $4,000. A simple CP power supply and a 1-pound spool-gun setup, complete with leads and flow meter, can be obtained for under $2,000. This is a good setup for a home workshop or for a shop anticipating only occasional aluminum welding. A rugged 300-amp inverter for a power source, such as a PowCon, costs about $2,400. A 1-pound spool-gun setup adds $850. A push-pull feeder/welding-gun setup costs between $2,000 and $4,000, varying by manufacturer. Since the price of equipment varies to such an extent, I recommend you contact a welding equipment supplier for suggestions on the type of equipment best-suited to your needs. If you are building only one boat, then renting equipment can be a good option. A welding power source (often a PowCon) with a wire feeder, gun, and an argon flow meter rents for about $60 a day, $125 a week, or $300 a month.

Welding wire sells by the pound. Wire on an 11-pound spool costs about $3.20 a pound; wire on a 1-pound spool costs about $5 a pound. Argon inert gas sells by the 100-cubic-foot unit. Prices vary regionally and by the amount you purchase, but use $50 per 100 cubic feet as a guide.

To assemble a fully functional MIG aluminum-welding outfit operating on 220-volt single-phase input power, as described above, the following components are required:

- A DC power source set for 208/230-volt single-phase 50-Hz input, with a power cord of adequate length and fitted with a male plug compatible with the electrical outlet to be used.
- A welding-wire feeder and a welding gun configured as either (1) a one-pound-spool gun fitted with a contact tip and drive rollers for .045-inch-diameter (3/64) filler wire and attached to the power source with a stretch at least 30 feet long, or (2) as a push/pull canister-type wire feeder connected to the power source with at least 20 feet of stretch and to a MIG welding gun for a push/pull system with a whip at least 15 feet long. Both the feeder and the gun should be fitted with drive rollers for .045-inch-diameter (3/64) filler wire, and the gun equipped with a contact tip for the same wire.
- A ground clamp on a lead at least 20 feet long to provide the negative ground.
- A compressed-gas bottle filled with argon, preferably at least 150 cubic feet.
- A gas regulator and flow meter with fittings compatible with those on the stretch.
- Six one-pound spools of .045-inch-diameter alloy-5356 filler wire or, if using a push/pull canister-type feeder, one 10-pound spool of filler wire.
- At least three spare contact tips for the welding gun.
- One spare welding-gun gas cup.
- If using a pistol-type welding gun, one gun-nozzle adapter kit for restricted-access welding and one spare curved contact tip.

Operator's Gear

To use MIG welding equipment, the operator must wear a full-face welding hood with a #10 or #11 lens for welding at or below 200 amps. A clean stainless steel hand wire brush is needed to remove contaminants and soot from the weld. Welding gloves and leather sleeves round out the welder's gear.

Testing the Welding System

The very best way to evaluate new equipment is to have a professional from the welding-supply house assist with the start-up of the system and the initial test welding *at your shop*. This will reduce the time to de-bug the equipment. Welding-supplier representatives are often highly qualified welders who can

FIGURE 6-5. Welding positions.

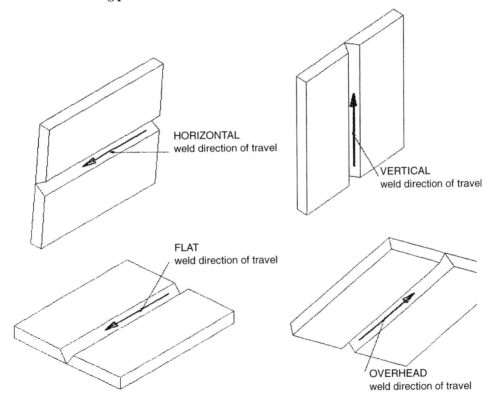

HORIZONTAL
weld direction of travel

VERTICAL
weld direction of travel

FLAT
weld direction of travel

OVERHEAD
weld direction of travel

offer sound advice for both the operation and the care of the equipment. Such a representative will provide the needed expertise to get the equipment on line and will suggest machine settings for the best results. (Recommended voltage, amperage, gas flow, and travel speed for MIG welding ⅛-inch and ³⁄₁₆-inch aluminum are also given in Table 6-1.)

If you have a friend who is an experienced aluminum welder, solicit his (or her) assistance. Keep in mind that a welder who does a professional job on his machine at his shop may be out of his element on your machine in your shop. See how your welder friend performs prior to asking him to do a critical weld for you. You may be able to do it better.

Select some small scrap pieces of aluminum, similar in thickness to what you'll be working with, and practice. Try different welding positions and various machine settings. Try both carefully cleaning the metal prior to welding and welding without cleaning the aluminum. Notice the difference between welding cold and hot metal. Look for crater cracks at the termination of your welds.

One of the single most important aspects of welding is for the person doing it to be as comfortable as practical, meaning the material to be welded should be placed in the easiest welding position. Since it's usually easiest to weld when the work to be welded is lying flat and about workbench high, try to position the work accordingly. (This is called the "flat" position in welding terms.) Make the welding-machine operator as comfortable as practical.

The welder should have full visual access to the weld area with the welding hood down, and free motion of the gun over the entire area to be welded. Make a dry run of the weld beforehand to be sure that the equipment is located in the correct position and that there aren't any restrictions to movement.

Welding Technique

Before welding, be sure you have a full-face welding hood with a proper lens, welding gloves, and long sleeves (preferably welder's leather sleeves). Check the welding hood for any light leaks and repair any you find. Be aware that exposed skin on your neck is subject to arc burn. For this reason, welders often attach a leather flap to the bottom of the welding hood. This piece of leather is usually about 6 inches square and is pop-riveted to the hood's base. Put on the hood and gloves before starting a weld.

Assemble the welding power source, feeder, power and ground leads, argon bottle, and argon regulator into a complete welding system. Plug the welding power source into a 220-volt, single-phase outlet. Prepare for welding by testing the machine settings for the welding position and the thickness of the material to be welded.

If you are using a PowCon DC inverter, set the short-arc puddle control to full hot, the range setting on high, and the LCD switch to amps. Set the weld power (amps) rheostat at about 15 for ⅛-inch material, 30 for ³⁄₁₆-inch material, and 45 for ¼-inch material.

Turn on the gas (argon) and adjust the rate of flow by turning on the power source and depressing the welding-gun trigger-switch, observing the rate of flow at the flow meter. Set the flow rate in accordance with Table 6-1.

Set the feed rate on the welding gun to fast. Connect the ground clamp to the work and try a welding pass. Turn down the rate of wire feed on the gun until you find a rate you're comfortable with.

The desired arc length is ⅛ to ⅜ inches between the work and the contact tip of the welding gun, and can be checked visually during welding. Move the tip of the welding gun either closer or farther from the work to adjust the arc length. Next, weld a sample pass, and observe the amperage draw on the LCD. (A helper is handy here, in that he or she can observe the amperage draw while the weld bead is being placed.)

Keep running test passes and adjusting the power settings by turning the weld-power rheostat until the amperage shown on the LCD is within the range of the specified amperage shown in Table 6-1. When the amperage is OK, change the switch on the LCD to volts and adjust the voltage reading by adjusting the puddle-control rheostat—again to be in the range shown in Table 6-1. Readjust amperage, voltage, gas flow, and wire feed as necessary, until the weld bead is being deposited at the desired gas flow, arc length, amperage, voltage, and rate of feed.

Listen to the sound of the welding process; it should be a consistent high-frequency buzzing with very little popping or crackling. While testing the machine settings, practice post-weld purging and reversing the direction of travel for about 1 inch at the end of a weld bead to prevent crater cracks.

Chances are that your test plate will be very hot by the time you get the machine adjusted. Try your settings on a piece of material of about the same temperature as the part you wish to weld and the same thickness. If the bead looks good, you're ready to weld.

When two plates are butt-welded, the back side of the first weld pass is usually contaminated in some manner, requiring removal of the contaminated weld from the weld zone. This contaminated metal is customarily *back-chipped* or *gouged* out with an air-driven hammer using a special chisel. On aluminum sheet ³⁄₁₆ inch and less, back-chipping is often accomplished by sawing out the contaminated metal. It can also be accomplished with a die grinder or an abrasive grinder, but any abrasive residue must be removed from the weld zone.

Because of crater cracking caused by rapid cooling and metal shrinkage, back-chipping is sometimes required at the termination of each weld bead to insure complete fusion, free from weld defects.

A simple method of back-chipping is sawing out defective metal with a Skilsaw. Retract the blade guard and lower the saw blade into the weld sufficiently deep to gouge out the defective weld deposit and expose clean metal. This procedure is so simple that for aluminum hulls, no other back-chipping technique will be required on the exterior plates. Welds in restricted areas can be back-chipped with a pneumatic chisel, a die grinder, or a small carbide-tipped circular saw blade fitted to a right-angle-drive-equipped die grinder (Figure 5-13).

Back-chipping is absolutely required at the termination of each weld pass, where the smallest weld defect can result in a leak. It isn't uncommon to put a pressure test on an aluminum tank, only to observe a leak at every start and stop of every weld pass. Aluminum will crater crack at the termination of a weld bead when the molten metal cools, then shrinks (see Figure 6-6). One method of solving this problem is to back-weld slightly at the end of a weld bead by reversing the direction of travel and welding back over the new weld bead about 1 inch before breaking the arc. This should ensure a sound, crack-free weld.

The preferred way of applying a weld is with a push motion with the tip of the gun sloped at about 10 degrees away from the direction of travel (Figure 6-7).

FIGURE 6-6. **Crater crack at the termination of a weld bead.**

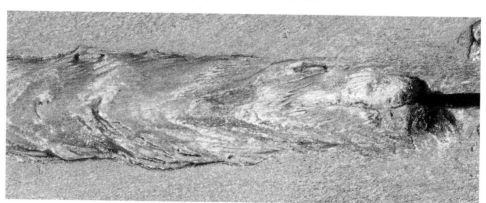

FIGURE 6-7. Pushing the weld bead.

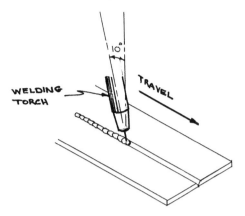

This is called pushing the weld bead. Applying the bead with a slight weaving motion will encourage good fusion and often gives a bead an excellent appearance.

When welding thin aluminum—⅛ inch or less—sometimes it's almost impossible to push the weld bead. When it's attempted on ⅛-inch material, the result is often blow-through (just what it sounds like). In these cases, especially in the vertical and horizontal welding positions, use a down-hand pass, in which the slope of the torch is the same as that shown in Figure 6-7 (about 10 degrees), but the direction of travel is reversed. In this circumstance you are actually dragging the weld bead, allowing a much faster rate of travel and, consequently, less heat build-up.

Heat build-up can cause the welded material to warp. To avoid the high heat build-up associated with a continuous weld bead and thus reduce weld-induced warpage, it's generally wise to follow a back-stepping welding sequence. Weld a bead between 6 and 12 inches long in a direction of travel away from you and terminate the bead with a 1-inch-long reverse (curl-back) in the bead to prevent crater cracking. Reposition the gun 6 to 12 inches from the start of this weld, and weld toward it (Figure 6-8). Overlap the first weld slightly (1") with the new bead. In effect, you're welding over the start of the first pass. Start a third bead 6 to 12 inches from the second one, and so on, repeating this back-step sequence until the entire seam is welded. The slightly higher weld-bead crown at the overlaps can be removed by abrasive grinding, die grinding, or sawing.

FIGURE 6-8. Back-stepping.

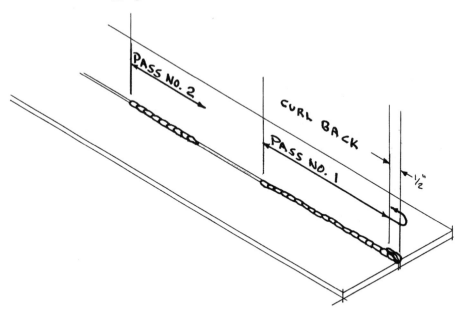

A high-crown weld bead is usually due to low heat, and flat, no-crown, or sunken weld beads are caused by too much heat. Figure 6-9 shows the difference in appearance between a cold and a hot weld bead. Weld heat can be reduced slightly by turning down the amperage.

Joint Preparation

The oxides and oils that coat all unfinished aluminum must be removed from the area to be welded and up to 1 inch each side of the weld. Do this initial cleaning of the surface with a power angle grinder fitted with a rubber backing pad and an 80-grit sanding disc or a Scotchbrite abrasive pad available from a welding supplier. Stainless steel wire brushes will rapidly remove aluminum oxide and dirt, but stainless steel brushes load up with oils from the aluminum surface and must be cleaned at regular intervals to avoid weld contamination.

The single biggest cause of weld contamination is oil on the work piece. Oils break down under the welding arc and create hydrogen bubbles that cause a very porous and weak weld. Solvent, such as acetone or alcohol, is a good

FIGURE 6-9. Weld bead appearance, left: too cold, right: too hot, below: good.

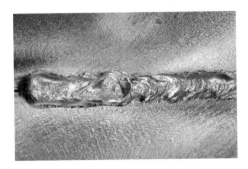 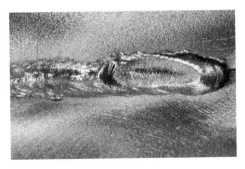

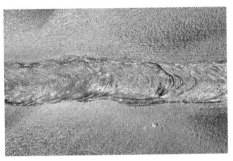

FIGURE 6-10. Butt-welding sequence.

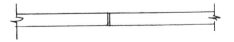

1. Fit-up for butt weld

2. First weld pass

3. Turn over & gouge back side
   of weld using "Skillsaw"

4. Second weld pass

degreaser for cleaning local areas for welding. Remove dirt and oxides by mechanical means, then wipe down the area with solvent and a clean rag just prior to welding. Dirt and other contaminants on poorly cleaned aluminum show up as dark spots in the weld.

It is rarely necessary on a small boat to bevel the edge of a plate for welding since the material is usually not more than ³⁄₁₆ inch thick. All butt welds are straight butts, without a bevel. Where full penetration is required, the material is butt-welded from one side, back-chipped to sound metal from the opposite side, then rewelded on the back-chipped side (Figure 6-10). Beveling plate edges only becomes important when the aluminum is more than ³⁄₁₆ inch thick.

When a large gap in a critical area must be filled, a stainless steel backing bar can help. The stainless bar is secured in position against the back side of the weld joint (Figure 6-11) to prevent blow-through of the weld metal. The bar is removed after the welding is completed.

An aluminum backing bar might be used, but it will fuse to the weld joint. This backing bar may be removed after welding (by sawing or grinding) or left in place as part of the joint. Do not leave aluminum backing bars at critical welds since they can foster the start of corrosion and cause high stress concentrations.

The welding procedures described above are the bare minimum requirements to effectively weld ³⁄₁₆-inch or thinner aluminum using the MIG process. Thicker material requires full-penetration welding, and the *Aluminum Welder's*

FIGURE 6-11. Stainless steel backing bar.

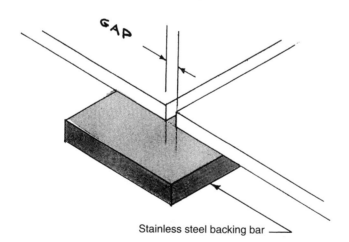

GAP

Stainless steel backing bar

Training Manual and Exercises (see reference listing at the end of this chapter) is an excellent guide to the additional requirements of full-penetration welding. More information on aluminum welding can be found in the other references listed at the end of this chapter.

Fit-up For Welding

Good fit-up is a requirement for quality welding just like it is for woodwork or pipe-fitting. The size of the gap between adjoining surfaces to be welded will greatly affect the quality of the weld. Weld joints with very little gap (1/16 inch or less) are much easier and faster to weld than joints with a large gap, and a tight fit reduces weld heat and heat-caused distortion. Neat, uniform gaps between surfaces to be welded will significantly contribute to the consistency and quality of the weld joint.

Butt-welding requires close attention to fit-up, particularly between shell plates. The adjoining surfaces must be in close alignment to ensure a fair surface. One method of ensuring close alignment is to place a flat bar on end straddling the weld seam. One corner of the bar is tack-welded—just sufficiently to hold it in place—to the *lower* of the two plates (Figure 6-12). Pressure is applied to the top of the bar to force the two plates into alignment, with the tack-weld acting as a hinge. Any slight misalignment can be detected by running your hand across the seam to be welded (Figure 6-13). After the plate edges are aligned, tack-weld them together sufficiently to hold the alignment in the immediate area of the bar/lever. Then pull the bar in the opposite direction, away from the weld seam, to break the hinge tack-weld, and remove the bar. Reposition the bar as needed to continue the fairing process, tack-welding along the butt seam until it is in 100% alignment. When all alignment and tack-welding is completed, grind off the remains of the hinge tack-welds and sand the areas to restore the surface fairness of the aluminum plate.

When more pressure is needed than a simple flat-bar-and-tack-hinge arrangement can provide, saddles or dogs, used with wedges, can be employed (Figure 6-14). Apply maximum alignment pressure by using a hydraulic jack in place of wedges. All of these procedures result in some damage to the plate surface and should be used only when necessary.

Plates to be welded must not only be the same height, they must be in the same plane (Figure 6-15). Temporary structural members called *strongbacks* can be tack-welded to the plates to hold them in alignment. Once the material is aligned, tack the seam securely, remove any saddles or other temporary alignment aids, and grind the temporary weld beads flush.

FIGURE 6-12. Using a flat bar to lever plates into alignment.

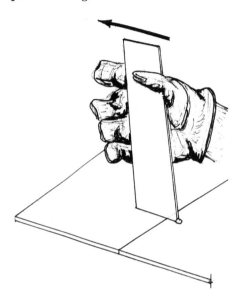

FIGURE 6-13. Checking plate alignment by feel.

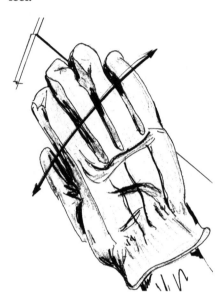

FIGURE 6-14. Saddle-and-wedge alignment

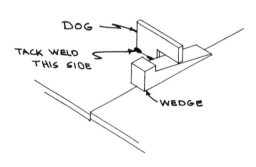

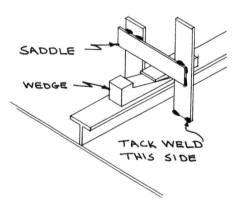

FIGURE 6-15. Aligning plates in the same plane.

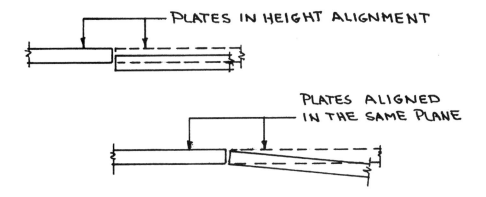

Controlling Weld-induced Distortion

Some distortion of the weldment is common to all welding processes. This is caused by stresses from weld heat and expansion being locked into the metal: the more heat build-up, the more severe the distortion. Aluminum expands approximately twice as much as steel, which can cause problems for a welder experienced primarily with steel. The welder must be aware of the rapid rate of aluminum expansion with the application of heat and not *overweld*.

Skilled welding-machine operators have learned how to control distortion by the use of various welding techniques. Other than heat control, restraint of the welded joint and following a specific weld sequence are the most effective methods of controlling distortion. Minimize warping by only lightly tacking the seams of the structure being assembled until *all* weld restraints are in place. Besides strongbacks, other weld restraints include structural members located near weld seams (or vice-versa) so they can serve dual purposes (Figure 6-16). Weld-induced distortion is also reduced by a careful fit-up—seam gaps of 1/16 inch or less—which reduces heat build-up, and by welding the seams in a sequence that tends to cause the individual distortions to cancel rather than accumulate.

To butt-weld two flat, unrestrained plates so that the welded plates remain in a flat plane requires following a procedure that minimizes the effects of weld-related distortion. This is accomplished by holding the metal in the desired position during the welding process and during the cooling period after welding.

Prepare suitable stongbacks to span the weld joint. Strongbacks can be any

FIGURE 6-16. Placing a weld seam near a structural member that will also function as a weld restraint.

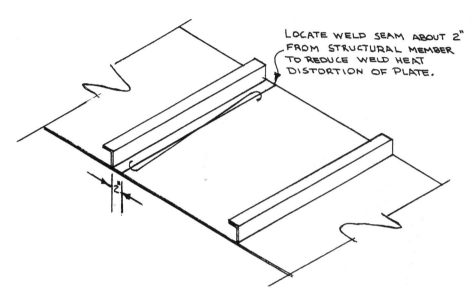

LOCATE WELD SEAM ABOUT 2"
FROM STRUCTURAL MEMBER
TO REDUCE WELD HEAT
DISTORTION OF PLATE.

2"

straight and stiff material but are usually cut from scrap aluminum. They must be straight on the edge that will butt to the plates to be welded. In addition, a notch cut-out, called a *rat hole*, is required where the strongback will cross a weld seam to allow access for the tip of the welding gun. The notch can be any shape, but it must be large enough to allow the tip of a welding gun to pass.

Clean the plate edges to be welded. Lay the two plates on a flat surface and butt them together at the edges to be welded. Place the strongbacks across the seams at about 12-inch intervals (see Figure 6-17). Be sure the plate edges are aligned and the strongbacks are firmly pressed down to ensure contact with both plate surfaces, then weld the strongbacks in place with 1-inch tack-welds. Place welds on only one side of the strongbacks to make it easier to remove them later.

After the strongbacks are in place, carefully align the plate edges between strongbacks using the techniques previously described, and place 1-inch-long tack-welds where needed to hold the alignment. Hand wire-brush these tack-welds between plates, and remove any crater cracks with a die grinder or a small saw. Weld the seam, working around the strongbacks, following the back-stepping sequence shown in Figure 6-8. (The 1-inch tack-welds are incorporated in the weld seam.)

Turn the joined plates over. Using a Skilsaw, back-chip the weld seam by sawing a kerf straddling the weld seam and sufficiently deep to remove all contaminated weld metal (Figure 6-10).

Weld the seam using the back-stepping sequence, power wire-brush it clean, and repair any defects. Power wire-brush the seam after welding to remove any soot, and inspect the weld. Repair any obvious defects, then turn the welded plate back over. Break the strongbacks loose by bending them toward their tack-welds. Grind flush any tack-weld remnants on the plate surface. Power wire brush the weld seam to clean it, inspect it, and repair any defects.

The above procedure controls weld distortion in an axis that crosses the weld seam but does not control distortion that is parallel to the seam. An additional strongback placed parallel to the weld seam and 2 to 3 inches away will provide adequate restraint to control this longitudinal distortion.

FIGURE 6-17. Temporary strongbacks.

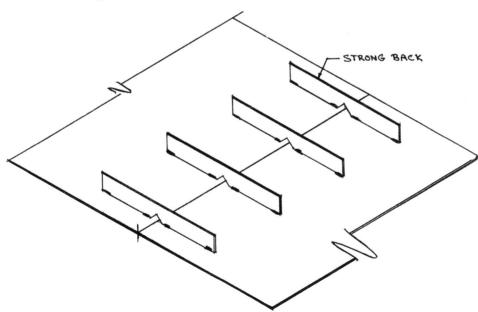

STRONG BACK

When butt-welding in place on the boat, use the boat's structural members for strongbacks where possible, adding temporary strong-backs as needed. Make your first full weld pass on the *inside* of the shell plate. Apply the outside weld after the seam is back-chipped to sound metal.

FIGURE 6-18. Permanent strongbacks.

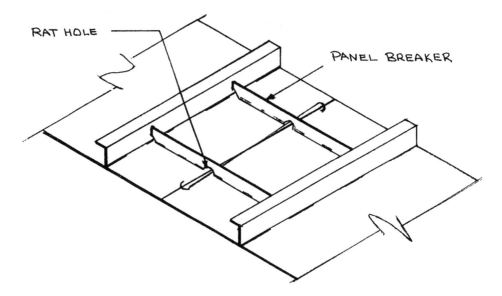

FIGURE 6-19. Direction of weld seam movement.

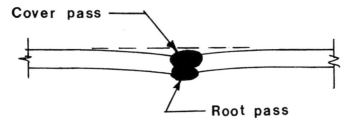

Permanent strongbacks may sometimes be incorporated to hold a structure fair (Figure 6-18). If they are later covered or otherwise out of sight, permanent strongbacks usually don't cause a problem.

It's important to note the direction the plate edges move in relation to the final weld pass. The most movement is away from the final (after back-chipping) pass, as illustrated by Figure 6-19. The hot weld metal shrinks when cooling, forcing the slight depression in the joint when viewed from the cover-pass side of the plates. This is usually the outside of the hull, and this shrinkage can be used to advantage to assist in shaping compound curve shell.

When positioning shell plates on the framework, secure the plates to the frame with *very small* tack-welds between the frame members and the plates to hold down weld-induced distortion. Do not put any plate-to-frame tack-welds within 6 inches of the chine, gunnel, or other sight edge. Too large a weld between a frame member and a plate can cause unacceptable distortion (Figure 6-20). The badly deformed plate sketched in Figure 6-21 is the result of heavily welding the plate to the structure before the abutting plate is welded in place. Alleviate this problem the same way: keep the tack-welds *small* and hold them back at least 6 inches from the plate edge.

To maintain a fair line at distinct sight edges where two plates meet, such as at the chine, a careful sequence of fit-up and tacking is required. Use longitudinal strongbacks parallel to the weld seam (about 2 to 3 inches from the joint) to both fair the seam and to hold the fair line for tack-welding. Stitch the seam on the outside using ¼-inch tack-welds at about 6-inch intervals, with the strong-

FIGURE 6-20. Excessive distortion at a plate-to-frame tack-weld caused by welding too close to the plate edge.

FIGURE 6-21. Distortion caused by tack-welding too heavily to structural members.

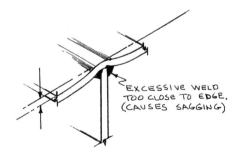

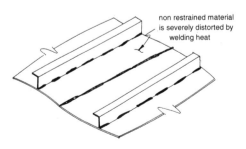

backs holding the plate edges in a fair line. This step is essential to prevent any unfairness in the sight edge, which will be very offensive to the eye. After the plates are securely tacked, complete the inside fillet weld, back-chip the outside (including removal of the original small tack-welds), and complete the weld from the outside.

When the surface finish of the aluminum must be maintained, welded-in-place strongbacks are not acceptable. The use of longitudinal strongbacks along sight edges can be minimized or eliminated by careful fairing and dressing the plate edges. Use a straightedge or a flexible batten to draw fair lines to aid in dressing the plate edges. Dress them with a power hand plane or by careful grinding. Often the dressed plate edges can be pulled together by hand. Align the plate edges by eye and tack-weld them to hold the fair line without the use of strongbacks. Alignment of the edges must be consistent, with one plate edge lapping the other a uniform distance. An example of improper alignment is shown in Figure 6-22.

The cumulative effect of weld-induced shrinkage can alter the final lines of a boat. On a sailboat, for example, the deck at the bow and stern will be slightly closer to the waterline than desired. This is caused by the large amount of weld-

FIGURE 6-22. **Alignment must be consistent.**

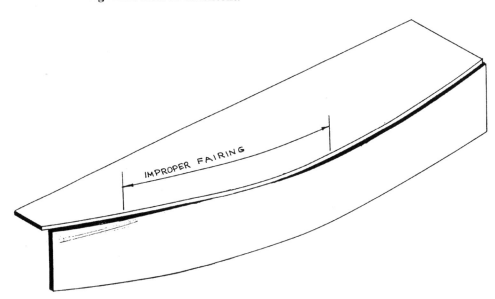

ing and the associated stresses being greatest along the longitudinal stem of the boat, which effectively arches the back of the boat. Since this arching is partially offset by the high stresses of a sailboat's rigging, it's normally disregarded.

Once weld-induced shrinkage is determined from a prototype boat, adjustments can be made on future identical boats to compensate for shrinkage. These adjustments can include changing the welding sequence, or actually changing the boat's layout dimensions slightly to allow for weld induced shrinkage.

On large ships, a shrinkage allowance, or *trim*, is included in the template to compensate for anticipated weld-induced shrinkage. This is typically 2 inches of extra material at the base and ends of large flat panels—to be trimmed off during fit up on the boat. On small boats, this trim allowance is reduced.

A rule of thumb you can use to estimate weld shrinkage is about $\frac{1}{32}$ inch per panel stiffener. A large flat panel that will have, for example, six stiffeners (Figure 6-23) will shrink in length about $\frac{6}{32}$ (or $\frac{3}{16}$) inch. It doesn't seem to matter if the welds are continuous or intermittent.

FIGURE 6-23. Shrinkage allowance for large panels.

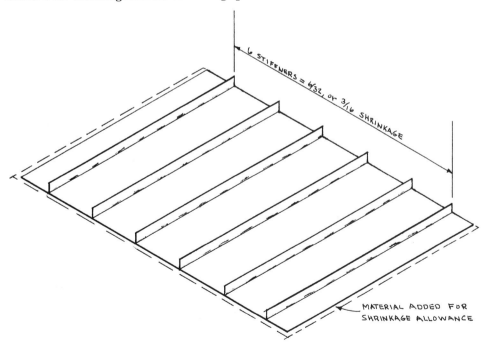

If a boat hull is not welded symmetrically—that is, a little welding on the port side matched by a little welding on the starboard side—then the hull can be out of true. When a boat starts to lose its true lines, tack-welds start breaking, and bulges and kinks develop in the internal structure. For these reasons, welding should always proceed in as symmetrical a manner as practical.

Post-Welding Clean-up

Cleaning up welds usually involves at least the removal of soot and unsightly excess metal. Welds may be ground down for a better appearance, and they're sometimes actually ground flush with the adjacent parent metal. The degree of post-welding clean-up often depends on how visible the weld will be. For example, welds on the inside of a boat that will never be seen under normal circumstances often aren't cleaned at all. At the most, they get a quick hand brushing with a stainless steel wire brush or a wash-off with a cleaning solution. Smoke on the surface of the parent metal alongside a weld is easily wiped off with a cloth.

Dirty or sooty-looking welds may require a cleaning solution, such as one of the aluminum brighteners sold in automotive stores. These chemically attack the aluminum and will change the surface texture to a uniform but somewhat duller finish than the mill-furnished bright finish. Streaking may occur if the cleaning solution runs down the surface; if this happens, applying the cleaning solution to the entire surface will result in a uniform finish. Repeated applications and rinses may be required to remove streaking. Small parts are often dipped into a cleaning solution to remove dirt and soot.

Grinding Welds

When a weld needs to be ground flush with the parent metal, the common tendency is to dig into the weld joint with the grinding disc and remove more metal than necessary. The reason for this is the slight inset of the parent metal at the joint, caused by weld distortion, as mentioned earlier (Figure 6-19). For a truly flat weld joint, this depression must be entirely filled with weld metal, then ground flush.

It's almost impossible to do a quality job of grinding with a guard installed on the angle grinder because the grinding disc needs to be nearly parallel with the work to give a good flush surface. Use a full-face protective shield and safety glasses.

FIGURE 6-24. Velcro holding pads ease frequent changes.

Grinding discs designed for aluminum all cut rapidly but leave behind a rough surface with deep scratches. The discs also wear down rapidly and require frequent replacement if there is much grinding to be done.

To finish a weld bead after grinding, use a circular sander with an 80-grit sanding disc to remove most of the deep grinder scratches, then follow this with a 120-grit disc. (The 120-grit disc will load up fairly quickly and require frequent renewal.) Another fine finishing tool is a surface-conditioning and deburring disc. Standard Abrasives combines these discs with a Velcro holder pad (Figure 6-24) to fit a 7-inch angle grinder. A similar product is manufactured by 3M under the Scotchbrite trade name.

For a large weld requiring a lot of metal removal, a Skilsaw used carefully can greatly speed the removal of the bulk of the weld bead. Place the front of the frame of the Skilsaw on the parent metal with just the tip of the blade over the weld bead. Retract the guard with your thumb, and start the saw. Hold the saw securely with the front of its frame on the parent metal and slowly lower the blade onto the weld to be removed. You can effectively plane off the excess weld bead by gently moving the saw from side to side on the weld bead.

Planing Welds

In some cases, a hand-held power plane can be used to smooth a weld bead, but only for edge welds—such as along the chine. A power plane should not be used on flat surfaces since the edges of the cutter will gouge the parent metal if the plane isn't held perfectly flat.

References

Guide for Aluminum Hull Welding. Miami, FL: American Welding Society, Inc., 1983.

Aluminum Welders's Training Manual and Exercises. Washington, DC: The Aluminum Association, 1986.

Welding Kaiser Aluminum. Oakland, CA: Kaiser Aluminum and Chemical Sales, Inc., 1978.

7

Aluminum Boat Lofting

Aluminum can be formed by bending, rolling, and other methods. Because of this, small aluminum boats can make greater use of formed parts than boats built of other materials. However, layout of parts to be formed often involves lofting techniques that are beyond the capability of most novice—and some professional—boatbuilders.

For aluminum-boat construction in the size range of 24 feet and under, certain lofting shortcuts are common to small welded-aluminum-boat builders in the Pacific Northwest. These typically include a lot of mock-up of a small boat to determine the shape of developable surfaces. It's not uncommon to find a small-boat manufacturer that first builds the boat by wrapping large aluminum sheets around some type of fixture to determine the boat's shape. Once the shape is established, templates for future boats are made from this mock-up.

A boatbuilder needs to understand the basics of lofting. Lofting goals, the terms used, and the techniques for laying down lines and fabricating templates are covered in this chapter in sufficient detail to construct a small aluminum boat. I would like to stress that time spent lofting the boat, when approached in a logical manner, will be more than offset by savings in time and improvement of quality of fit.

All fabrication projects require layout work—measuring and drawing lines on the material to ensure it is cut to the correct size and shape. Projects with straight sides and square corners can be laid out directly from the construction drawings, or blueprints, without any intermediate steps, but the long, sweeping curved lines of most boat designs are almost certain to complicate the layout process.

A construction drawing could be drawn showing a boat's layout dimensions, but such a drawing would be so cluttered with dimensions that it would be nearly unreadable. For this reason, a number of critical layout dimensions are almost always omitted from construction drawings. The actual dimensions are developed in an intermediate step of full-size layout, commonly called *lofting*.

Lofting is simply drawing the desired part full size so it can be laid out accurately. The entire boat is drawn first, then each part is drawn to fit within the parameters of the boat. Myriad small details can be incorporated into the full-size lofting, minimizing the potential for error.

Since boats are usually larger than a drawing board, plywood is laid on a floor to make a large drawing surface, called a *loft floor*. The boat is drawn full size on the plywood loft floor, and from these lines templates are constructed for cutting out the various parts.

With recent developments in a working interface between computer-assisted design (CAD) and automatic aluminum-cutting equipment, some lofting is now being done on a computer. Full-size parts are being cut from the CAD data without the need for conventional lofting.

To take advantage of CAD lofting, the boat must first be accurately drawn using a CAD system. Once this is accomplished, various aluminum suppliers can use their plasma cutting equipment to convert the drawings into parts. A few naval architects have some stock designs that have been drawn on CAD—mostly for boats designed for steel construction. If a stock design for steel meets your needs, discuss with the architect the possibility of using the CAD drawings to have parts cut for an aluminum version of the boat.

Unless a design already on CAD is selected, CAD drawing and automatic parts cutting is usually beyond the capability of the novice boatbuilder. Most small boats will be manually lofted. (If you want additional information on CAD, ask your local aluminum supplier or talk to a naval architect.)

Sovereign Yachts, 7814 8th Ave. South, Seattle, Washington 98108, operates a commercial aluminum plasma cutting center in addition to constructing custom aluminum boats. They also offer a limited selection of precut aluminum boats intended to be supplied in a kit form.

Preparing the Loft Floor

The area where you will do your lofting should be well-lighted and dry and sufficiently spacious to allow full-size lofting of the boat's lines drawing without the interference of columns or posts. The floor should be reasonably flat, so that a string pulled taut across the floor can define a straight line. Ideally a bandsaw and a table saw should be located adjacent to the loft floor for cutting the wood templates and patterns.

The loft floor can be a layer of ¼-inch AC plywood or other suitable drawing surface, tightly abutted, and well nailed down to provide a smooth surface. A coat of white latex paint is helpful for better line contrast.

The loftsman should *always* wear knee pads. It's no coincidence that the condition of very sore knees caused by kneeling on them for long periods is known as "loftsman's knees." Knee pads should be nonmarking (*not* black rubber) and soft. An ideal knee pad is a 12-inch-square pillow of soft 1-inch foam rubber secured by Velcro straps both above and below the knee. Since the profusion of lines and data the loft floor may eventually include can require weeks to develop, loft-floor etiquette also requires shoe removal prior to walking on the floor to avoid dirt and scuff marks that might obliterate markings.

When you lay down a new loft floor, allow at least 1 to 2 feet between the loft area and the wall at the baseline side of the loft floor. This provides you with a narrow walking lane and an area for the loose end of a flexible batten to carry into during fairing of long lines. Since this lane is along the baseline, it allows you to see the loft floor from the same viewpoint as the lines drawing.

The length and width of the loft floor area must be large enough to draw the full-size boat lines. Minimum length and width of the loft floor is the boat's overall length and its half-breadth, plus about 1 foot additional around the perimeter. Additional room at the stern for development of a flat pattern for the transom and sufficient height for a superstructure, radar mast, or other items high above the DWL needing layout is a plus if the area is available.

If the available area is not large enough to loft the boat you're building full size, the lofted lines may be to a smaller scale, or the longitudinal axis may be to some scale other than full size. Another technique for a large boat is to loft half the boat length, then double back and loft the other half. These techniques are for limited loft-floor space and shouldn't be used unless absolutely necessary.

Laying Down the Lines

After the loft floor is sized and the plywood nailed down and painted, the process of laying down the lines from the boat's lines drawing can begin. Start with the basic reference lines, such as waterlines and station lines. These lines are called the *grid*, and since the grid lines are permanent, lay them out in black ballpoint. There will be numerous occasions to erase lines that cross the grid as lofting progresses, but if the basic grid reference lines are drawn on the floor with a ballpoint, they should remain intact.

The first line down is the baseline. Pull a taut chalkline near the edge of the loft floor and "snap" a line. Follow up with a straightedge and a ballpoint pen to harden the line. Next, select a point on the baseline about halfway down the loft floor (not on a plywood seam) and lay out a vertical line 90 degrees to the baseline to represent a midships station. Double check the initial loft-floor layout very carefully, since all reference lines will be laid out from these two lines. Waterlines will be drawn parallel to the baseline, and station lines will be drawn parallel to the midships station line.

The spacing between station lines will be shown on the lines drawing. Calculate the cumulative measurements from the lines drawing, and starting at the midships station, work both forward and aft to lay out and draw the station lines. Identify each line with its station number at both top and bottom, using a wide-tip felt-tip marker, making the labels about 2 inches high.

Measuring up from the baseline, lay out and draw in the required waterlines parallel to the baseline. Identify each waterline with 2-inch-high figures at each end of the loft floor. This completes the basic grid.

Lofting a Drift Boat

A simple, flat-bottom, McKenzie-River-type drift boat will serve as a good example for an introduction to lofting. Figure 7-1 is a reproduction of the lines drawing for this drift boat. You've already seen this drawing back in Chapter 4 (Figure 4-5). Most boats will require considerably more detail on the loft floor than the drift boat, but the basic techniques are similar for all boats.

Laying Down the Loft Floor

The floor area needed to loft the drift boat is 4 x 16 feet, which will allow the boat's lines to be drawn full size. Level the floor as best you can, and paint it with one coat of flat white latex paint.

FIGURE 7-1. Lines drawing for a McKenzie River drift boat.

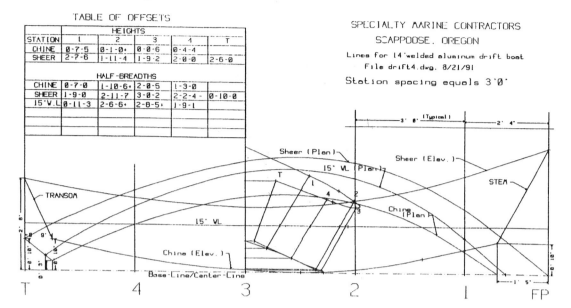

TABLE OF OFFSETS

HEIGHTS

STATION	1	2	3	4	T
CHINE	0-7-5	0-1-0+	0-0-6	0-4-4	
SHEER	2-7-6	1-11-4	1-9-2	2-0-0	2-6-0

HALF-BREADTHS

	1	2	3	4	T
CHINE	0-7-0	1-10-6+	2-0-5	1-3-0	
SHEER	1-9-0	2-11-7	3-0-2	2-2-4-	0-10-0
15"V.L	0-11-3	2-6-6+	2-8-5+	1-9-1	

SPECIALTY MARINE CONTRACTORS
SCAPPOOSE. OREGON
Lines for 14'welded aluminum drift boat
File drift4.dwg. 8/21/91
Station spacing equals 3'0"

Laying Out the Basic Grid

The first step to full-size loft any boat is, as described above, to draw the basic grid. The lines drawing for the drift boat shows the station lines 3 feet (3' 0") apart. One waterline (15" WL) located 15 inches ABL (above baseline) and one buttock line located 15 inches off CL (centerline) are shown.

Transfer these lines to the loft floor:

- Start with the baseline (labeled base-line/center-line on the lines drawing) and draw it on the floor, locating it about 6 inches in from one edge.
- Lay out station 3 near the midpoint of the loft floor; all the other vertical stations will be laid out from this line. Position this station line at least 2 inches away from any loft-floor seam.
- Draw all the shown waterlines and buttock lines onto the floor. In this case, there is only one waterline and one buttock line given.
- Draw vertical lines parallel with station 3 for all station lines. Doublecheck all layout lines for accuracy, and correct any errors; any error at this point will affect the shape of the boat.

This completes the basic grid for the drift boat.

Lofting the Profile and Plan Views

To loft the profile and plan views, use the table of offsets (TOE) found on the lines drawing (Figure 7-1). The table of offsets is actually two tables, one labeled "heights" and the other one "half-breadths." Using the offsets from the tables, locate the positions of the chine and sheer at each station. These dimensions are measured up from the baseline and marked on the loft floor. Locate and mark the terminal ends of the chine and sheerline on the profile view. Connect these points with a smooth curve.

The procedure is as follows:

- Starting at station 1, the chine height is given in the heights table (Figure 7-1) as 0-7-5, or 0 feet 7⅝ inches above the baseline (ABL). Mark this point on station line 1. Locate and mark the sheer height (2-7-6) on station 1 at 2 feet 7¾ inches ABL.
- Continue the layout for both chine and sheer until all station lines show the location of the chine and sheerline in profile. Remember that a + at the end of a dimension adds ¹⁄₁₆ inch; e.g., the 0-1-0+ station 2 offset for the chine designates 0 feet 1¹⁄₁₆ inches.
- In the profile view, draw in the points defining the bow and stern. Connect these points with a straight line.
- Use a flexible batten to connect the points defining the chine and sheer, fairing the lines into smooth continuous curves. (Fairing a line with a flexible batten is described in Appendix IV.)
- Follow a similar procedure, this time using the offsets from the half-breadths table, to draw the plan view of the chine, sheer, and waterline on the loft floor. The profile and plan view should look like Figure 7-1 when completed.

Lofting the Body Plan

The body plan is a view from the front (or rear) of the boat showing one half of the stations, all stacked one on top of the other. This is the view that's used to develop the outline of the boat's frames, and it's the last primary view drawn on the loft floor. Only half of each station is drawn because the stations are symmetrical around the centerline; all needed information can be developed from these half-breadth views, and they save both time and loft-floor space. Half-breadth templates will later be constructed over the body plan, and these will be flopped around the centerline during the layout process to lay out both sides of the part.

FIGURE 7-2. Using paper calculator tape for picking dimensions from the loft floor.

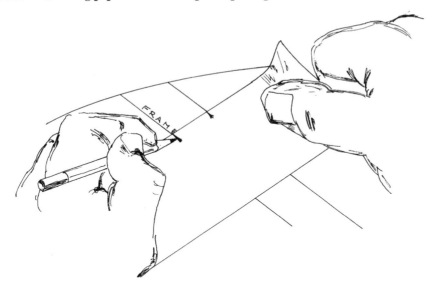

Locate the points for the half-breadth views by taking the dimensions from the loft-floor profile and plan views, and draw the body plan full size on the loft floor. The actual method of picking up the measurements can be by tape measure or, for better accuracy, using a *pickup stick*. The pickup stick is a flat, straight strip of ⅛-inch wood about 1 inch wide and of some convenient length that is squared at one end. To use the stick to pick up a chine half-breadth dimension at station 1, select the loft floor plan view, place the squared end of the stick on the centerline at station 1, and place a mark on the stick where station 1 crosses the chine line. Use the distance between the end of the stick and the mark to transfer the chine half-breadth to the body plan view by placing the squared end of the pickup stick at the centerline of the body plan view and marking the loft floor adjacent to the mark on the stick.

Calculator paper tape can be used for the same purpose, with one end carefully folded over square, and the tape rolled out and marked in a similar manner as the pickup stick, as shown in Figure 7-2.

Fairing the lines of the profile and plan views (originally laid out using the table of offsets) with a batten removed any minor high or low spots from the curved lines and corrected any minor misalignments, so the dimensions you will pick up from the faired lines on the loft-floor plan and profile views will be more accurate than those provided in the table of offsets.

FIGURE 7-3. The body plan for the McKenzie River drift boat drawn on the loft floor.

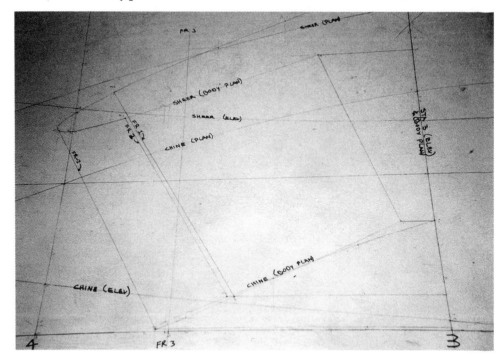

After the points representing the chine, sheer, 15-inch waterline, and 15-inch buttock line locations at each station in the body plan have been located, connect them with a smooth curve. If a continuous fair curve can be drawn through these points (fairing the sheer and chine curves in the body plan will require a selection of battens, from very stiff to very limber), the lines are fair in all three views (Figure 7-3). This checks the accuracy of the lofting.

This completes the lofting of the basic lines. You can put the lines drawings aside.

Lofting Structure

After you have the lines drawn on the loft floor, it's time to determine the actual location of each frame shown on the construction drawing (Figure 7-4), and to draw them in their proper locations on the loft floor so patterns can be constructed. *The frames are not located at stations.*

FIGURE 7-4. Construction drawing for a McKenzie River drift boat.

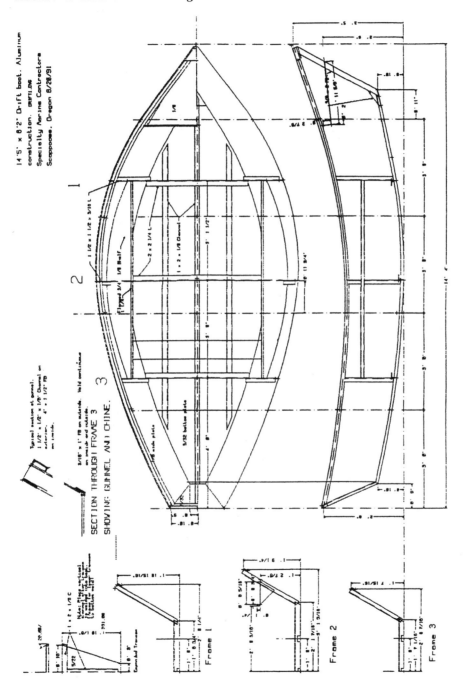

Frames

It so happens that a welded-aluminum McKenzie River drift boat has no frames, but for the purpose of illustration—to show how frames are lofted—I've incorporated frames in the construction drawing.

To locate the frames on the loft floor, first study the construction drawing to find each frame's location in reference to a station line. Draw in a single line—the *molded line*—for each frame in the profile and plan views. The molded line (Figure 7-5) is simply one side—the layout side—of the frame; the centerline of the frame (if you need it) is determined by the thickness of the material.

After the frame lines are drawn on the loft floor in the profile and plan views, the location of the chine and sheer for each frame in the body plan is determined by the intersection of the frame lines with the sheer and chine lines. Transfer these points to the body plan and draw in the half-breadth frames. The actual transfer of layout points for frames in the body plan from the plan and profile views involves drawing a light, temporary line parallel to the centerline in the body plan view at the chine half-breadth distance, then drawing another temporary line parallel to the baseline at the chine height. Where these lines cross is the actual defining point of the chine in the body plan view. The same procedure—picking dimensions and locating defining points—is used to locate the sheer. (The chine and sheer points of each frame should land on the fair lines that

FIGURE 7-5. **The molded line of a frame or bulkhead.**

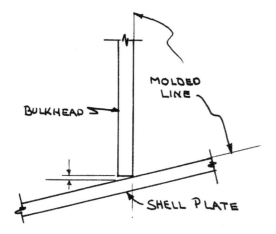

represent the chine and sheer in the body plan.) These half-breadth frames in the body plan are full size, and a construction template can now be made directly from them.

Transom

Unlike the frames, the transom isn't vertical. The slope of the transom means it isn't shown in its true size in the body plan. To draw the transom ready for template making, it's first necessary to draw it in its true size, or flat pattern.

The flat-pattern layout can be developed around the transom line in the profile view, as illustrated in Figure 7-6. The line that represents the transom in the profile view on the loft floor is the true length of the transom at the centerline. The transom half-breadth at the top and bottom can be picked directly from the plan or profile view. Lay out the lines representing the top and bottom of the transom at 90 degrees to the transom centerline. Connect the end points of these two lines to complete the transom flat pattern.

FIGURE 7-6. **Developing a flat pattern for the transom.**

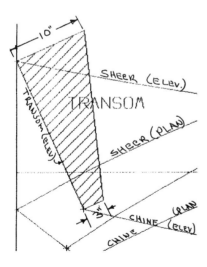

Shelf at 15-inch Waterline

The side shelf is located on the 15-inch waterline, with the outer edge of the shelf against the shell plate, and the inboard, flanged face 24 1/16 inches from centerline, as shown in the section view of Figure 7-7. The 15-inch waterline already drawn on the loft floor defines the curved outer edge of the shelf, and a line drawn 24 1/16 inches from and parallel to the centerline in the plan view will define the inboard edge. The shelf ends are located at frames 1 and 3. This defines the shelf in true size in the plan view. However, note the formed inboard edge of the shelf. To include material needed to form the edge, simply add material to the inboard face (Figure 7-8).

FIGURE 7-7. Section view.

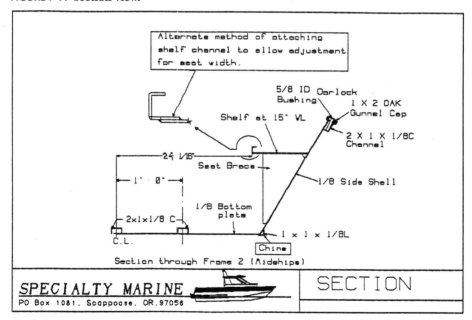

FIGURE 7-8. Shelf at the 15-inch waterline.

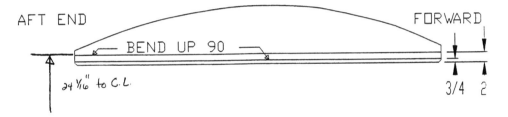

Flat Pattern Development

Other parts of the boat, including the small foredeck and the bottom and side plates, cannot be templated directly from the loft floor as presently drawn since none of these parts is shown in its true flat pattern size. Each must have an auxiliary view developed before they are shown in true size.

One of the most important aspects of lofting for a metal boat is a clear understanding of how to develop an auxiliary view required for picking off a flat pattern. Sometimes it is unclear if the view is a true-size view. A test for a true-size view of a flat object is to view the object when rotated 90 degrees to the existing view. If the object appears to be a straight line (edge on), the flat object is shown in true size. A good example of this is a station shown in the body plan view. When a station is viewed in either the profile or plan view, which is 90 degrees to the body plan, it appears as a straight line. For this reason, only objects located on a plane that is parallel with a waterline plane, buttock-line plane, or station-line plane can be picked directly from the loft floor without development of an auxiliary view.

The various methods of developing a true-size auxiliary view include the use of folding lines, rotating the member about some axis, measuring girths to assist with layout of curved surfaces, calculating true size dimensions, and triangulation. One of these, or a combination of methods, will allow development of an auxiliary view that meets the test for true size. Selection of the simplest method requires a little thought.

Folding Lines

The true-size view of the transom for the example drift boat was developed using the folding-line method. In this case, the true-size transom was laid out by placing an imaginary folding line on the centerline of the transom in the profile view. The new auxiliary view of the transom was then drawn 90 degrees to the profile view. This meets the test for true size. The formed edge for the shelf at the 15-inch waterline was also a folding-line development, in that the vertical and horizontal portions of the formed edges were folded at 90 degrees in relation to each other.

The small foredeck on the drift boat is not in any plane shown in the basic three loft-floor views; it slopes aft and down when viewed in the profile view. To develop the outline of the foredeck for a flat pattern, it is first necessary to draw it on the loft floor in all three views, then project from these views to draw an auxiliary view showing the deck in true size. Draw the foredeck in the profile view since it can be easily drawn with straight lines, using dimensions given in Figure 7-4. However, it cannot be drawn in the plan or body plan view until the slightly

FIGURE 7-9. Folding line method: locating a common point along the hull/intersection line.

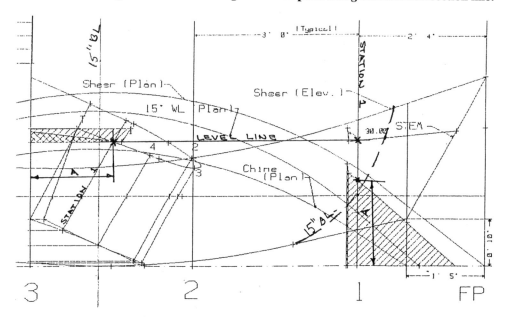

curved foredeck/hull intersection line is located. This is accomplished by locating a series of points along this line, then with the assistance of a flexible drawing batten, connecting them with a smooth curve.

Using Figure 7-9 as a guide, pick the height from the loft floor at the intersection of station 1 and the foredeck in the profile view, and transfer this height to station 1 in the body plan view. Make a small mark on station 1 to show the point. After the point is located on the body plan view, pick the half-breadth of the point (A) and transfer it to the plan view at station 1 and make a small mark. This will locate one point on the foredeck/hull intersection in both the plan and body plan views.

One point is not sufficient to draw in the foredeck/hull line. The 15-inch buttock line/deck intersection will locate another point. Additional station lines can be drawn in that cross the foredeck line at convenient locations, and points on

FIGURE 7-10. Folding line method: developing a true-size view.

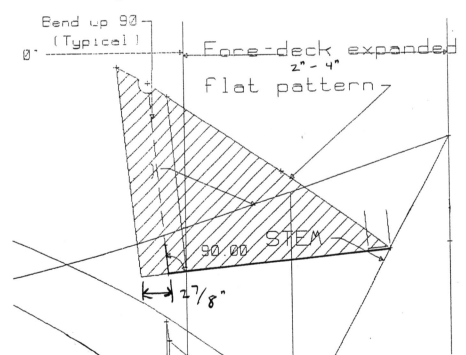

these additional stations can be used to locate additional points. When sufficient points are located, use a drawing batten to draw a smooth curve through all points that will define the foredeck/hull intersection line in both the plan and body plan views.

The foredeck has a 2⅞-inch formed lip that turns up on the aft end. To establish the extreme half breadth of the lip, draw a section cut, similar to a station slicing through the boat, with the formed lip on its surface. Draw this section as a straight line in the profile view, 90 degrees to the deck centerline. A body plan view can be projected from the profile view, then the plan view can be drawn by picking up offsets from the body plan view. This will complete the drawing of the foredeck and its lip in the three basic loft-floor views.

The foredeck is not shown in true size in any existing view. However, an auxiliary view can now be projected from existing views to show the foredeck in true size. To draw it in true size, proceed in the same manner you used to draw the true size transom. The centerline length of the foredeck is in true length in the profile view and is a convenient starting reference line. Using this reference line as a folding line, project station lines at 90 degrees to assist with development of the true-size view (Figure 7-10). Pick half-breadth dimensions for the defining points of the foredeck/hull line from the plan view, and plot the half-breadth of each station on the new true-size view. Connect the points with a smooth curve to complete development of the foredeck/hull curve in the true size view.

The lip is added to the flat pattern by drawing a line 2 ⅞ inches from and parallel to the aft edge of the foredeck. The extreme half-breadth of the lip is picked from the body plan. This lip is later bent up 90 degrees.

Rotation

A true-size view can often be developed by rotating a plane about a known axis. This involves looking at the plane edge-on so it appears as a straight line, then rotating the plane around an axis, which will appear as a single point. As an example, this technique can be used to develop the flat pattern for the seat-locker box shown in Figure 7-11. From the side view of the locker box, the box end is rotated 60 degrees until it's in the same plane as the bottom of the box, as shown in the box end view (Figure 7-11). This technique is similar to the folding line but faster in some applications.

FIGURE 7-11. Rotation method: a locker seat.

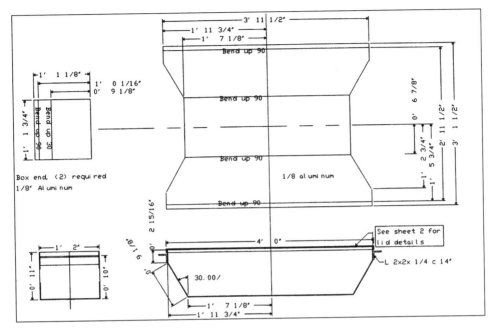

Girths

Curved surfaces can often be developed into flat patterns by measuring along the perimeter, or girthing the curve, a simple method of developing a flat pattern for a curved surface free of twist, such as the drift-boat bottom. To confirm that the bottom is free of twist, look at the body plan view and you'll see that the station lines on the boat bottom are parallel. This proves that the bottom is cylindrical, as opposed to being conical or a nondevelopable surface. As discussed in Chapter 4, a cylindrical or conical surface can be developed from a flat pattern. (Cylindrical does not necessarily mean circular, which is a special case.)

Girthing is accomplished by placing a flexible batten along a curved line, shown in its true length, and marking the batten where it crosses reference marks. When the batten is straightened out, the distances between the reference marks reflect the true distances along the girth of the arc.

Expand the drift-boat bottom plate into a flat pattern by first girthing the true-length line representing the bottom of the boat in the profile view. Place marks on the girthing batten for each location where the batten crosses a station line, and at the bow and the stern ends of the bottom. A convenient place to

FIGURE 7-12. Marking girth using a batten.

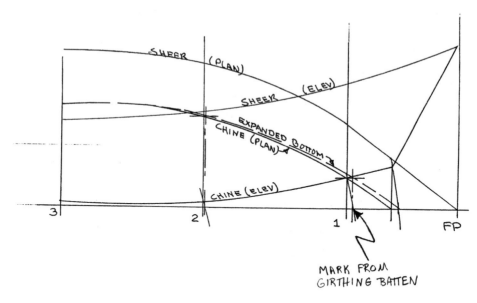

MARK FROM
GIRTHING BATTEN

lay out the flat pattern for the bottom is over the loft-floor plan view of the bottom. Place the station 3 mark on the girthing batten on station 3 on the loft floor at the boat centerline as a starting point. Mark the girths representing station locations on the loft floor from the batten (Figure 7-12), expanding the longitudinal axis of the bottom to compensate for its curvature. Draw new station lines on the loft floor representing the true-size view station lines.

Since the boat bottom is flat in the transverse axis, station lines are shown in true length in the plan view. Therefore, the half-breadth dimensions do not change at each station in the true-size view. Project half-breadths to the true-size station lines, locating reference points to draw a true-size, or *expanded*, bottom half-breadth view.

Calculation

True-size patterns can often be laid out using calculated distances. Cylinders can be developed into flat patterns by calculating the circumference. Various geometric shapes can often be developed by mathematical methods. Flat patterns for forming are often developed by calculating material stretch-out, as described in Appendix II.

Mathematical methods for calculating true lengths are often faster and more accurate than other methods. Using mathematical methods to determine distances and angles is usually combined with other methods to develop true-size views.

Triangulation

Developing true-size patterns for shell plate is often accomplished by *triangulation*. This technique can be used to develop very close approximations of a true-size developed surface that is difficult or impossible to develop by other methods. The procedure is to first break the developable surface into workable-size segments, break these segments into triangles, and then determine true lengths of each line segment that define the triangles. An arc of radius equal to the true length of a line segment is swung from a starting reference point on a straight line to intersect with the line at some point. From the original starting point and this new point, other similar arcs are drawn, and the third point is located to define a triangle where these arcs intersect. The lines representing the triangle are then lightly drawn on the loft floor through these points. By swinging arcs, with the center of each arc located at the corners of this initial defined triangle, adjoining triangles are developed and drawn using the same technique. This process is continued until the entire network of interconnecting triangles forms one large surface. The points of each triangle located on each edge of the large surface are later joined by either straight or curved lines to develop the true-size flat pattern.

When a curved surface is laid out using triangulation, there is some error. This is because the method of determining the length of curved lines, to be used as the radii for drawing arcs for triangulation, actually reflects the lengths of the chords of the arcs, not the distance around the arcs. It's obvious that in an area of extreme curvature, the difference between the chord length and arc length can be significant. To minimize error, the distance between the arc and the chord of the arc should not be more than 2.5 percent of the chord length, as illustrated in Figure 7-13. This will result in a chord length not less than 99.8 percent the length of the corresponding arc. If the divergence is greater than 2.5 percent, it can be reduced by dividing the curved line into a greater number of intervals, thereby reducing the length of each chord/arc segment.

Another method to reduce error in areas of extreme curvature is to actually measure arc lengths by girthing. However, for all practical purposes chord lengths are adequate to approximate the length of segments of a curve when expanding shell plate if intervals between segments approximate station line

FIGURE 7-13. Allowance between arc and its chord should not exceed 2.5%.

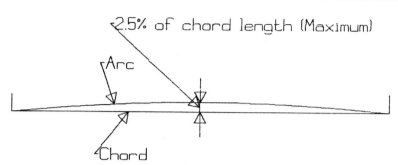

spacing. This should result in about 9 or 10 segments for a typical small-boat shell plate expansion.

The side shell plate of the drift boat is a developable surface in that it is a portion of a cylinder, as is evident by the station lines being parallel in the body plan view of the lines drawing. Another test for a developable surface is that all the station lines, if extended, will meet at a common point. This indicates that the shape is conical. Often the station lines are not parallel, nor do the station lines meet at one common point on the lines drawing, but the surface may still be developable, as explained in detail in Appendix III.

To develop side shell plate for the drift boat, first determine if the spacing between stations will be adequate to allow accurate triangulation of the side shell. On our example drift boat, station spacing was much too far apart to allow accurate side shell plate development into a flat pattern. I shortened the interval by adding an additional station between each existing station, resulting in 9 segments. Each of these segments was then divided into triangles, as shown in Figure 7-14.

Before starting the actual process of drawing arcs, true lengths of triangle sides to be used as arc radii must first be determined. A careful analysis of the loft floor will reveal which lines are shown in their true length and which aren't. It's more common than not that the true length of a line is *not* shown in any existing view on the loft floor. When a true length is not shown, it can be determined by drawing an auxiliary view of the line showing it in its true length.

The length of the station sides, as shown in the body plan view, (Figure 7-1) are in true length and can be picked directly from the loft floor for arc radii.

FIGURE 7-14. Adding stations will allow for more accurate triangulation.

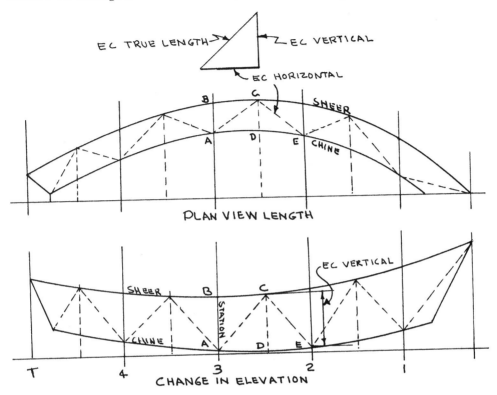

The only other side shell line shown in true length is the stem of the boat, shown in the profile view. All other line segments must be developed into their true length.

A rapid method of drawing an auxiliary view of a line in true length is by measuring the length of the line in the plan view and the change in elevation of the same line's end points in the profile view. These two distances are used as the base and altitude of a triangle, with the resulting hypotenuse of the triangle being the true length of the line (Figure 7-14). This true length is the arc radius used for triangulation.

Drawing the Drift Boat Side Shell in True Size

I selected a point about 6 inches above the baseline on station 3 in the profile view as a convenient starting point to triangulate the side shell into a true-size view, or as more commonly called in shipbuilding, the *shell plate expansion*. This starting point is labeled point A in Figure 7-15 and is the point where the side shell at the chine intersects station 3. A line superimposed over station 3 in the profile view now can be considered station 3 in the expansion view. The shell plate expansion will expand both forward and aft, up and down, from station 3 and point A.

To locate the point on the plate expansion representing the side shell at the sheer at station 3, pick the true length of station 3 between chine and sheer from the body plan, and swing an arc equal to this distance, with the center of the arc at point A, to intersect with station 3 on the loft floor expansion view. This new intersection locates the point where the sheerline intersects station 3. Label this point B, as shown in Figure 7-15.

FIGURE 7-15. Shell plate expansion.

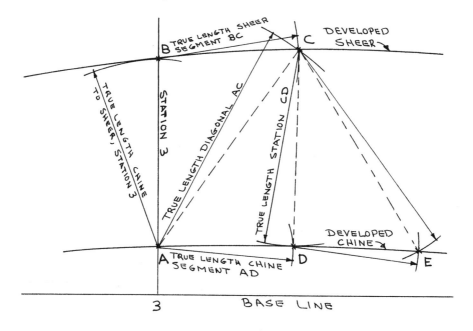

FIGURE 7-16. Side shell expanded flat pattern.

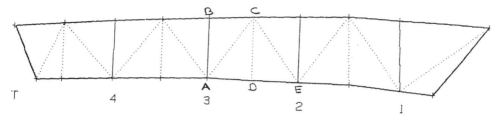

From point B, swing an arc with a radius equal to the true length of sheer segment BC. (Since the chord of the curve BC is not shown in its true length in any existing view, its true length must be developed by using the plan view length and change in elevation as the base and altitude of a triangle; the hypotenuse of the triangle will be the true length of the straight line chord BC.) From point A, draw an arc with radius equal to the true length of diagonal AC. (The true length of AC must also be determined.) These two arcs intersect at point C. From point C, draw an arc with true length radius CD, and from A, draw an arc with true length radius AD, intersecting at point D. Repeat this process, using true lengths for segments of the chine, sheer, stations, and diagonals until all points defining the perimeter of the flat pattern are located. Connect the points located by this triangulation with smooth curves for the chine and sheer, and by straight lines for the stem and transom. This will result in a pattern for the expanded shell plate that looks like Figure 7-16.

Templates

The development of flat patterns, or templates, is the end result of the lofting process. The body-plan view gives a clear exterior outline for transverse frames. As you draw additional parts of the structure on the loft floor, you can determine the location of frame cutouts for through-passing longitudinal members and the location of decks and other lofted structures. With one eye on the construction drawing of the part to be templated and the other on the loft floor, you can develop templates that will include all required data to lay out the part.

Developing templates is uncomplicated for flat parts, but parts that will be formed must take into consideration bend radii and resulting stretch-out.

Flanges

Often aluminum boat frames and other components are fabricated out of sheared or sawed plate with a flat-bar face-plate, or flange, welded to one edge to form a T or an L section. This results in a strong composite section but is subject to distortion caused by the heat of welding, and straight or uniform lines are not always simple to maintain. Forming the metal plate into an L section with a press brake in place of welding can speed up production and improve quality. The L section bent from flat plate is commonly called *flanged plate*. It's often more economical to bend a lot of material into flanged plate in some standard length at one time.

A simple flanged plate to be formed into an outside dimension of 5 inches x 2 inches using ³⁄₁₆-inch aluminum plate will not have a 5-inch and a 2-inch leg to obtain the desired dimensions because the aluminum material requires some minimum bend radius or it will fracture. In the case of ³⁄₁₆-inch aluminum in alloy 5086-H32, this bend radius is 1.5 to 2.5 thicknesses (Appendix II), or .28 inch to .47 inch, depending on the grain of the material. The grain usually runs the long dimension of the plate, with bends in this axis requiring the larger bend radius. Therefore, in this case, a .47-inch (rounded up to .5) bend radius was

FIGURE 7-17. Flanged plate layout for 5- x 2- x 3/16-inch angle (alloy 5086-H32).

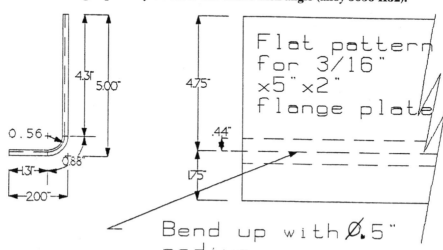

selected (Figure 7-17). Also, the neutral axis of formed aluminum plate is about ⅓ the thickness of the material, measured from the inside face, as shown in Figure 7-17.

The dimensions, as viewed in the cross-section of the flanged plate and measured along the neutral axis, are the true length, or flat-pattern dimensions, to be used for layout. (See Appendix II for laying out for press brake bends.)

The true-size flat pattern to form 5-inch x 2-inch x ³⁄₁₆-inch flanged plate out of aluminum alloy 5086-H32 is 6½ inches wide, with the centerline of the bend 1¾ inches in from one side (Figure 7-17).

Template Construction

Templates can be constructed from any available flat material, including cardboard, plywood, nailed together strips of wood, Masonite, or metal. A good all-around template material for aluminum construction is thin plywood, preferably with one A-grade face. Plywood is easily cut with a jig saw, or other hand or power tools commonly found in a home workshop.

Templates must be constructed and marked consistent with shop fabrication capabilities. This means that templates are of little use if the process required to fabricate the part with the template is beyond the capability of the shop that will build the boat. Since most individuals or small boatbuilders do not have a press brake on premises, they need to know the capability of the press brake at the shop that will do the forming for the boat. An example is the length of the brake; if the bed can only brake a piece of metal 6 feet long, it doesn't make much sense to develop a template for a piece of metal that requires a formed flange 20 feet long. If no press brake will be available for the project, templates should be modified to allow for fabricated instead of formed items.

The shape of each template and the markings on it will determine the characteristics of the part. Templates must be clearly marked with such critical information as the part identification, the quantity of finished parts required per hull, the material type and thickness, and references to the boat centerline and at least one waterline. If forming is necessary, the template will need a notation of the centerline of the bend, as well as the radius, angle, and direction; notes such as "bend up 90 degrees" or "bend down per template" are essential. On bends of larger radius than the press-brake male die, "start bend" and "end bend" references are needed, as well as the radius of bend.

A complete set of templates for a welded-aluminum McKenzie River drift boat is shown in Figure 7-18. The templates include the expanded side shell

FIGURE 7-18. A complete set of templates for a McKenzie River drift boat.

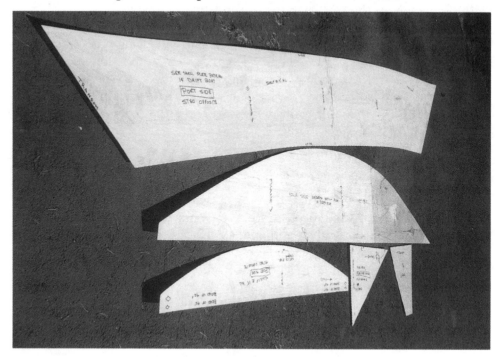

plate, the side shelf with allowance for press-brake stretch-out, and half-breadth templates for the expanded transom, the bottom plate, and the foredeck.

It's not uncommon to have a template for the outline of the entire half-breadth of a frame plus individual component templates for the parts required to assemble the frame. Figure 7-19 shows a frame half-breadth template along with templates for the individual frame parts for a 23-foot sportfishing boat.

All templates should be carefully cut out, dressed, and marked as to specifics required to complete the part. It's a good idea to bundle templates in a logical manner to maintain accountability for each template.

Picking Up Lines

A number of methods are commonly used to pick up the lines from the loft floor and transfer them to template material. To minimize the time required for this job, you are likely to use a combination of two or more of the following techniques.

FIGURE 7-19. Frame half-breadth template and corresponding component templates for the individual frame parts for a 23-foot sportfishing boat.

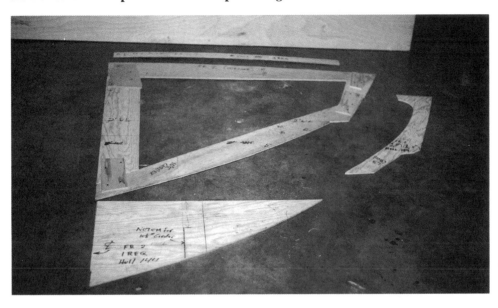

FIGURE 7-20. Carpet tacks used to pick up lines from the loft floor.

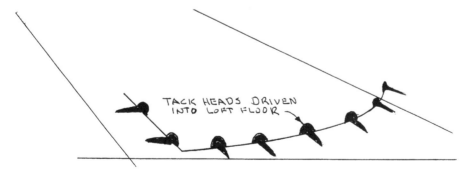

Tracing. You can trace the shape to be templated from the loft floor onto paper. Place the tracing on the template material, and make a series of punch marks on the traced lines to transfer them to the template material.

Carpet tacks. Place the heads of carpet tacks or small box nails on the lines to be picked up, and drive one edge of the tack heads into the loft floor (Figure 7-20). Put the template material on top of the imbedded tack heads, and apply sufficient pressure to impress the marks of the tack heads into the backside of the template material. Connect the marks with a drawn line.

Pick-up batten. Secure a batten in position on the loft floor by driving finish nails alongside the batten. Fabricate several batten holders and place them over the pick-up batten as shown in Figure 7-21. Drive a finish nail through the small end of each batten holder and into the loft floor to hold the holder in position. The slots in the batten holders will grasp the batten and hold it sufficiently firm to retain its shape. After all batten holders are in place, remove the nails from alongside the batten, letting the batten holders hold the batten in the required position. Lift the batten and the free end of the batten holders slightly, and slip a piece of template material under the batten. Trace the batten line onto the template material.

Straightedge. Use a straightedge to transfer straight lines to template stock by laying the straightedge along the line to be picked up. Place the template material over the straightedge so the ends of the straightedge extend from

FIGURE 7-21. **Picking up a line using a batten and holders.**

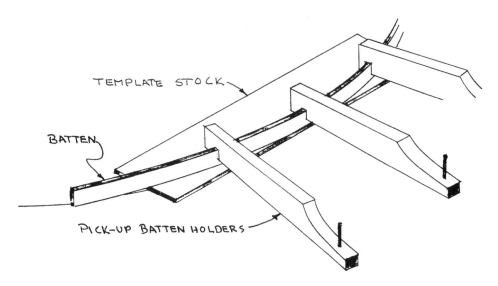

beneath the template material on both sides, and draw a straight line on the template material, aligned with the extended ends of the straightedge.

Lofting Miscellaneous Components

Lofting of a boat does not stop with the development of the basic hull framing and shell plate. Other components that must be fabricated and attached to the hull in some manner often require additional lofting in special areas. On the drift boat, additional lofting was needed to lay out the seat-locker box, and lofted lines were consulted to lay out the oarlock installation. On boats more complex than the drift boat, special lofting projects can continue during the entire construction process. Access to the loft floor is needed for layout of engine beds, cabins, propeller struts, fuel tanks, and any number of special add-on needs.

Engine Bed

To properly install the main propulsion engine and gear, the engine bed and centerline of the propeller shaft must first be laid out to suit the engine and the engine location. Factors to consider are location of the engine to best suit the vessel arrangements, shaft angle and location, engine gear angle (if any), adequate clearance of the engine from boat structure (2-inch minimum is a good rule of thumb), and access to the engine for oil change and service. To accurately locate the engine mounts at the desired location within the hull, a trip back to the loft floor is required.

Dimensions required to accurately locate the engine mounts within the boat are taken from the engine and gear drawings—furnished by the engine dealer—and located on the loft floor at the desired engine location. Draw the centerline of the shaft on the loft floor in the profile view, and also locate the engine and gear centerlines on the floor. Next draw the location of the engine mounts on the engine and gear on the loft floor. If adjustable flexible engine mounts will be used, their height must be considered when setting engine bed elevations.

Draw a level line on the body plan view representing the base of the engine flexible mount. Draw a vertical line in the body plan view representing the half-breadth distance to the center of the engine mount. The intersection of these two lines is the location of the engine mount base.

Once the base of the engine mounts is located on the loft floor, you can confirm adequate clearance, determine engine accessibility, and complete the actual design of the engine bed. For structural strength, the engine bed girder will usually have a stout top flange welded in place. In order to increase the depth of the engine girder, and for ease of access to the engine-mount bolts, the flange atop the engine girder is toed outboard. (This requires moving the engine gird-ers toward the centerline about 1 inch so the engine mount bolts can penetrate the flange.) Access, or "lightening" holes are often cut into the sides of the engine girder for access to the bottom of the engine.

Transverse structures in the way of the engine and engine bed often require modification to suit the engine installation. Any modifications are accomplished on the loft floor, then incorporated in the affected part.

Earlier, I touched on the development of shell plate into a flat pattern by triangulation. This technique can be expanded upon to include any developable surface in the boat's structure, including twisted chine bars, longitudinal frames, hull stiffeners that curve in space to remain normal to the shell plate, and other applications that previously were developed by mocking up. The techniques needed to accomplish this type of lofting can be found in reference books about drafting and sheet-metal layout.

Additional lofting information is included in several appendices at the back of this book. Appendix II, Calculating Material Stretch-out for Brake Bending, has already been mentioned. Appendix III details lofting techniques required to ensure a surface is developable from flat material. You can find lofting tech-niques needed to develop larger and more complicated boats in *Lofting* by Allan H. Vaitses (International Marine Publishing, 1980). *Ship and Aircraft Fairing and Development*, by S. S. Rabl (Cornell Maritime Press, 1941) includes meth-ods to develop shell plate and other complex boat structures.

References

Vaitses, Allan H. *Lofting*. Camden, ME: International Marine Publishing Company, 1980.

Rabl, S. S. *Ship and Aircraft Fairing and Development*. Cambridge, MD: Cornell Maritime Press, 1941.

8

Aluminum Boat Construction Sequence

Fabricating the components and assembling them into a complete boat can progress rapidly and accurately if you incorporate a little forethought. *Before* the detail lofting of the components, you must first determine how the boat will be assembled. You can then loft, template, and fabricate the boat's component parts to conform with your assembly plan. Templates should incorporate proper assembly references such as clearly defined waterlines and buttock lines. These reference lines will be transferred to the component part fabricated from the template and used later during the assembly of the structure.

As with any assembly project, an adequately rigid, level, and square assembly platform will greatly expedite building a boat. Assembly platforms, or *jigs*, vary widely, depending upon the size of the boat and the assembly sequence you'll use. Except for production boats constructed with extrusions, aluminum boats are generally assembled inverted to make positioning and welding the bottom and side plates easier. The complexity of an assembly jig is inversely related to the extent of the boat's permanent framing structure.

Small production-built planing boats using chine and keel extrusions are usu-ally assembled rightside up in a cradle-type jig. The hull bottom material is forced down into the jig where it's welded to the keel extrusion, to form a "V" bottom.

Larger boats and boats constructed without the use of extrusions at the keel and chine usually have both transverse and longitudinal framing. Since this frame structure develops the hull form, a jig isn't needed for that purpose. Such boats are called *self-jigging* designs and are usually assembled inverted, typically with minimal jigging.

Design of an Assembly Jig

An assembly jig can be as simple as a flat plate on the floor with uprights tack-welded to it at frame locations, or it can be as complicated as those found on the assembly lines in production shops. For most single-boat projects (one-off), a simple rigid framework with some provision to hold the components in position during assembly will do. The jig should also provide for the rapid and accurate alignment of the various parts to a reference waterline and to the boat's center-line. A well-thought-out jig is usually simple, and greatly speeds the boatbuilding process.

Often during the assembly stage, it becomes advantageous to move the boat in the shop. With this in mind, construct the jig in such a manner that the entire structure can be moved about on the shop floor without damage to jig or boat. Pipe rollers or a heavy dolly under a sturdy jig can be used to reposition the boat to the desired location, or even to move it outside temporarily. On larger boats, the assembly jig base can be used as a moving dolly. Construct the jig with two parallel main beams about 8 feet apart, and the jig with a boat sitting on it can be skidded to a crane for turning rightside up. The jig base spacing of 8 feet allows the jig to be skidded onto a flat-bed trailer without additional framework.

Access to the boat's interior while it's on the jig is another factor in jig design. Allow adequate height for a workman to crawl between the gunnel and the shop floor while the boat is inverted on the jig.

A waterline that will be used for a common height reference while assembling the boat is selected early on in the project. We call this the *assembly reference waterline*, and it should be selected so it will be at some convenient distance from the shop floor during assembly of the boat. If the boat is assembled inverted, this must be taken into consideration. As a general rule for larger boats, the assembly reference waterline would be about chest-high from the shop floor for easy reference. Once this waterline is determined, every component of the boat that must be located for height should show the assembly reference water-line. If the component is located in such a position that the assembly reference waterline will not fall on it, then some other waterline must be located on the part to determine its proper elevation.

Design and mark the jig so the centerline and the assembly reference water-line can be rapidly and easily located at any position on the jig.

Self-jigging Boats

Most home boatbuilders will not feel comfortable developing the flat patterns for shell plate. If the required flat patterns are not available, an aluminum boat constructed as a one-off project—such as a home-built boat—should be designed with some internal framing, which can become a rigid skeleton for the boat. With a rigid skeleton, the shell plate can be patterned directly from the boat framework. This rigid framework often is stiff enough to allow the bottom and side plates to be attached without the need for additional jigging to develop the boat's shape. This type of self-jigging design requires only that the boat framing is located and held securely in position until the shell plate is in place.

A boat framework with husky transverse and longitudinal members will likely develop adequate strength to prevent any frame twisting during the installation of shell plate. A hull with this type of longitudinal framing requires an assembly jig only rigid enough to hold the frames in position until the longitudinal members are installed (Figure 1-6). Once framing members are in place, the jig need only hold the boat in a level position for plating.

The assembly of an aluminum boat with self-jigging framing usually involves erecting prefabricated frames, a stem/keel, the transom, and any other members necessary to complete the framework. Each part is clearly marked with reference lines for the centerline and some common waterline. During assembly, these reference lines are placed in alignment to ensure the proper alignment of the framework.

Even with a self-jigging framework, some type of assembly platform is needed to hold the parts in position until they can be welded. The boat shown in Figure 1-6 was assembled over a floor area covered with ⅜-inch surplus aluminum plate. The boat's plan-view location of the frames was drawn on the aluminum plate. Vertical aluminum members, similar to posts, were stood at each frame location and tack-welded to the aluminum-plate floor. Then the boat's frames were simply clamped to the posts to start the assembly sequence.

Production Boat Fixture

A number of small professionally built welded-aluminum boats have minimal interior framing. Such boats require some type of jig to hold the bottom and side plates in position during assembly. The jig must be strong enough to hold the parts sufficiently rigid to provide accurate alignment for assembly and adequate restraint for welding.

Assembly Jig Material

The assembly jig can be constructed from any available material. If it's economically feasible, use aluminum for the jig so you can tack-weld temporary boat-to-jig braces to it.

The cost of jig material for a large boat can be significant. For boats over 30 feet, consider a rigid structural-steel I-beam base. You can bolt aluminum upright members to this rigid base to support boat framing during the hull assembly.

Fabricating Boat Frames

Each transverse frame of an aluminum boat usually consists of a number of pieces, each one templated from the loft floor with sufficient detail to fully define it. If the part is to be formed or flanged, the template should be for the flat pattern so that all the pieces can be laid out on the aluminum sheet and cut at one time. Figure 7-19 shows a typical set of frame templates consisting of a half-breadth exterior outline template and the individual parts templates needed to construct frame two of a 23-foot sportfishing boat.

You will need a layout slab to assemble frames accurately. This is nothing more than a piece of aluminum plate large enough to lay out the entire frame. A large section of the bottom shell plate is commonly used for this purpose. The working side of the slab will be marred by grinding and welding, so you'll most likely want to turn that side inward when you later install the plate on the boat.

Lay out a centerline and the reference waterline on the slab at right angles to each other. Use these to accurately position the half-breadth exterior outline template for the frame to be assembled and trace the perimeter of the template to draw the frame outline on the slab—both port and starboard sides. Place the cut-out individual parts on the outline, and align the waterlines and buttock lines drawn on the parts with the slab reference lines.

It's important to note that often the parts do not fit exactly as desired and may require a little trimming to fit both the frame outline and the reference centerline and waterlines. The cumulative effect on the parts of small inaccuracies in lofting, templating, and cutting causes these discrepancies. Correct them at this time, and ensure that the reference layout lines all line up accurately.

A production expedient for maintaining the proper exterior shape is to tack-weld small angle clips to the slab around the perimeter of the frame half-breadth template. Holding the individual frame parts in contact with the clips assures the correct exterior shape.

Once the frame parts are positioned, tack-weld them to the slab in preparation for assembly welding. After all the joints are welded, break the tack-welds loose by grinding, and turn the assembled frame over. Back-chip the welds, and weld the back side. Attach any required welded-on flanges *after* the frame is assembled. Once the frame is completed, check the reference waterlines and centerline, and correct their locations on the finished frame, if necessary. Remove any temporary alignment clips from the slab, grinding the weld beads flush, and proceed to the next frame. When all frames are fabricated, clean the slab of all welds, and return it to your stock for later use as the boat's bottom plate.

Check each notch cut into the frames for proper size prior to completing the frame assembly. Aluminum to aluminum has a very high coefficient of friction; it's not possible to force-fit aluminum flat-bar into a notch that is slightly too narrow. Check all notches and cutouts for proper fit with a sample piece of material before calling the prefabricated frames complete. This is especially important for the interlocking *egg-crate* type of transverse and longitudinal structure.

Erecting the Framework

Some small aluminum boats can be assembled by simply pulling the parts together and tack-welding them in place, as is the case with the McKenzie River drift boat shown in Figure 8-1. Two pieces of ½-inch plywood to assist in positioning the bottom and side plates are the extent of the simple jig. But as a boat's design becomes more complex, so does the assembly jig.

Most aluminum boats built in limited quantities have interior framing that is assembled prior to the placement of shell plate. The frames, keel, and other critical parts that will define the boat's hull form need to be precleaned and clearly marked with reference waterlines and centerline before they're erected—usually inverted—on the assembly jig. Use a level to mark the reference waterline on the assembly-jig uprights (the water level described in Appendix VI is an excellent tool for this application). Establish the boat's centerline on the jig and string a taut line to represent it. Align the frames with the reference waterline and the centerline, and temporarily secure them to the assembly jig.

Next, locate the stem bar, keel, transom, longitudinal members, and sometimes the chine bars on the erected framework and lightly tack-weld them in position, being careful to observe the distortion precautions detailed in Chapter 6. You may need temporary additional strongbacks and restraints to maintain alignment and a fair structure. Pay particular attention to the chine bars and stem bar, since these items are normally sight edges. Tack-welding additional flat-bar

FIGURE 8-1. **Assembling a McKenzie River drift boat.**

strongbacks the full length of the chine bars and stem bar (Figure 8-2) until after the adjoining shell plate is securely tacked into position will reduce any tendency for the chine or stem bar to be out of alignment.

After the basic boat framework has been erected, install additional items requiring careful fit-up, such as formed gunnel parts, engine-bed girders, cockpit wells, etc. These are easier to install, because of better accessibility for welding, before the shell plate is attached.

Fairing the Structure

When all boat framing has been erected, place a slender strip of thin wood at various locations along the framework, using it as a flexible batten to ensure that the boat is fair and the framing has no pronounced high spots. If any high spots are found, check the position of the offending frame member to be sure it's properly aligned with the reference waterline and centerline. Fair in any remaining

FIGURE 8-2. Temporary strongback tack-welded to the chine bar.

high spots with a batten, mark the part for metal removal, and either grind or plane it down to the desired height. Pay particular attention to the ends of longitudinals for fairness with the stem bar.

If longitudinal framing members are too low, the result will be a gap between the shell plate and the longitudinal member. You can eliminate the majority of these low areas after shell plate is positioned on the hull by using a saddle and wedge as explained in Chapter 6 (Figure 6-14). Since the positioned shell plate is very rigid, the framework will usually bend to fit the shell plate, not the other way around. If the framing member is so rigid that the shell plate is actually pulled in, then relieve the framing member by making a few temporary cuts in the member to facilitate pulling it into place. After the member is pulled into position and tack-welded in place, reweld the temporary cuts in the framing member.

During the fairing process of a hull that is being developed from flat plates, use a straightedge to make sure the framing is consistent with a developable surface. If the shell plate is developable, the orientation of the straightedge should be easy to locate by moving it about the hull surface. In the forward third of a planing hull bottom, a straightedge oriented at—as a general rule—about 45 degrees to the centerline will touch both the keel and the chine, with all framing members in contact with the straightedge. If the framing is in contact with a straightedge oriented in the correct direction, the hull should develop out of a flat sheet of material. A line drawn on the structure where the straightedge lies will be the location of a ruling; if there are local high spots on the ruling, grind them down until the straightedge touches all members along the ruling. Use a flexible batten to fair in adjacent areas.

If a straightedge cannot be oriented to lie flat on the hull surface in at least one direction, then the shell plate will not develop. Appendix III provides one method of modifying the boat's lines to conform to a developable surface.

Limber Holes and Rat Holes

It will be far easier to make all cutouts in framing members located adjacent to the shell plate before the plate goes on. Structural members in contact with the shell plate should have limber holes where entrapped moisture would tend to collect when the boat is rightside up. Rain, spray, and condensation should be able to pass through framing members to the bilge. Before the shell plate is installed, analyze the structure to determine the need for limber holes and their locations. Cut half-circles with a radius of about ½ inch in the structural member at the desired locations. Be sure insulation or other parts won't plug lim-

FIGURE 8-3. Rat holes in the framing provide weld access.

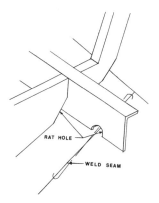

RAT HOLE

WELD SEAM

ber holes and restrict the free passage of water. You may want to enlarge limber holes located along the keel in the bilge area to provide a less-restricted flow to the bilge pump.

Rat holes are similar to limber holes but are cut into structural members in the way of shell-plate butt-weld seams. Their purpose is to allow 100 percent access to the inside of the seam to ensure proper welding (Figure 8-3). After all weld seams have been tested and repaired, rat holes may be plugged.

Fit-up of Shell Plate

The shell plate should be installed in a manner that minimizes warping of the boat framework. On larger boats, that will require more than one plate to cover the hull bottom. Install the larger, flatter portions of shell plate first; they will cause little movement of the framework while imparting considerable stiffness to the structure. Distortion of the framework is minimized if shell plate requiring more twisting while being pulled into place is installed only after the flatter sections of shell plate have been securely tacked in place.

Because the bottom plate of a chine boat is usually flat and relatively large in the after portion of the boat, it's normally installed before the side plates. Accessibility to the inside surface of the bottom (the hull is inverted) is also much easier before the side plates are installed. The curvature forward in the bottom plates of modern planing boats is gradual enough that the plate material can usually be pulled into position manually without the need to preroll the plate.

The sequence of installing shell plate on smaller boats can differ because the bottom plate often is one piece. Experience has shown that it's easier to fit the pointed forward end of the bottom plate first. If the wider portion of the bottom shell plate is clamped to the boat framework first, then the bow end is pushed down to contact the boat framework; the shell plate will assume an increasing rate of curvature as it moves forward. This normally results in the forward portion of the shell plate touching the framework only at the tip of the bow end of the plate, with a gap between the bow end and the clamped down portion. It can be difficult to force the shell plate down to meet the framing to eliminate this gap, often requiring some preformed curvature in the shell plate. On the other hand, if the pointed bow end of the shell plate is clamped to the frame first, the plate will usually wrap around the structure with considerably less gap when pushed down into position, and preforming won't be required.

To fit up the bottom plate, starting at the bow end, align the pointed end to the proper location on the framework, and either clamp it in place or weld a saddle or dog to the framework to secure the end in place using a wedge (see Figure 6-14). Don't tack-weld it yet: some side-to-side movement of the plate may still be required during fit-up. Apply gentle downward pressure—assisted by gravity—to the shell plate suspended aft of the bow, until it comes in contact with the framework. Slight side-to-side movement may be required to maintain the correct alignment with the stem bar. As fitting progresses toward the stern, clamp the plate to the framework to hold it in position. When the entire length of the bottom plate is in proper alignment, tack it securely to the framework, and remove the clamps.

Shell panels on small planing boats can often be cut from a single large piece of material, requiring no seams other than on the perimeter. This requires that the hull framing be designed and constructed to comply with the requirements of a developable surface.

Where a hull is not fully developable, the hull panels can be broken up into smaller panels, using butt-weld seams between them to complete the plating. As a rule of thumb, use the largest hull panels that are practical to minimize welding. The hulls shown in Figures 8-2 and 8-4 are not fully developable and have a number of shell-plate butt seams.

Shell plate can be cut to the approximate size by first making a template of the area to be plated. This is easily done on small boats by draping a large piece of corrugated cardboard over the structure and marking it around the panel perimeter with a pencil. (Suppliers often pad aluminum shipments with corrugated cardboard; save this material for templates.) Cut the cardboard template out with a knife. Typically you can use the same template to lay out the shell plate for both sides of the hull, but it's not uncommon for boats to be slightly out of symmetry, so fit the template carefully to the opposite side, and note any adjustments before you cut the material.

For large surfaces, construct a shell-plate template from strips of plywood placed over the framework. Mark the strips from the framework, trim them to fit, clamp them in place over the boat framing, and nail them securely together. Add diagonal braces to ensure the template retains the correct shape. When the template is complete, lay it on the floor. If it lies flat, it's a developable surface; if it has a bulge or won't lie flat, the panel isn't developable, and you should reduce its size.

After the shell plate is cut out to fit the template, clean the inside surfaces for welding to the framing, and clean around the perimeter for welding to adjacent plating. Check the boat framing for adequate limber holes and welding rat holes in the area to be plated (Figure 8-3), and if needed, cut them in before proceeding. Position the panel on the boat's precleaned framework, and temporarily secure it in place with clamps. After the piece is clamped in position, it must be worked into contact with framing and adjoining shell plate while maintaining an overall fairness (techniques to align plates are detailed in Chapter 6). Each piece of shell plate may require a different sequence of fit-up and tacking, depending upon the judgment of the boatbuilder. Special clamps, such as woodworker's furniture clamps that fit on long lengths of pipe, can be used to clamp difficult areas. Portable come-along pullers, pry bars, mallets, and plain old-fashioned muscle power are commonly employed to obtain the desired fit-up. Don't overlook the assistance of a helper to briefly hold two plates together while they are tack-welded. Remember to make the tack-welds only large enough to hold the plate in position, located so as to minimize distortion.

On larger boats, saddles can be placed on the inside surface of the shell plate straddling internal framing, and wedges used to force the shell plate into contact with the plating. Use the flat bar/lever technique shown in Figure 6-12 and the strongback techniques shown in Figure 6-15 to fair abutting plate edges together. Keep in mind that these techniques will damage the plate surface finish.

Once one shell plate has been fitted and tack-welded in place, fit adjacent plates. The gap between the adjoining plates should not exceed ⅙ inch.

Hull Weld-out

After the fit-up, start welding the shell plate on the seams inside the boat. Following a prescribed welding sequence, as outlined in Chapter 6, weld all watertight hull seams inside. After the inside hull seams are 100 percent welded, back-chip the welds from the outside, and weld the outside of the seams (Figure 6-10). Weld the shell plate to the framework only after all hull-plate butt welds are completed. This welding sequence reduces weld-heat-induced distortion.

On an aluminum hull, start the final shell plate weld-out by welding the transverse butt seam closest to midships, starting at the keel and welding outboard on both the port and starboard sides. This allows the unrestrained shell plate to be drawn toward the welded transverse seam. Next move to the transverse seam immediately forward of the one just welded, and weld it out in the same manner. Move to the transverse seam immediately aft of the midships transverse seam, and weld it out. Repeat this process until all transverse shell plate butt seams are welded.

After the transverse seams are welded, start the longitudinal seams by starting midships on the keel seam, and progress both forward and aft. This lets the bottom plate slide sideways toward the keel when the plate-edge-to-keel weld cools and shrinks. After the keel weld is complete, weld the next longitudinal seam outboard from the keel, both port and starboard, starting midships and working both ways. Next weld the bottom plate to the chine bar or to the side plate at the chine, depending on the chine design. This allows the bottom plate to pull the side plate toward the keel slightly instead of locking in high stresses. By following this sequence, weld-heat-induced stresses are not allowed to accumulate, minimizing locked-in stress.

Visualize the hull plate as a sheet that can slide over the framework to compensate for shrinkage at the weld seams and not cause the framework to buckle because of locked-in stress. It should be obvious that a lot of welding along one side of a plate will warp it. It should also be obvious that if both sides of the plate are welded in some symmetrical sequence, distortion should be considerably reduced. A weld sequence that follows this line of thought will minimize distortion.

The general rule for the welding sequence in metal-boat building is to weld the transverse seams first, followed by the longitudinal seams. Start midships and work both ways, welding a little bit on each side at a time, progressing symmetrically fore and aft, inboard to outboard.

Welding the Framework to the Shell Plate

After all the watertight hull-plate seams are welded, weld the frames and longitudinals to the shell plate. These welds will show a definite shrink mark through the hull side, but the marks can be greatly reduced by holding the welds small and skip-welding. For a watertight bulkhead that must be continuous-welded to the shell plate, put a 100 percent fillet on one side only and skip-weld the other side. A double continuous fillet weld to the shell plate will be very distinct on the outside hull surface and should only be used if absolutely required.

The weld between longitudinal members and the hull bottom can, in most cases, be intermittent. Use a welding sequence that includes reversing the direction of weld-bead travel at the end of each stitch weld, traveling back over the just-welded bead for about 1 inch to prevent crater cracks (see Chapter 6 and Figure 6-8). Continuous-weld at least one side of the forward third of the longitudinals on the bottom shell plate of a planing hull; slamming induced stress will often cause a zipper-effect weld failure on stitch welds in this area. Be sure to weld around the ends of all framing to discourage the start of weld cracks.

Turning the Boat Over

On a small boat, the hull can be carefully turned over after the shell plate is only tacked in position so the inside hull-seam welding can be done with the boat rightside up. This allows the smoke from the welding an easier escape to the atmosphere, eliminating a lot of welder discomfort. The easier access, better lighting, and flat welding position will speed weld-out. When the inside welding is complete, turn the hull over once again to complete the outside welds. Resituating the hull lets you do most of the welding in the flat position.

On larger boats that can be difficult to turn over, it's desirable to complete the bulk of the hull-bottom interior welding prior to turning the boat over, since dirt and debris will fall into the bilge area when the boat is upright and complicate the weld-out of the interior framing. This is contrary to the procedure used for small boats that can be easily turned repeatedly. Once the larger boat is turned upright, it will not be turned upside down again. This is another reason to complete the interior welding while the boat is inverted, so that the exterior welding, particularly on the bottom, can be accomplished in the flat position.

FIGURE 8-4. **Turning the hull over.**

Turning a boat over that's less than 40 feet can usually be accomplished without a crane if the task is carefully thought out. If the shop ceiling is high enough, the boat can often be rolled over inside, using automobile tires as padding between the hull and the shop floor, and overhead beams and rafters as attachment points for come-alongs and small hoists (Figure 8-4). Larger boats are usually moved outside and turned over with a mobile crane. Mobile cranes with two hooks can be rigged so the boat can be rolled over in the air without touching the ground.

Watertight Testing of Welds

A soapy-water bubble test is the most common method of checking for pin holes in watertight welds. Soapy water is brushed over the weld to be tested. An air hose (from a compressor) is used on the opposite side of the plate from the soapy water to blow directly on the weld being tested. This is called an *air-wand*

FIGURE 8-5. An assembled air wand for testing hull welds for watertightness.

test. An air wand is simply an on/off valve with a short piece of pipe of some convenient diameter and length used as the wand (Figure 8-5).

Proper use of the air wand results in a small increase in air pressure at the weld. Air bubbles will appear in the soapy solution on the opposite side of the plate from the air wand if air can pass through the welded area. Test all weld seams that are required to be watertight in this manner, and mark any detected leaks for repair. Conduct a final air-wand test after all repairs have been made.

Final Metal Work

After all watertight hull welds have been tested and repaired as necessary, the boat is ready for the additional metal work needed to complete the project.

FIGURE 8-6. Scribing-in a panel to fit.

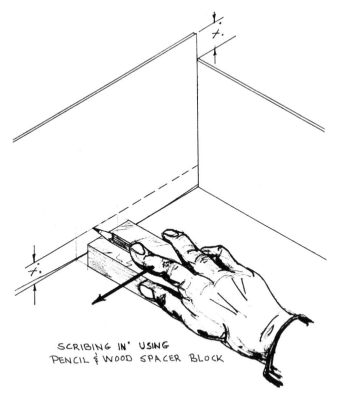

SCRIBING IN' USING
PENCIL & WOOD SPACER BLOCK

Some items that make up the boat can be more economically prefabricated independent of the hull. Since a boat hull or deck will have some distortion caused by welding, prefabricated items, such as a center operator's console or a cabin, may not fit exactly to the desired surface. This distortion is compensated for by a small amount of additional metal, called *trim*, incorporated in the prefabricated item (see Chapter 6). This additional material is cut to fit during the scribing-in of the part to the boat structure (Figure 8-6). If 1 inch of trim was added to the base of the item to be joined to the deck, then the scribe line should be 1 inch above the deck line so that when the console is trimmed in, it will be at the correct height, and there won't be any welding gaps.

To complete the boat hull, finish the gunnels and install the decks. Attach all trim, including rubrails, pad eyes, and other miscellaneous weldments. If an aluminum cabin or console is required, install it at this time.

Reference

Guide for Aluminum Hull Welding, ANSI/AWS D3.7-83. Miami, FL: American Welding Society.

Sailboats

Most aspects of sailboat and powerboat construction are identical, but in some areas, sailboats demand more skill and time. This is particularly evident in the shape of the hull. Most sailboat designs call for round bilges, so a nondevelopable shell is common—in contrast to the conically developed plating on most planing powerboats. Sailboat hulls are almost always self-jigging, with the shell plates welded over a skeleton of transverse and longitudinal members. The methods of constructing a self-jigging hull with nondevelopable shell are found in Chapters 5 through 8. The only additional tooling needed is a bending roll (Figure 5-20) to preform shell plate.

Aluminum Masts

Sailboat masts have traditionally been wood. A number of boats still have wood masts, and there are still some wood-mast builders around, but the vast majority of sailboat masts manufactured today are made of extruded aluminum. Cost and efficiency of an aluminum mast are its primary positive factors; and while a wood mast takes time and effort to maintain, an aluminum mast is almost maintenance free.

The aluminum spar has evolved from the rather large cross section and relatively thin-walled extrusions of 25 years ago to the smaller and thicker extrusions of today. The larger, thin-walled masts were slightly lighter but had more wind

FIGURE 9-1. **Typical mast cross sections. (Courtesy Forespar.)**

Section	Shape	Depth	Width	Wall	lbs./ft.	Moments of Inertia I_XX	I_YY
095	B	3.75	2.75	.085	1.35	1.92	1.15
110	C	4.75	2.75	.100	1.50	2.40	1.10
128	B	5.00	3.00	VAR.	1.70	4.80	1.90
130	D	5.00	3.50	.120	2.08	4.22	2.43
135	B	5.31	3.75	.115	2.20	7.16	3.17
150	D	6.00	4.00	.140	2.75	8.91	4.40
152	B	6.00	4.00	.130	2.80	11.50	5.60
165	A	6.52	4.10	.147	3.33	14.41	6.78
166	B	6.50	4.00	VAR.	3.30	16.00	5.70
180	B	7.15	4.50	.148	3.57	18.50	7.44
181	A	7.15	4.50	.148	3.57	18.50	7.44
185	B	7.15	4.50	.170	4.21	19.50	10.00
200	B	7.69	4.86	.180	4.54	27.40	11.45
202	B	8.00	4.25	VAR.	4.46	34.60	8.60
205	B	8.06	4.88	.180	4.76	32.20	12.00
220	B	8.55	5.40	.188	5.20	39.00	16.60
5484	A	8.55	5.40	.188	5.20	39.00	16.60
5890	A	9.00	5.80	.188	5.30	49.25	23.40
232	B	9.19	4.86	VAR.	6.19	63.70	15.60
6210	A	10.00	6.20	.188	6.15	70.54	29.75
280	B	11.00	5.88	VAR.	10.04	132.91	34.57
6911	A	11.00	6.88	.190	7.50	88.00	48.20
7512	A	12.00	7.50	.200	9.10	132.61	60.20
061	E	2.25	.61	.070	.38	.13	.01
081	E	3.25	.88	.100	.79	.54	.06
121	E	4.75	1.25	.130	1.50	2.18	.24
171	E	6.75	1.80	.130	2.19	6.51	.77

resistance, and the thin walls presented some difficulties when drilling and tapping for threaded fasteners. The smaller and thicker modern mast section offers less wind resistance and more readily holds a tapped-in threaded fastener. Welding is also easier on the thicker mast.

Various mast manufacturers have aluminum extrusion dies designed for their products. Typical mast cross sections are shown in Figure 9-1. Mast sections can be round, oval, or some special shape, and generally include a slot for the luff of the sail. The aluminum alloy used is usually 6061-T6 or -T651. The T6 temper gives the alloy its high strength; any temper lower than T6 will not be as strong (see Chapter 3). Welding on the spar is limited in scope and location to protect the T6 temper.

Aluminum masts may also be constructed of preformed and butt-welded sheets (composite construction), but this is typically limited to masts too large to practically fabricate with a standard extrusion, or to masts with long tapering sections.

Mast Loads

Masts are subject to high compressive loads and, as with any long, slender column, failure from buckling can occur. Intermediate spreaders and shrouds (guy wires) reduce the tendency of a mast to buckle. The spreader locations are support points that resist buckling. Masts are most subject to failure by buckling in the center of the span between support points, with the longest span between support points normally being between the main deck and the spreaders. Consequently, this is the critical section where a mast might buckle. If you construct a mast from two or more lengths, locate the splice at other than this critical section to reduce the possibility of the joint, stiffened by the use of a sleeve, contributing to a load failure.

Mast Modifications

A mast extrusion may require cutting, welding, drilling, fastening, and other fabrication operations before it's ready for installation aboard the boat. Modifications to the basic extrusion can be fairly simple or quite extensive, depending on the size and complexity of the boat.

Splicing

Mast extrusions can be manufactured to any length by special order, but as a practical matter, the upper limit is usually about 40 feet—the longest extrusion that can be economically handled and shipped. Any mast over 40 feet long usually requires a splice.

Splicing is usually accomplished by welding, but because of the annealing effect of weld heat, 6061-T6 looses considerable strength in the weld zone. To minimize the loss of mast strength, fit an internal sleeve inside the mast centered on the weld seam (Figure 9-2). The length of a splice sleeve should be not less than eight times the maximum mast width. In a pattern similar to that shown in Figure 9-2, drill the ends of the mast that are to be over the sleeve with holes about 1 inch in diameter to be used for plug welding. Slide the sleeve inside the

FIGURE 9-2. Using a sleeve at a mast splice.

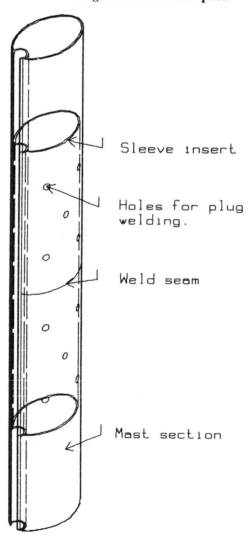

Sleeve insert

Holes for plug welding.

Weld seam

Mast section

mast sections and butt-weld the stub ends of the mast together. Plug weld the mast to the sleeve through the drilled holes.

The ends of the sleeve inside a spliced mast can create potential stress points and should be scalloped or tapered for a mast that will be subject to bending or used for racing.

FIGURE 9-3. **Straight mast taper.**

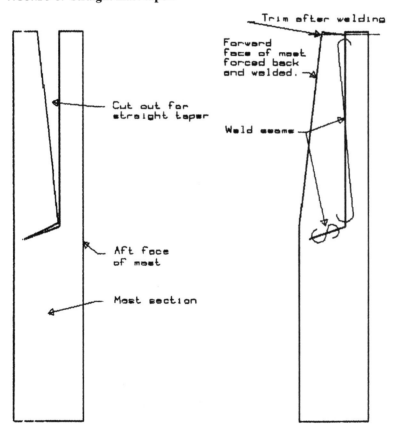

Taper

Tapering a mast at the top is aesthetically pleasing and improves efficiency by reducing weight aloft and decreasing windage. Masts are always tapered on the forward side to leave the straight sail track on the aft side unaffected. A common practice is to taper the upper 20 percent of the mast.

Tapering can be either *straight* or *cambered*. For a straight taper, remove a slender triangle from each side of the mast and force the forward face of the mast back to abut the aft edges of the cutout. Butt-weld the abutting edges of the

FIGURE 9-4. **Cambered mast taper.**

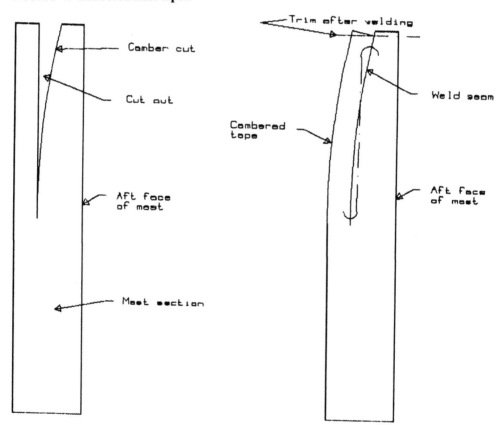

FIGURE 9-5. **Cutout for spreader compression member. Note hole for tang through-bolt.**

FIGURE 9-6. **Cutout for internal halyard exit.**

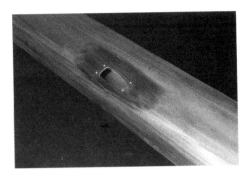

cutouts together. For the taper to begin properly, a small triangular section may have to be removed from each side of the mast to allow the forward portion to *hinge* back, as illustrated in Figure 9-3.

A cambered taper also requires removing pie-shaped sections from the mast, but in this case give the aft leg of the cutout a gentle camber (Figure 9-4). This technique eliminates the need for the additional triangular cutout required for a straight taper; when you force the forward side of the mast back for welding, it will take a gentle camber.

Other more-complex tapers are used on racing-boat masts, depending upon the boat design criteria.

Mast Cutouts

All holes, slots, and cutouts in a mast must be made properly, or they can be the start of a crack. There must be no sharp corners; the corners of all cutouts for spreaders, sheaves, shrouds, etc. must have a smooth radius. Gently radius all sharp edges as well by sanding or other means. Figure 9-5 shows a cutout for a spreader compression member and a hole for a tang through-bolt. The cutout in Figure 9-6 is for an internal halyard exit. Note the buffing marks on the mast. The buffing not only removes all sharp corners but it also removes dirt and oxides in areas that may later require welding.

Mast Attachments

Items such as spreaders, masthead fittings, winch bases, and tangs must be attached to a mast to make it functional. Attachments to an aluminum mast can be made by welding, through-bolting, drilling and tapping for threaded inserts, or by riveting.

Spreaders

Mast spreaders are commonly an airfoil-shaped aluminum extrusion. Spreader extrusions are available in a number of sizes, usually in alloy 6061-T6. The method of attaching spreaders must be well thought out. Welding to the mast itself must be held to an absolute minimum to avoid annealing the metal with weld heat. Make any weakening cutouts or attachment holes in areas subject to the least stress—usually along the sides (port and starboard) of the mast.

Rigging tension puts high compression loads on the mast section at the spreaders, and the working of the mast results in minor movement between it and the spreaders. It's a common practice to insert a stout piece of aluminum through the sides of the mast at the spreaders to relieve the compression load and to reinforce the spreader-to-mast joint. Special extrusions available for this use (Figure 9-7) are inserted through carefully cut slots in the mast (Figure 9-5) and lightly tack-welded in place. The spreader extrusions slip over the compression member and are through-bolted to it to attach the spreaders to the mast (Figure 9-8).

FIGURE 9-7. **Special extrusion for spreader attachment.**

FIGURE 9-8. **Spreaders attached over internal compression member.**

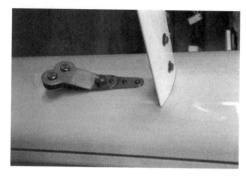

FIGURE 9-9. Spreader attachment using traditional pad and clevis.

FIGURE 9-10. Conventional spreader-mast end fitting.

While the above method of spreader attachment is clean and strong, it is also difficult to repair without access to an experienced sparmaker. If you anticipate extended bluewater cruising, consider the more traditional method of spreader attachment shown in Figure 9-9. Fasten the attachment fitting to the mast at the spreader location by drilling and tapping into the mast section.

On masts with thin walls, often found on older boats with aluminum masts, it is wise to through-bolt the spreaders to the mast attachments and utilize compression tubes to prevent crushing the mast section.

The rigid attachment fitting distributes the spreader loads over a larger area of the mast. A rectangular-shaped piece fits into the inboard end of the spreader extrusion (Figure 9-10) and is bolted into the mast attachment (Figure 9-9), attaching the spreader to the mast.

At the outboard end of the spreader, insert a piece of solid aluminum—slotted to receive the shrouds—and weld it to the extrusion (Figure 9-11). Small holes drilled through the insert block allow the shrouds to be lashed to the ends of the spreaders with a number of wraps of seizing wire pulled tight with pliers.

When designing any through-mast spreader member, keep in mind that normally electrical wiring (and often halyards) are routed inside the mast. Not only is a wire route necessary, but moving wire-rope internal halyards can cause extensive wear to an internal aluminum member. One method of minimizing damage to this member is to place a wear strip on it. Look carefully at the member shown in figure 9-7. It is designed for a small stainless steel wear bar to fit into the fore and aft edge of the member to act as a chafing strip.

FIGURE 9-11. Outboard end of speader.

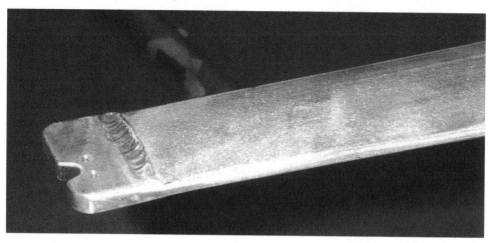

Tangs

Mast tangs are usually through-bolted. A typical tang installation is shown in Figure 9-12. In order to adequately tighten the tang attachment bolt and not collapse the mast section, insert a pipe sleeve through the mast—a ½-inch ID by ⅝-inch OD tube for a typical ½-inch attachment bolt—to act as a compression member for the through-bolt. Drill a ⅝-inch diameter hole through both sides of the mast (Figure 9-5) and fit the sleeve into the mast flush with the outside faces. When you bolt the tang in place, the bolt will tighten against the sleeve instead of crushing the mast section. An additional benefit is that the sleeve provides a slightly larger bearing area to support the tang. Screws may be added to prevent the tang from rotating and to increase the joint strength; screw them into drilled and tapped holes in the mast.

Mast Internal Wiring

Internal wiring should be secured to the mast to prevent the wiring from moving around and chafing on the internal surfaces and halyards. Accomplish this by enclosing the internal wiring in a piece of plastic (PVC) pipe conduit rivetted at about 3-foot intervals to the inside surface of the mast (Figure 9-13).

Electrical wiring should be marine quality, such as *Ancor Marine Grade* wire and cable. The conductor should be tinned type 3 with heavy and durable insu-

FIGURE 9-12. Typical aluminum mast tang installation.

FIGURE 9-13. PVC conduit for internal wiring.

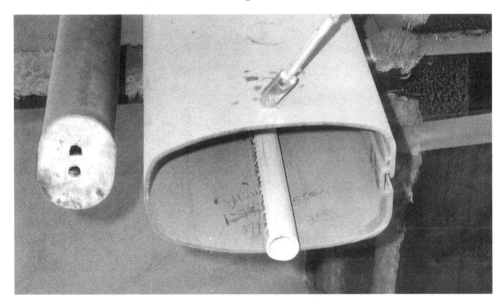

lation. Entry and egress points for the wire should have soft grommets to prevent chaffing of the insulation. Wires should exit keel-stepped masts just below the main deck level; wiring that exits in the low portion of the mast is more subject to damage from chafing, dampness, or sea water.

FIGURE 9-14. Welded aluminum masthead fitting.

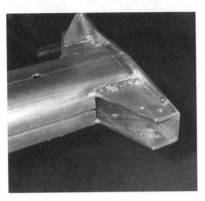

FIGURE 9-15. Aluminum masthead fitting showing sheave.

FIGURE 9-16. Mast-mounted winch base.

FIGURE 9-17. Mast light installation.

Masthead Fitting

Most masthead fittings are fabricated of aluminum and welded to the top of the mast. Notch the masthead fitting into the mast rather than butt-welding it to the top only (Figures 9-14 and 9-15).

Mast Attachments

Weld flat plates to the mast to provide winch bases (Figure 9-16). Pop-rivet small items like mast lights (a popular alternative to spreader lights—see Figure

9-17), or attach them with screws into drilled and tapped holes. Use only stainless steel or aluminum fasteners in the mast, and coat threaded fasteners with a *never seize* compound. For threaded fasteners you expect to repeatedly remove and replace, use stainless steel Heli-Coil inserts—available at automotive suppliers.

Special Applications

Welding modifications to a mast can result in weld-heat-induced distortion. Distortion is controlled by a careful welding sequence and, in some cases, by the use of special stress-relieving techniques. The large mast used on the *Aoranji II* (Figure 9-18) was constructed using an aluminum extrusion and provided with a slight taper over the upper portion. A stress-relieving system involving induced vibration was employed during the welding of the taper, resulting in very little weld-heat distortion.

The main boom for the *Aoranji II* was constructed in two halves from alloy 5086-H32 and then butt-welded longitudinally. Careful adherence to a predetermined welding sequence resulted in a straight boom, free from any objectionable weld distortion.

FIGURE 9-18. *Aoranji II's* **mast and boom.**

Mast Peripherals

A number of additional related items are needed to both support the mast and to complete the rig of a sailboat. Many of these can be fabricated out of aluminum, either as an integral part of the boat or as a separate, independent piece. Because of the inherent strength of an aluminum deck, hardware can often be bolted directly to it without additional under-deck reinforcement. When a special equipment foundation, such as a winch base, is required, it can be fabricated and welded in place with a minimum of deck reinforcement.

Mast Step

Masts may be stepped on deck or on the keel. A deck-stepped mast needs a compression member from the deck step to the keel to transmit compressive forces to the keel. Trim the butt end of the mast square, and construct the mast step compatible with a square mast butt.

If the mast is stepped on the keel, the step can be constructed with a collar on the outside of the mast, i.e., so that the mast slips into the mast step. Deck-stepped masts usually fit over a male step extension, providing a clean and protuberance-free joint. This requires drilling and countersinking the mast and drilling and tapping the step for the flathead screws that will fasten the mast to the step. Whatever the design of the step, it should provide for proper venting and drainage of the mast.

For masts that pass through the weather deck, a boot is required to maintain watertight integrity. The neoprene rubber boot (a section of inner tube can make an excellent mast boot) should be protected from sunlight by a canvas cover, which also presents a neat and finished appearance.

Chainplates

Rigging on a welded-aluminum hull is normally attached to fabricated chainplates approximately abeam the mast (for the shrouds), an extension of the stem bar at the bow for the forestay, and an extension of a stout centerline stiffener at the stern for the aft stay. Construct chainplates of aluminum alloy 5086 and weld them to the boat's framework. Tremendous forces are transmitted through the chainplates and stay fittings, requiring material that is considerably thicker than the shell plating. The holes through aluminum chainplates are subject to egging out, so it is advisable to swage in stainless steel hole bushings.

The strength of welded chainplates is demonstrated by the common practice of lifting the entire boat by using the chainplates as the pick points (Figure 9-19).

FIGURE 9-19. Using welded aluminum chainplates as pick points to lift a boat.

Toerail

A slotted deck-edge rail is often used for securing rigging. Such rails can simply be flat bar that is drilled or punched and then welded in place (see Figures 9-19 and 9-20). This also makes a good toerail, a sturdy attachment point for stanchion sockets and a natural outside edge of a deck-edge gutter.

Winch Foundations

A short length of pipe slightly larger in diameter than the winch base makes one of the simplest and most professional-looking winch foundations, but since large-diameter aluminum pipe is quite expensive, circular winch bases are usually rolled out of plate. Cap the base with a circle of aluminum plate of adequate thickness to hold the mounting bolts for the winch. Scribe the circular winch base to fit the contour of the deck and to obtain the desired orientation of the winch in relation to the deck. When the winch base fits, but prior to welding it in place, cut a large hand-access hole through the side of the base, then weld the base into position on the boat (Figure 9-20).

FIGURE 9-20. **Aluminum winch base.**

Miscellaneous Sailboat Deck Items

Boom traveler supports, boom crutches, dorade boxes, foundations for deck hardware, and other miscellaneous items can be rapidly constructed from aluminum and welded to an aluminum deck. Such items can look very professional and are relatively easy to construct.

Ballast Keel

The ballast keel of a welded-aluminum sailboat is often constructed hollow with ballast carried internally, as discussed in Chapter 4. If the ballast keel is fabricated of aluminum separate from the hull, installing the ballast is greatly simplified. If it isn't practical to have a separate keel section, consider leaving a small section of the boat's shell plate off until the ballast is placed: it's much easier to place ballast through a hole in the shell than to carry it down through a hatch. After the ballast is placed and sealed, weld the omitted plate in place over the opening.

Internal ballast is placed into a hollow keel in predetermined amounts and locations. The location is commonly by compartment, which is the space between framing members. The location of the ballast and the amount to be placed in each compartment is usually determined by the naval architect. The ballast is carefully weighed and recorded as to location as it is placed in the boat. Ballast can be lead, iron, or any other heavy material, and it can be either solid or, as with molten lead, poured into the keel.

Internal Ballast Materials

Lead is the most desirable ballast material because of its high weight—708 pounds per cubic foot. The melting point of lead—621 degrees Fahrenheit—is well below marine aluminum (1,200 degrees), allowing molten lead ballast to be poured into a hollow aluminum keel. Lead ballast is the highest-density ballast that is economically practical. To discourage the use of exotic ballast materials that can be prohibitive in cost, the International Offshore Rule for racing sailboats does not allow ballast with a higher specific gravity than pure lead.

Interestingly, since 100 percent pure lead is very hard to find, some avid racing sailors would determine the difference between pure lead and the actual specific gravity of their particular lead ballast, and make up the difference by inserting a small amount of tungsten (which weighs 1,205 pounds per cubic foot) or exotic and even heavier by-products of nuclear reaction.

Older cruising boats have commonly been fitted with cast iron or steel ballast (491 pounds per cubic foot) bolted to the exterior of the keel. Some cruising boats use internal steel ballast—steel punchings, small pieces of scrap steel or iron, or small cast pigs placed cold inside the keel cavity.

Concrete does not make a good ballast when compared with other available materials. The weight of concrete is only 144 pounds per cubic foot, as compared to aluminum, which is 169 pounds per cubic foot. However, concrete can be used if sufficient volume within the keel area is available. Melted down zinc anodes are a poor choice, in that zinc, at 446 pounds per cubic foot, weighs less than steel.

Lead Ballast

Lead can be purchased from salvage metal dealers. Be advised that salvage lead can contain a high percentage of other elements, which in most cases will result in an alloy with a specific gravity less than pure lead. Because of the high cost of *pure* lead, most boatbuilders use salvage lead for ballast. Take some specific gravity tests during the pouring of the lead to satisfy yourself that the lead is nearly 708 pounds per cubic foot.

For a fee, a lab can test your lead to determine its specific gravity, or you can do it yourself if you have access to a chemist's balance-beam scales and some

FIGURE 9-21. **Apparatus to determine specific gravity of a lead sample.**

weights calibrated in grams. The process is to first weigh a lead sample suspended in the air by a thin thread. Next, weigh the suspended lead sample submerged in a beaker of water, as shown in Figure 9-21. The difference in the two weights equals the amount of water displaced and is the volume of the lead sample in cubic centimeters—since one cubic centimeter of water weighs one gram. Divide the lead sample weight (in grams) by the volume (in cubic centimeters) to obtain the specific gravity of the sample. The specific gravity of pure lead is 11.3423 grams per cubic centimeter.

Molten Lead

Lead can be poured directly into a hollow aluminum keel, it can be packed in cold, or a combination of molten lead and cold pieces can be used. When you work with molten lead, safety precautions are absolutely essential. Lead emits toxic fumes in the molten state that can cause lead poisoning if inhaled. Special respirators are available for filtering out the lead particles—*ordinary paint respirators will not suffice*.

Lead in the molten state can also cause severe burns. Protect the molten lead from all water or liquid: water splashed into molten lead will cause an explosion that will throw the molten lead into the adjacent area. Never work with molten lead without safety goggles, a full face shield, heat resistant gloves, and full length coveralls or work clothing—no exposed skin. Contact your local safety supply outlet for the appropriate respirator and other protective gear.

Working with molten lead is very hot work. Be careful of overheating, and be sure you have good ventilation and plenty of fresh air.

Cutting Lead

If large cast *sows* of lead are obtained from the salvage dealer, they must be reduced in size to fit into a melt-down pot, but cutting lead can be very frustrating. It clogs up saws, and it won't burn like steel. The simplest method of cutting it is to use a rosebud type of oxyacetylene torch and melt off chunks. Some boatyards use chain saws.

Melting Pot

A steel chamber about 2 feet in diameter and 3 feet high mounted on legs so the bottom of the pot is about 30 inches above the shop floor makes an excellent melting pot. A trip to a salvage yard will usually locate a suitable container that can be modified with a steel-cutting torch to do the job. If the

pot has fairly thick walls, ¼-inch or heavier, it will better retain heat and sim-
plify the job of melting lead. (A standard 55-gallon steel drum is too light.)

Install a valve in the bottom of the pot for tapping off the molten lead—an
ordinary household faucet can be used for this even though the packing will burn
out. Since most impurities will rise to the top, the molten lead drawn from the
valve should be relatively pure.

Use a large rosebud torch, fueled by either oxygen-acetylene or propane, to
play the heat directly on a small amount of lead in the melting pot until the lead
melts. Continue to hold the torch flame in contact with the lead in the pot and
add additional solid lead to the molten lead until the pot is about half full of
molten lead. To maintain the lead in a molten state, keep the flame in near proximity to the molten lead, either holding the torch or carefully placing it on top
of the pot.

Pouring Bucket

You will need a pouring bucket strong enough to handle molten lead. It
should be constructed of ¼-inch or heavier steel to retain heat. Fit it with a pouring lip and a handle to tilt it for pouring. The lifting bail should be similar to a pail
handle, allowing the bucket to be held up and dumped at the same time. A pouring bucket about 18 inches in diameter and 18 inches high will contain 1,300
pounds of lead when 70-percent full! Use an overhead hoist attached to the lifting bail to move the bucket to the pouring area. A sketch of a lead-pouring
bucket is shown in Figure 9-22.

Pouring Molten Lead

When sufficient molten lead is in the melting pot, open the pot valve and
fill the pouring bucket to the desired level. Weigh the bucket and molten lead.
Move the pouring bucket over the keel cavity and dump the lead into the keel.
Now weigh the empty bucket to determine the net weight of the lead you just
poured into the keel. Repeat this process until you have poured in the required
amount of ballast.

It is not important that the layers of lead solidify between pours (effectively
forming a cold seam). It's more important not to overheat the keel aluminum,
so numerous small pours are better than a few large pours.

Molten lead solidifies quickly once it's poured into the keel, so it's a bad idea
to place a large amount of solid, cold lead into the keel cavity and pour molten
lead over it to fill the voids. The rapid solidification of the lead may result in air
gaps between solids. On the other hand, careful placement of some solid lead to

FIGURE 9-22. Lead-pouring bucket.

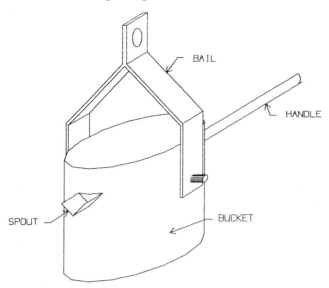

ensure that no voids will be formed when the molten lead is poured is a satis-factory method of filling the cavity and reduces the amount of melting required.

Preparing the Keel for Molten Lead

Hot, molten lead will cause the aluminum keel to expand rapidly. Exterior strongbacks welded to the keel and located not more than 6 inches apart are required to hold the keel sides in the desired position until the lead cools. When the lead has cooled, remove the strongbacks, and grind and sand all welds flush.

Sealing the Lead

If water enters the keel in proximity to the lead, it will provide the electrolyte to foster corrosion between the lead and the aluminum keel. To prevent this from happening, prior to placing the lead ballast, seal the keel cavities that will contain ballast with temporary aluminum plates and air-test the structure to about 3 psi. Repair any leaks that are found. Remove the temporary cover plates for pouring the lead. Be sure to leave adequate room between the lead and the cover plate to allow the plate to be rewelded—lead that melts and flows into the area of the seal

FIGURE 9-23. Mold for casting triangular lead ingots, made from aluminum angle.

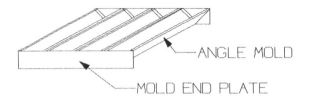

ANGLE MOLD FOR POURING
TRIANGULAR LEAD INGOTS

weld will contaminate the weld area and make seal-welding impossible. After the lead is poured, weld the cover plates in place and air-test the seams, repairing them if necessary.

Solid Ballast

Lead or steel ballast can be placed into a hollow keel in solid form. Pack the ballast as densely as possible, then restrain it. A common method of restraining solid ballast is to pour molten tar over it.

To isolate the solid ballast from the aluminum keel, first line the bottom of the cavity with a layer of heavy roofing felt, then place a layer of ballast over the felt and not in contact with the aluminum keel sides. Pour hot tar over the ballast until it is firmly held in position. Pack additional ballast into the cavity, and again pour hot tar over it to lock it in place. Repeat this process until all the ballast is installed, then weld cover plates over the ballast area to seal it from bilge water.

To minimize air gaps between ballast solids, triangular bars can be cast that allow very close packing. This works particularly well with lead since it's easily cast into triangular ingots. A simple casting mold can be fabricated from either steel or aluminum angle, as shown in Figure 9-23.

Propulsion Systems and Controls

Modern propulsion systems for boats can be reciprocating or turbine engines, gasoline or diesel fueled, and inboard or outboard mounted. Power can be delivered through conventional propellers, inboard/outboard units, or water jets. And the wide range of horsepower ratings and suggested applications for each system requires some difficult choices. First determine the performance you'll need, then work backward to arrive at the best system for the application.

Engine Selection

If a propulsion system is selected primarily for speed, reduced reliability and fuel economy usually result. If it's selected for power, speed and fuel economy are sacrificed. If the primary consideration is fuel efficiency, speed and power will be sacrificed. The boatowner and the designer must work together to identify the propulsion system that will provide the best compromise between performance and efficiency for a specific boat.

Another consideration is the intended uses of the boat. A boat to be operated in shallow water and rivers and subject to grounding may be best served by a water-jet unit. For offshore operations requiring a high level of reliability, good fuel economy, and minimum fire hazard, a diesel engine is indicated. If a large, clear area in the stern of the vessel is needed, a midship engine installation may be required. And if the boat is to be constructed by a novice, ease of installation may be a major consideration, suggesting outboard power.

The initial out-of-pocket cost of a propulsion system can be a big factor. For example, although diesel engines have a number of advantages over gasoline engines, the initial cost of a diesel engine can easily more than double the cost of the propulsion system over one using an equivalent gasoline-fueled engine.

Only after performance objectives, operating parameters, and budget implications have all been considered can the right propulsion system be selected.

Diesel Engines

Diesel is almost always selected for reliability and operating economy, and the much lower fire hazard of diesel fuel is a major consideration when operating offshore. Diesel fuel costs less, and diesel engines are usually more fuel-efficient than gasoline engines.

Diesel engines can be naturally aspirated, turbocharged, or turbocharged with after-cooling. By altering the amount of fuel an engine can efficiently burn, these various configurations provide a range of horsepower ratings.

Naturally aspirated. In a naturally aspirated engine, the amount of fuel that can be efficiently burned is determined by the volume of air drawn into each cylinder by a downward stroke of the piston. The engine horsepower rating is limited by the amount of air available.

FIGURE 10-1. Lugger L6140A turbocharged and after-cooled marine diesel engine.

L6140 A - with heat exchanger cooling, PTO and aft exhaust outlet

Non-service side features:

1- Liquid cooled turbocharger for power and safety.
2- Air filter/silencer.
3- 90/10 cupro-nickle heat exchanger in cast tank.
4- Gear oil cooler.
5- Pump mount PTO with electric clutch.
6- Alternator. Choose 24 or 12 volts in various amperage outputs.
7- Dipsticks available both sides.
8- 12 or 24 volt starter placed high and dry.
9- Your choice of marine reverse gears.
10-Thermostatically controlled stainless steel oil cooler.
11-Cast iron, freshwater cooled exhaust manifold.
12-Individual, four valve cylinder heads.

Turbocharged. A turbocharger delivers increased air volume into the cylinders, but compression of the air by the turbocharger also increases the air temperature. The horsepower rating of a turbocharged engine is limited by the turbocharger speed and the internal temperatures.

Turbocharged with after-cooling. The addition of a water-cooled after-cooler between the turbocharger and the engine's intake manifold provides cooling for the hot compressed air from the turbocharger. Cooling the air increases its density and allows more fuel to be burned. Horsepower rating is limited by internal temperature limits, turbocharger speed, and the structural limits of the engine. Figure 10-1 shows a typical after-cooled turbocharger configuration on a diesel engine.

Diesel engines are commonly given horsepower ratings at specified RPM settings. It's important to compare rating definitions for each manufacturer's ratings to obtain a true comparison. Technical data furnished by diesel engine manufacturers is usually much more complete than that provided by gasoline engine manufacturers. Supporting data for the Lugger L6140 A (the engine in Figure 10-1) is shown in Figure 10-2.

When comparing diesel engines, contact engine dealers in your area for information on specific brands. Ask the dealers for product information to include rated horsepower, weight, fuel consumption, gear ratios and availability, and any other pertinent data.

For the first-time builder, it's very nice to have a prewired instrument panel and a prebundled wiring harness. If you plan to operate the vessel in salt water, you'll need to make sure the engine you select is freshwater cooled and equipped with the required heat exchanger and seawater circulating pump.

Gasoline Engines

Most small powerboats (less than 30 feet) are powered by gasoline engines, either inboard or outboard. Gasoline engines are both safe and reliable when installed, operated, and maintained correctly. The principle advantages of gasoline engines are lower initial cost, high horsepower-to-weight ratios, and the ready availability of maintenance facilities. Factory-available options usually include freshwater cooling, prebundled instrument harnesses, and prewired instrument panels. Larger alternators or dual alternators can be supplied mounted to the engines for increased electrical capacity. Power-take-offs for various applications may also be available.

Gasoline engines generally turn at much higher RPM than diesel engines to obtain rated horsepower. Most U. S. marine engines are automobile engines

FIGURE 10-2. Manufacturer-supplied performance data for the Lugger L6140A diesel engine.

PERFORMANCE DATA

Duty Rating	High Output	Medium Duty	Continuous Duty
Rated Output	600 hp (444 kW) at 2100 rpm	550 hp (407 kW) at 2100 rpm	470 hp (348 kW) at 1800 rpm
Shaft Output	579 hp (429 kW) at 2100 rpm	530 hp (392 kW) at 2100 rpm	453 hp (336 kW) at 1800 rpm
Maximum Torque	1730 ft lbs at 1400 rpm	1577 ft lbs at 1300 rpm	1540 ft lbs at 1500 rpm
Fuel Consumption	17.8 at 1800 rpm	16.4 at 1800 rpm	12.8 at 1500 rpm
Gallons per hour based on prop draw hp	21.2 at 1900 rpm	19.4 at 1900 rpm	15.5 at 1600 rpm
	25.0 at 2000 rpm	22.8 at 2000 rpm	18.7 at 1700 rpm
	29.2 at 2100 rpm	26.7 at 2100 rpm	22.2 at 1800 rpm

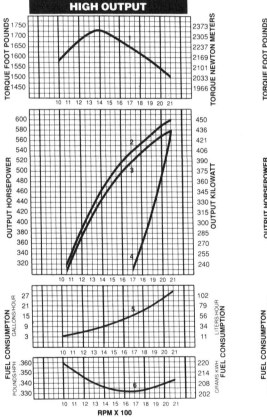

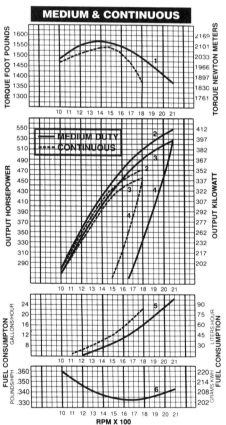

FIGURE 10-3. **Kodiak 350 HO marine gaso-line engine.**

FIGURE 10-4. **Manufacturer-supplied per-formance data for Kodiak 350 HO.**

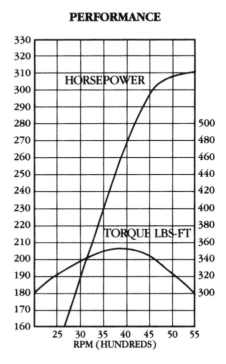

PERFORMANCE

converted for marine use. This conversion usually includes water-cooled exhaust risers, raw-water circulation pump, marine carburetor with backfire protection, and all requirements to meet federal regulations concerning small-craft electrical, fuel, and ventilation systems. Freshwater-cooled heat exchangers are a common option when operation in sea water is anticipated. Figure 10-3 is an example of a marine engine manufacturer's *marinized* gasoline engine (in this case a Chevy V-8) fitted with a heat exchanger and exhaust manifold risers.

Gasoline engines are rated by cubic-inch or liter displacement and by horse-power at maximum RPM. As with diesel engines, compare the standard and conditions used to determine horsepower and engine efficiency when evaluating relative engine performance. Fuel consumption data is not readily available in brochures but can be obtained from the manufacturer's representative. Performance information for the Kodiak 350 HO (the marine gasoline engine in Figure 10-3) is shown in Figure 10-4.

Turbines

Turbine engines using jet fuel have been successfully used for special marine applications. The turbine is used in place of a reciprocating engine and drives a propeller or a water jet through a reduction gear. Jet turbines have been used primarily on larger boats, usually military. Because of high fuel consumption, the turbine is used for sprint speed only; conventional diesel engines are used for cruising and fuel economy. Jet turbines have fallen out of favor due to their fuel consumption, and in recent years lightweight high-speed reciprocating diesel engines in the larger size ranges have all but replaced the jet turbine.

Drive-train Systems

The propulsion system includes the propulsion engine, transmission, propeller shaft and bearings, strut, and propeller or water-jet unit. Drive-train system refers to all the components of the propulsion system except the engine and transmission. The most common drive train systems for aluminum boats are conventional shaft and propeller, inboard/outboard (I/O), outboard, and water jet, and each one has specific advantages. The intended use of the boat will greatly influence the selection of the drive train. Other considerations are cost, ease of installation, and reliability.

Conventional Shaft and Propeller

A conventional propulsion system is an inboard engine delivering its power through a transmission with reverse capability, and a preset reduction gear. The components of the drive-train system are a propeller shaft with a through-hull stuffing box, a shaft log, shaft bearings, and a propeller. The drive train also commonly includes a strut with a bearing for additional shaft support (Figure 10-5).

A conventional drive system affords the designer more freedom to customize the installation than do other drive systems. The system is simple; consequently, it's very reliable. The cost of materials is low when compared with other drive systems. However, the conventional shaft-and-propeller system is also the most labor intensive to install because it requires a separate rudder, which isn't required for outboard, I/O, or water-jet systems.

Mounting the engine. The Mercruiser MIE 5.7L inboard gasoline engine with a Borg-Warner in-line gear, as shown in Figure 10-6, is a good example of a readily available inboard gasoline engine. The forward engine mounts are located

FIGURE 10-5. Conventional shaft-and-propeller drive train.

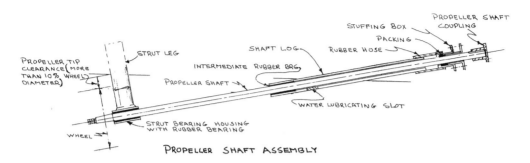

FIGURE 10-6. Mercruiser 5.7 liter inboard with Borg-Warner gear.

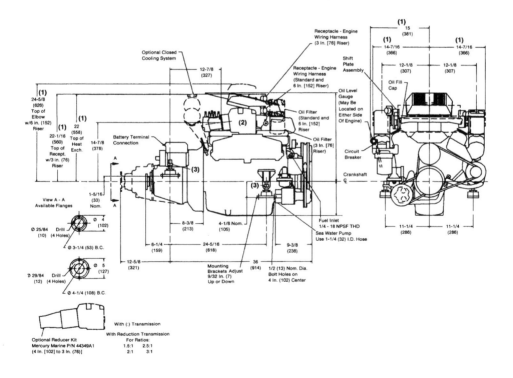

on the engine block, and the aft mounts are on the gear housing—a typical configuration. In aluminum boats, flexible engine mounts should be used for electrical isolation and for vibration and noise abatement. Purchased separately from the engine, isolation mounts consist of a cast housing with a rubber interior. They are installed between the boat's engine bed and the mounting brackets on the engine, and when installed properly, they effectively "rubber mount" the engine.

Any inboard engine installation should take into consideration the accessibility of the engine for service. Provisions for changing the engine and gear oil must be considered. Ready access to belts, spark plugs, and other items that can reasonably be expected to need periodic servicing should be provided.

Marine transmission. Again, your transmission will depend on how you will use your boat. High-speed boats—ski boats, for example—require high propeller RPM for maximum acceleration. Work boats are more likely to require pulling power and will generally use lower RPM at the prop to maximize torque.

Another transmission selection consideration is shaft angle. A large deviation from horizontal by the propeller shaft will cause a loss of thrust. If the crankshaft is out of level more than 15 degrees, engine oil will run to the low portion of the oil pan, possibly causing oil scavenging problems that can result in engine damage. When excessive shaft angle is evident, consider an alternate transmission configuration, such as a down-angle gear (Figure 10-7) or a V-drive (Figure 10-8), to reduce the engine inclination.

Choose the best gear configuration for your application based on the relative importance of speed, pulling power, and fuel economy. Consider propeller size and pitch prior to finalizing the gear ratio, since the propeller acts as an additional gear in the drive train.

Propeller shaft. Propeller shafts on aluminum boats are usually stainless steel in alloy 17-4PH. Other special alloys developed by manufacturers specifically for aluminum boats can be obtained from shafting suppliers. Other shafting materials, including commercially available alloys of stainless steel (other than 17-4PH) and copper-bearing alloys (bronze, for instance) should not be used.

When determining propeller-shaft diameter for light pleasure-boat service with the prop protected by a skeg, a design strength safety factor of 2:1 is acceptable. Methods for calculating shaft sizes can be found in ABYC section P-6, "Materials, Size, and Installation of Propeller Shafting Systems."

For race boats, work boats, and diesel-powered boats, higher safety factors of 5:1 to 10:1 are recommended by the American Boat and Yacht Council guidelines. Another factor in the design of a propeller shaft is the diameter of

FIGURE 10-7. Hurth 630A down-angle gear.   **FIGURE 10-8. Borg-Warner V-drive.**

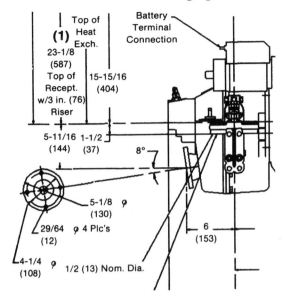

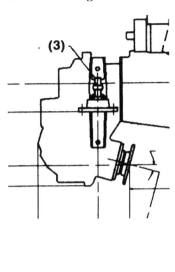

the propeller, which should not exceed the propeller shaft diameter by more than 15:1.

When the material type, boat use, safety factor, and propeller size are all considered, the process of propeller-shaft design can get complicated. For this reason, let the engine manufacturer's representative, the propeller shop, or the naval architect design your prop shaft.

Shafting needs to be straight, but since absolute straightness is almost impossible, acceptable amounts of variance have been established over the years by experience. Permissible variances are well specified in applicable published standards. (For additional information on straightness, and on shaft diameter, see ABYC Section P-6, *Materials, Size and Installation of Propeller Shafting Systems.*)

Aside from inherent straightness variances, unsupported lengths of a shaft will deflect under their own weight and can require intermediate bearing support. Boats up to about 40 feet LOA seldom have shaft lengths long enough to require supports other than at the rigid shaft coupling at the reduction gear and a bearing at the propeller strut. This is called a *two rigid bearing* arrangement.

Determine the *actual* length of the propeller shaft after the strut is welded in place and the main engine with gear is located in the hull and aligned by eye. Measure the distance from the face of the gearbox output flange to the aft end of the propeller strut, and provide this information to the propeller-shaft shop; they will determine the shaft length from this measurement.

The propeller shaft should be prepared by an experienced propeller shop familiar with the standards and calculations required. The prop shop will add to the measured distance the additional shaft length for the propeller hub, threads for the nut, and clearance between the strut and the propeller hub, in accordance with established standards. The shop will machine the coupling provided with the engine gear to suit the shaft diameter. A keyway will be cut into the propeller shaft and in the gear coupling for the installation of a key to prevent the shaft from rotating within the coupling. A standard taper with a key and threads for a propeller nut will be machined on the aft end of the shaft. Standardization and tolerances for propeller-shaft ends, propeller hubs, and shaft couplings should be in accordance with applicable standards (SA Standard J755 *Marine Propeller-shaft Ends and Hubs* and J756 *Marine Propeller-shaft Couplings*, and ABYC P-6-4.e.[1] and P-6.4.e.[5]). Having the same shop prepare the shaft and provide the prop will reduce the potential for error.

Propeller shaft bearings. On small aluminum craft, a nonmetallic water-lubricated rubber bearing is the simplest and least expensive shaft bearing. The bearing consists of a nonmetallic outer sleeve with a rubber lining bonded inside it. The rubber portion has molded grooves for water lubrication.

Install the shaft bearing into the propeller strut with a light press-fit. Shaft bearings are normally secured by two stainless steel setscrews, and the bearing sleeve will be slightly drilled to promote a good mechanical grip by the retainer setscrews.

Ample water must be available to lubricate rubber bearings. Strut bearings exposed on both ends to free-flowing water are adequately cooled. Bearings located within or at the end of the shaft log must have provision for free-flowing water to lubricate and cool them. Water entering only from the aft end of the bearing is *not* sufficient: a raw water inlet and scoop forward of the bearing is often used to establish the necessary flow. For bearing installations entirely within the shaft log, lubricating water may be supplied by the discharge flow from the main engine raw water pump to ensure bearing lubrication during engine operation.

Intermediate bearings. Water-lubricated rubber bearings are not used for intermediate bearings that support the shaft inside the hull; for this function, choose either a ball-bearing pillow block or a flange-type bearing rated for marine service.

Bearing strut and housing. Since aluminum shrinks considerably more than steel when welded, welded-aluminum boats require special attention to the alignment of the strut. The best way to ensure an accurate alignment between the strut and the reduction gear output coupling is to *line-bore* the assembly after all welding is finished. Line-boring requires a special setup with a long boring bar that machines the inside of the strut-bearing housing in perfect alignment with the engine, and the strut is machined only after all welding in the vicinity of the engine and strut that could cause distortion has been completed. This method is regularly used on large ships but, because of the expense, is seldom used in modern small-boat building.

A suitable alternative to line-boring is fitting the strut-bearing housing to a dummy shaft installed in the required position in the hull. Slide the strut-bearing housing over the dummy shaft, place the prefabricated strut legs into position on the hull, and weld them in place. (Strut legs usually pass through the shell plate and are welded to internal framing. The step-by-step procedure to align the strut with a dummy shaft is detailed in Appendix V.) Adjustments during final engine alignment, after the boat is in the water, will compensate for any minor misalignment that may exist.

Shaft log. The propeller-shaft log is usually a section of heavy-wall aluminum pipe sufficiently long to pass completely through the hull. The alloy of the shaft log should match the adjacent hull material, but the pipe's wall thickness should be thicker than adjacent shell plate to allow for possible machining during final alignment of the propeller shaft. Enough of the shaft log must protrude into the hull through the bottom plate to allow attachment of the rubber hose that connects the log to the stuffing box (Figure 10-5).

Locate the shaft log with the same dummy shaft used to locate and install the strut. Cut away sufficient hull material to slide the shaft log through, use temporary bushings or shims to center it around the dummy propeller shaft, and tack-weld the log in place. Complete the final weld-out of the shaft log at the same time as the final weld of the propeller-shaft strut—after all other welding in the vicinity is finished.

Alignment of the shaft log isn't critical unless it includes a bearing. The propeller shaft should have at least ⅛ inch clearance all around inside the shaft log.

Stuffing box (packing gland). Economical aluminum or stainless steel stuffing boxes are not readily available. Available stuffing boxes are generally made of bronze and are *not* compatible with aluminum hull construction.

A stuffing box can be fabricated from aluminum (Figure 10-9) and sealed with wax-impregnated flax packing. As an alternative to the conventional bronze stuffing box, shaft seals (Figure 10-10) constructed of rubber and stainless steel and using O-rings to maintain watertight integrity (such as the units offered by Lasdrop, 10131 NW 46th St., Sunrise, FL 33351) are more compatible with aluminum.

Engine installation. Lofting the engine bed to consider the location of the shaft, access to service the engine, clearance of structure, etc., was covered in Chapter 4. After the engine bed has been installed in the hull and all work that will be difficult to accomplish after the engine is installed or that can damage the engine or related parts (such as welding in the immediate area) is complete, the installation of the propulsion system can start.

To install the inboard engine, rig a sling to suspend the engine (with gear attached) at approximately the angle it will assume after installation. Position the nuts on the flexible engine mount's adjustment screws for equal up and down travel—to ensure adequate adjustment in either direction during engine align-

FIGURE 10-9. Fabricated aluminum stuffing box.

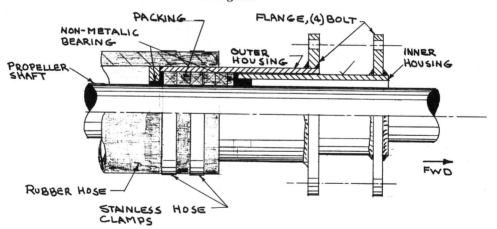

FIGURE 10-10. **Shaft seal. From Boatowner's Mechanical and Electrical Manual by Nigel Calder,** *International Marine,* **1990.**

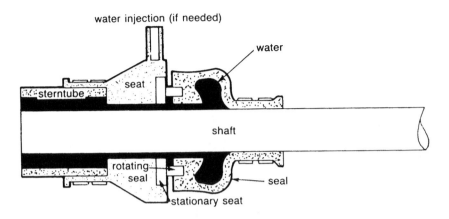

ment—and bolt the mounts to the engine and gear. Carefully position the engine mounts over the engine bed and lower the engine until no engine weight is on the hoist. Then perform the following alignment steps:

- Set the main propulsion engine and gear onto the engine bed.
- Position the propeller strut and shaft in the hull and temporarily align the shaft with the engine.
- Mark the engine bed girders for drilling of engine-mounting-bolt holes. Remove the shaft and the engine.
- Drill engine-mounting holes and relocate the engine on the bed.
- Weld the propeller strut in place, re-install the shaft, and re-align the engine to the shaft.
- Install and tighten engine-mounting bolts. This completes the alignment of the main engine while the boat is in the shop. (For more detailed engine installation and alignment instructions, see Appendix V.)

Perform the final alignment with the boat in the water—after its temperature has stabilized, its fuel tanks are full, and a normal load is aboard.

Inboard/Outboard

The inboard/outboard, commonly called an I/O, is probably the most popular small-boat inboard gasoline propulsion system available today. This popularity is based on low price, ease of installation, and the capability of raising the propeller (lower unit) for trailer transport. Most I/O units have a built-in exhaust system that discharges through a hollow propeller hub, eliminating the need to fabricate and install an exhaust system. The outboard portion of the I/O unit swivels for steering, eliminating the need for a separate rudder assembly, and it's installed in the very stern of the boat, which is where you want it for most planing boats.

The complete I/O package from the dealer will normally include an inboard engine, the I/O unit equipped with power tilt, and all purchased options, which might include a prewired instrument panel with a harness, freshwater cooling, a larger alternator, and power steering.

I/O units are available for gasoline and diesel engines in a broad range of horsepower ratings. They are available with a single propeller, with dual contra-rotating propellers, and as heavy-duty units intended for commercial work and diesel power.

I/O Installation

Installation of a standard I/O unit is one of the simpler propulsion-system installations, providing the boat was designed for I/O power. Check the installation drawing provided with the I/O unit for proper layout of the engine beds and transom.

Design for I/O. To fit the geometry of the I/O unit, the transom of the boat must rake aft at about 12 degrees where the unit will be installed. Most I/O units require a transom of 2-inch minimum to 2¼-inch maximum thickness. The aft engine mounts normally found on the gearbox aren't used; instead, the engine is bolted securely to the portion of the installed I/O unit that is inside the hull.

Installation of the transom-mounted unit. Since the transom material on an aluminum boat is likely to be considerably less than 2 inches thick, you will need to build up the transom with some type of filler to achieve the 2- to 2¼-inch thickness I/O units require for a proper watertight seal. The watertight seal is between the I/O unit and the transom exterior face; the filler material used to bring the transom thickness up to 2 inches is placed on the inside of the boat and does not have to be watertight. Some boatbuilders have filled this space with scrap aluminum. Others have used aluminum channel, sculpted to fit the cutout contour. Some have even used wood—an especially poor choice since the wood rots and can contribute to corrosion of the aluminum.

The best spacer is an aluminum casting (Figure 10-11) made specifically for this application. (Such castings are available from Baywood Manufacturing Company, 3841 Sound Way, Bellingham, Washington 98226.) Simply place the casting against the back side of the transom plate and weld it in place. A cast spacer makes for a very neat and simple installation and has much to recommend it.

Use the mounting template supplied with the I/O to mark the transom for the cutout and for the location of the mounting-bolt holes. Make the cutout and install the transom filler, then drill the mounting holes through both the transom and the filler. Assemble the I/O transom-mounted unit to the transom by following the manufacturer's instructions.

FIGURE 10-11. **Cast-aluminum spacer to provide adequate transom thickness for an I/O installation.**

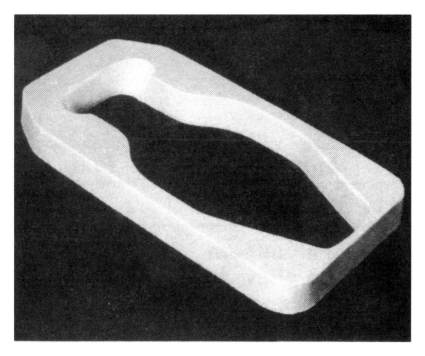

I/O engine installation. Prepare the engine for installation by following the detailed engine preparation data provided by the engine supplier. Ask your I/O dealer for the use of the special alignment tool required to align the engine and the transom-mounted I/O unit. This tool is a rod about 2 feet long designed to pass through the I/O unit and into the engine coupler spline.

Install the I/O engine as follows:

• Mount the I/O unit on the transom.
• Set the engine on the engine bed in approximate alignment with the I/O unit and mark the girders for drilling of the isolation-mount bolts.
• Temporarily remove the engine, drill the mount holes, and reset the engine.
• Pass the special alignment tool through the I/O unit into the engine coupler spline for final alignment.
• Tighten down engine-mount bolts.

The balance of the engine installation is done by following the manufacturer's instructions.

Because the I/O dealer has the expertise, not to mention special drill templates and alignment tools, you may consider having him install the unit in your boat, but if you're mechanically inclined, you can do it yourself without many problems.

Water-jet Propulsion

The water jet is one of the simplest and most reliable of the propulsion systems. The principle is simply to squirt water out of a nozzle, causing the boat to move in the opposite direction to the water flow. Contrary to popular belief, the water-jet outlet does *not* have to be underwater. Water-jet propulsion operates on the principle *force = mass x acceleration* and does not need "something to push against." Loosely defined, *force* in this case is the thrust pushing the boat, *mass* is the weight of the water pumped, and *acceleration* is the change of velocity of the water between entering and leaving the pump.

One very simple water-jet system is a gasoline-driven water pump in the boat with its suction hose overboard and the discharge water squirting out over the stern. This will propel the boat forward, and some small drift boats used for steelhead fishing on the Northwest rivers have actually been powered this way.

Principle advantages of a water jet are its ease of operation in shallow water and its ability to survive an impact with the bottom and continue operation. Because water jets can ingest small rocks without any apparent damage, they are ideal white-water boats. Boats with rugged and lightweight aluminum hull construction and water-jet propulsion systems have proved to be the most popular on Pacific Northwest rivers over the past 20 years.

Water-jet boats have the additional advantages of a clean bottom with no prop to foul and exposing swimmers to minimum danger. Because of the water jet's simple construction—basically a water pump—it has proved very rugged and maintenance free. The water-jet unit doesn't require a gear box in the drive train since the reverse function is accomplished by deflecting the water stream exiting the jet unit. This reversing deflector, often referred to as the *bucket*, is integral with the jet unit. In special applications where a power-take-off is used (such as a high-velocity fire-fighting pump), a gear may be included to disconnect the jet unit from the engine.

Since water-jet boats are often used in rough, white-water, it's not uncommon to fit them with a foot throttle to allow quick RPM reduction when the boat is airborne.

Water-jet Hull Design

C. W. F. Hamilton of New Zealand, one of the leading manufacturers of water-jet propulsion systems, recommends (see reference listing at the end of the chapter) a planing hull with a nearly constant deadrise angle—i.e., keel and chine lines parallel—in the after ⅓ of the hull, a deadrise angle of more than 10 degrees at the stern, and a stem that gradually rises as it approaches the bow. The company further recommends that the boat's weight not exceed 22 pounds per horsepower for best performance.

The hull bottom should have a flat area in the stern for mounting the flat intake screen. It should also be clean—free of a keel or strakes that will disturb the water flow to the intake—for a minimum of 6 feet forward of the intake.

Water-jet Installation

A 1⅟₁₆-inch hull thickness in the area of the jet intake is standard for axial-flow jet units like Hamilton and Kodiak. (Hamilton was a pioneer in water-jet units, and its designs have become somewhat of a standard for axial flow units.) Since aluminum boats used for white-water work rarely have bottoms thicker than ³⁄₁₆ inch, a bottom plate filler must be installed, similar to the transom filler for an I/O unit. One easy solution is to use ⅞- or 1-inch-thick by 2-inch-wide aluminum flat-bar and fabricate a *picture frame* to suit the jet intake opening. Drill and tap this frame and install stainless steel Heli-coil inserts to match the bolt size and pattern for the jet intake. Cut the boat bottom away to suit the jet unit inlet, and weld the picture frame mounting base around the cutout. This installation avoids any leakage around the intake mounting bolts since they do not pass through the hull's bottom plate.

Mounting bases are also made of cast rubber (available from Kodiak Marine, Portland, Oregon). This type of base is simply placed on the hull plate in the area of the water-jet intake and through bolted to the hull. Use the data supplied by the manufacturer of the propulsion unit to locate the intake and transom cutouts.

Install the inboard engine by setting it on the engine bed in close alignment with the water jet. Short drive shafts, or *spicers*, with universal joints are commonly used to connect the engine to the water-jet unit.

Outboard Propulsion

The outboard is the single most popular method of powering a small boat. The outboard's principle advantages are almost nonexistent installation labor, the additional interior room provided by mounting the engine outside the hull, and the ability to raise the propeller for ease of trailering. Because of the outboard's self-contained and portable nature, a boatowner can use the same motor on more than one boat. This in itself is a major cost savings for anyone with different boats for different applications.

Outboards can be fitted with water-jet lower units.

Designing for an Outboard

Like an I/O, the outboard requires a minimum and maximum transom thickness for the outboard mounting. Consult your dealer for recommended transom thickness, cutout location, and clearances for your particular outboard. (ABYC *Outboard Motorboat Transom and Motor Well Dimensions*, Section S-12, establishes recommended standards.) The height of the transom, measured from the deepest point of the hull bottom to the sill of the outboard motor cut-out, should be 15 inches for a short-shaft outboard or 20 inches for a long-shaft—up to 35 h.p. Transom heights for motors over 35 h.p. are 19½ inches and 24½ inches for short- and long-shaft motors, respectively.

Installing the Outboard

Small-horsepower outboards are installed by simply clamping them securely in position. Larger-horsepower units are through-bolted to the transom to ensure proper attachment. The weight of a large outboard may also require mechanical assistance when lifting it onto or off the transom, necessitating a special eyebolt screwed into the top of the motor for the lifting attachment point. These are obtained from the dealer.

Routing the various controls to an outboard motor may require cutting some holes. Use the installation information provided with the outboard to locate and size these openings.

The correct height of the propeller in relationship to the bottom of the boat is a factor of boat speed and propeller selection. Select the optimum height, in relation to the anti-ventilation (or cavitation) plate located on the lower unit above the propeller, as follows:

- *Work application* (heavy load, slow speed): one to two inches below the bottom of the boat
- *Normal duty* (average load, average speed): flush with the bottom of the boat.
- *Sport application* (water skiing, etc.): one to three inches above the bottom of the boat
- *High performance* (maximum-speed application): Four inches or more above the boat bottom

Controls

When both the throttle and the forward/reverse gear are operated by the same control lever, this is called single-lever control, and it's the control system most often installed on small boats. A number of manufacturers supply both control heads and control cables. Control heads and the surface they're mounted on should be able to withstand a force of 75 pounds in any direction, and the throttle and gear lever (or levers), should not be closer than 2 ½ inches from the steering wheel for proper hand clearance.

Controls should operate in the *natural* direction: that is, the lever should move forward to engage the engine gear in *forward* and back to engage *reverse*; when the throttle is advanced, engine RPM should advance, and when it's pulled back, RPM should decline. The same concept applies to trim-tab installations: raising the trim switch to the up position should raise the bow, and lowering the switch should lower the bow.

For dual-engine control stations, the port-engine control will be on the port side, the starboard control to starboard. On single-engine boats with a dual-control head, the starboard (right) lever should be the throttle, the port (left) lever the gear. For dual-engine installations with separate throttle and gear levers, the throttle levers should be alongside each other so they can be operated together with one hand.

The ABYC recommends that the throttle be identified by a red knob or some other means (surface texture, shape, etc.) to distinguish between throttle and gear. Shift controls will include a neutral position indication, usually a detent, and start-in-gear protection should be included to prevent starting an engine with the prop engaged.

Control cables are normally commercially available push/pull types designed for marine applications and sized to suit the specific controls. The control cable for the throttle should be color-coded red. Color coding can be accomplished with red tape placed at the quadrant end of the cable to mini- mize the possibility of accidentally crossing throttle and gear cables during maintenance work. Install control cables with a minimum number of bends— none with a tighter radius than specified by the cable manufacturer—and securely fasten them in place. Cables should not be close to the engine's exhaust system.

Pay particular attention to electrically isolating engine controls; stray volt- age can flow through the controls (and the metal console) to the hull. Electrically isolate the controls from the hull to ensure engine isolation from the hull. This is required to maintain a single-point negative ground of the boat's electrical system, as detailed in Chapter 12. Some thought is required to isolate metal controls from a metal hull. The simplest method is to mount the control head on a nonconductive surface, such as wood or plastic. If you mount the control head to a metal console that is in electrical contact with the hull, use isolation gas- kets and bushings around the mounting bolts. Be sure you also electrically isolate the control cables, including any attachment clips, from the hull.

Steering

The helm unit may be a reel type, a rack-and-pinion, or a rotary hydraulic pump. Steering systems may be motor mounted or hull mounted. A motor- mounted steering system is rigidly mounted to the propulsion unit, transmitting most of the steering stress to the engine mounts. An example of this is an out- board-motor steering unit that threads into the framework of the outboard; only the steering cable or hydraulic lines are attached to the hull. Conversely, a hydraulic cylinder attached to the rudder and the hull is an example of a hull- mounted steering system, transmitting steering stresses directly to hull structure. A hull-mounted steering system must be capable of sustaining a considerable load in either direction along the axis of the steering output mechanism, requiring appropriate consideration to the hull structure supporting the steering gear.

Helm units and the steering wheel itself must be capable of withstanding a considerable force, such as a 200-pound operator thrown against them during a rough ride. Slamming forces on a pleasure boat can reach 4 g's at the bow and 2 g's at the center of gravity, so it's not unreasonable to expect 3 g's at the steering station during a fast run in rough water. The helm and the structure supporting it must be capable of withstanding these high potential forces.

Pay particular attention to the mounting of free-standing steering consoles. The loads at the helm are compounded at the base of the console because of the lever effect of the height of the console. Free-standing consoles have a bad habit of breaking loose during a rough ride and causing operator injury. Steering consoles must not be simply bolted to the floorboards; weld or through-bolt them securely to the boat's framing.

Selection of a Steering System

A small-powerboat steering system might be either the manual tiller of a small outboard or a remote steering wheel controlling a rudder, an I/O, a water jet, or a (typically large) outboard. Remote steering is commonly a hardware item purchased separately from the propulsion system, and for a small boat you might select a reel-type helm unit with push/pull cable, a rack-and-pinion helm unit with push/pull cable, or a hydraulic steering system comprised of a rotating hydraulic pump helm and a hydraulic cylinder, all three ultimately pushing and pulling at the steering attachment point for the rudder, outboard, I/O, or water jet. Cable-over-pulley steering, once common, is very seldom used on newer boats and isn't recommended for boats of over 50 h.p. (Recommended guidelines for cable-over-pulley steering can be found in ABYC P-18 [1], dated 1-21-83.)

Whether a steering system will be motor- or hull-mounted depends on the steering configuration provided with the propulsion system. Outboard motors, I/O units, and water jets usually have provisions for engine-mounted (propulsion unit) steering systems. Conventional inboard installations require a rudder, which is a hull-mounted steering system. Whether you choose cable-and-reel, cable-and-rack-and-pinion, or hydraulic steering is a matter of the boat's intended use, personal preference, and your budget. Large-horsepower installations require heavy-duty steering systems such as rack-and-pinion units with heavy duty cables or hydraulic steering systems. As a general rule, a reel-type steering system with a push/pull cable is least expensive, followed by a rack-and-pinion helm with a push/pull cable. The most expensive is hydraulic, but if multi steering stations or considerable change of direction of steering cables is required to avoid interferences, hydraulic steering may be the most economical selection. Steering systems and cables come with detailed assembly and installation instructions, and they're sized to suit the boat size and horsepower.

Propellers

Propellers used on aluminum boats should not be constructed of a copper-bearing material, such as bronze, because the sacrificial nature of aluminum to copper will result in hull corrosion. Stainless steel propellers are favored for aluminum boats.

There are many considerations in selecting a propeller, or in boating vernacular, the *wheel*, and no known formula to automatically give the ideal propeller size for a given boat. Most major marine-engine manufacturers can provide excellent propeller selection data upon request, but your best selection data will come only from actual tests with various propellers. Most prop shops have loaner propellers just for this purpose.

You need to be familiar with a few terms to discuss wheel selection with your prop shop:

- *Diameter*—The diameter of the circle scribed by the propeller blade tips.
- *Pitch*—The distance the propeller would travel in one revolution if it were rotating in a solid—like a screw through wood. The theoretical distance traveled (in inches) in one minute is calculated by RPM x pitch.
- *Slip*—Since the propeller is rotating not through a solid, but a liquid, the loss of forward motion through the water is known as slip. Slip is the difference between the theoretical distance a propeller of a given pitch would travel in one revolution and the actual distance it travels, usually expressed as a percentage.
- *Pitch ratio*—The pitch of a propeller divided by its diameter.

As a general rule, select the largest diameter propeller—within practical limits—that you can turn at its most appropriate turning speed.

These limits are:

- Size of the propeller aperture.
- Type of operation (workboat, planing boat, etc.).
- Shaft angle required for a larger propeller—a large propeller may require an increased shaft angle to provide adequate clearance between the hull and the blade tips.
- Weight of the propeller, shaft, and gear relative to boat size.
- Minimum boat draft requirements.

Outboard and I/O propellers are usually configured with a hollow center for the engine exhaust outlet.

An excellent 43-page publication on propeller selection, *Everything You Need to Know About Propellers*, is available from Mercury Marine, Fond du Lac, Wisconsin 54935.

Exhaust Systems

Exhaust systems for outboards and I/Os are included with the machinery and require no additional fabrication; engine exhaust exits through the hollow center of the propeller. Commercially-available marinized automotive engines, as typically used with water-jet units, are commonly equipped with water-cooled exhaust *risers*. The risers are raw-water cooled and mix the water with the exhaust at the outlet, allowing the use of rubber exhaust hose downstream of the cooling-water inlet. Complete the exhaust installation for engines mounted above the waterline and equipped with water-cooled exhaust risers by simply installing a muffler in the nonmetallic section of the wet exhaust line and routing the exhaust overboard—preferably through the transom.

Conventional engines not equipped with wet exhaust risers and engines mounted below the waterline require some special provisions to get the exhaust safely out of the boat. Either a wet or a dry exhaust system may be installed. (Voluntary standards for engine exhaust systems can be found in ABYC, Section P-1, *Installation of Exhaust Systems for Propulsion and Auxiliary Engines*.)

A wet exhaust system cools, or partially cools, the exhaust gases and exhaust line with water entering into the exhaust stream. Flexible materials, such as neoprene, may be used for exhaust pipe in the water-cooled section of the exhaust line; dry sections of the exhaust system are constructed of high-temperature-resistant and corrosion-resistant materials.

A fabricated muffler for a typical wet exhaust system for mounting below the waterline is shown in Figure 10-12. Fabricate the hot sections and the

FIGURE 10-12. Fabricated exhaust muffler with cooling water inlet.

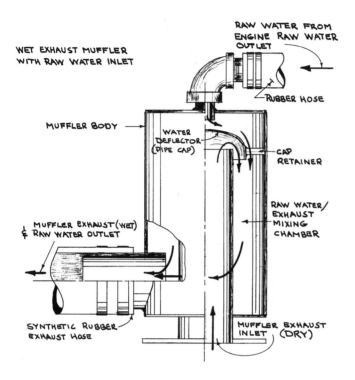

muffler in an aluminum boat exhaust system from stainless; beyond where the cooling water enters the exhaust system, usually at the muffler, use nonmetallic materials. On maximum-performance boats, where weight savings are more important than cost, titanium has been used with excellent results for both the wet and dry sections.

Install a section of flexible metal pipe, called *flex* or *wrinkle belly*, between the exhaust manifold outlet and the start of the dry section of the exhaust pipe. This flexible pipe keeps strain from developing on the exhaust manifold from the movement of the engine. A custom shop can make up the flex with a flange on each end to attach it to the exhaust system.

Insulate hot sections of the exhaust system in areas subject to fire hazard and, to prevent burns, in all exposed areas that exceed 200°F. Hot-pipe insulation is usually fiberglass and can be obtained for this application, preformed to suite the pipe, from a refractories supplier or through your engine dealer.

A considerable amount of heat will be generated by a dry exhaust pipe, and you'll need to incorporate some provision to carry this heat overboard. Heat can be carried away from the exhaust by providing suitable air vents from the outside to the engine exhaust area to assist with flushing the hot air out of the compartment. This can be assisted by a forced-air blower. Movement of the hot air overboard can be by natural convection if the hot pipe is encased in a sheet metal shroud that is provided with a provision to then vent overboard at a location higher than the exhaust pipe.

As with the engine controls, the exhaust system needs to be electrically isolated from the hull to protect the single-point negative ground. High-temperature insulation, in addition to the thermal protection it affords, can also provide excellent electrical isolation between the metal exhaust pipe and the exhaust system supports. Rubber exhaust hose doesn't require further electrical isolation.

When attaching rubber exhaust hose with hose clamps, be careful not to overtighten the clamps. Exhaust hose has a steel wire wound into the hose to prevent collapsing, and an overtight hose clamp can cut through the rubber of the hose and make electrical contact with the hose clamp, potentially breaking the electrical isolation of the system.

References

Caterpillar Application and Installation Guide. Peoria, IL: Caterpillar Tractor Co.

Safety Standards for Backyard Boatbuilders, COMDTPUB P16761.3. Washington, DC: U. S. Department of Transportation (U. S. Coast Guard), 1985.

Standards and Recommended Practices for Small Craft. Millersville, MD: American Boat and Yacht Council, Inc., 1991.

The Perfect Boat. Christchurch, New Zealand: C. W. F. Hamilton & Company, Ltd.

Everything You Need to Know About Propellers. 3rd ed. Fond du Lac, WI: Mercury Marine (Brunswick Corporation), 1987.

Gerr, Dave. *Propeller Handbook*. Camden, ME: International Marine, 1989.

Fuel Systems

Of the two standard marine engine fuels—gasoline and diesel—gasoline is by far the more regulated due to its more explosive nature. The proper design and installation of a fuel system is well documented in the American Boat and Yacht Council (ABYC) publication *Standards and Recommended Practices for Small Craft*. These standards incorporate the U. S. Coast Guard regulations and offer additional nonmandatory specifications to provide a safe and reliable fuel system. The USCG regulations are intended to prevent the most serious fuel-related hazards in boats carrying gasoline: fire and explosion. The fuel system, along with ventilation and electrical requirements associated with it, is one of the few areas that the Coast Guard has firm regulations concerning small craft (USCG *Safety Standards for Backyard Boatbuilders*, COMPTPUB P16761.3). Basically, the engine compartment and any other area that might contain gasoline fumes must have positive ventilation—a blower—to remove explosive vapors and must be protected from electrical sparks.

Gasoline Fuel Systems

The fuel system is comprised of the tank (or tanks), its fill, vent, and supply lines. The supply line should have a shut-off valve near the tank, and the system should include an anti-siphon valve to prevent fuel from draining into the bilge in the event of a broken fuel line. A separate fuel filter is required between the fuel tank and the engine mounted fuel filter, and a length of flexible fuel hose installed in the supply line prior to its connection to the engine prevents engine movement from damaging the fuel line.

Fuel Tanks

Fuel tanks are subject to U. S. Coast Guard inspection. A boatbuilder can fabricate fuel tanks, but the requirements for testing them to comply with the regulations make it uneconomical for the occasional tank builder. A professional fuel-tank builder can provide fuel tanks at a reasonable cost that will meet all required standards.

Fuel tanks constructed from marine-alloy aluminum are the best choice for aluminum boats. The tanks must be a minimum of .090-inch-thick material, and should use fittings manufactured of aluminum alloys 5052, 5083, 5086, 6061, or 6063, or 300-series stainless steel. Never use copper-bearing alloys, such as brass, in direct contact with aluminum.

Except for the fuel supply fitting, gasoline fuel tanks must not be fitted with an outlet such as a drain valve for withdrawing fuel; and *all* openings in a fuel tank must be at the top. Fuel tanks must be designed to prohibit standing water from accumulating on them. Adequate provisions for secure mounting—such as bolt-down clips or straps—must be included. Tanks that will contain gasoline cannot be integral with the hull or be used to support any boat structure or deck.

Fuel tanks may require slosh baffles with suitable openings at the top for air passage and at the bottom for fuel. All threaded tank fittings must be tapered pipe thread (NPT). A label bearing the manufacturer's name and address and the statement *This tank has been tested under 33 CFR 183.580* is required (USCG COMPTPUB P16761.3). The tank should also be labeled with the date of manufacture, the maximum test pressure, the material specifications, and the type of fuel to be placed in the tank (per ABYC [H-24] recommendations).

Because of the high g-forces experienced at the bow of a planing boat, the Coast Guard has placed restrictions on locating fuel tanks in the bow unless the tank has met certain rigid test standards. Fuel tanks labeled *Must be installed in the aft portion of the boat* may not be used in the bow area (see USCG 33 CFR 184.584).

Gasoline Fuel Lines

Fuel lines may be either hose or metal pipe and must comply with USCG requirements. Hose used for the fill pipe, vent line, or supply line to the engine must be USCG *type A* or USCG *type B*. Metallic fuel lines may be seamless annealed copper, copper-nickel, or nickel-copper. Unfortunately, copper-bearing alloys must be carefully isolated from the aluminum hull and tanks to minimize galvanic corrosion problems. Stainless steel, which does not cause galvanic corrosion of aluminum, is an excellent choice for fuel lines for an aluminum boat even though it isn't one of the approved fuel line materials listed by ABYC or the USCG. ABYC does authorize stainless steel in the 300 series for galvanic barriers (ABYC H-24.6.b) and for certain fuel line fittings. Contact your local U. S. Coast Guard inspection office for approval prior to using stainless steel for fuel lines.

On small boats, nonmetallic hose is often used for the entire fuel and vent lines, eliminating the potential of galvanic corrosion.

Metallic fuel lines must be secured to the hull structure with nonabrading and galvanic-isolating clips, such as electrical line support clips with synthetic rubber cushioning. Flexible fuel lines can be secured to hull structure similar to electrical conductors, using "snap-ties" or some other type of nonabrading attachment.

Fuel Tank Vent

The fuel vent originates at the highest point of the fuel tank. It should run to the outside of the hull—well above the waterline to prevent water intrusion—and be fitted with a suitable flame arrestor screen that can be cleaned. The minimum inside diameter (ID) for a vent *pipe* is $7/16$ inch; for a vent *hose*, it is $9/16$ inch.

Fuel Fill

The fuel fill must be located so that any fuel that may be spilled during fueling does not run into the bilge area and create an explosive hazard. The metallic fill neck is usually mounted to the aluminum hull structure in such a manner that it is electrically bonded to the hull and does not require a separate bonding conductor. The minimum ID of fuel fill hose is 1 ½ inches.

Fuel Valves

Manually operated fuel-system valves must be of a design suitable for the marine environment. They must have positive stops in both the open and closed position and be easily recognized as open or closed. Electrical fuel-selector valves of the automotive type may not be used (see *USCG Boating Safety Circular 71,* dated April 1991).

Fittings

Most readily available fuel-line fittings are of copper-bearing alloys, which should not be used in direct contact with the aluminum fuel tank. The available

FIGURE 11-1. Galvanic isolation of a brass valve attached to an aluminum tank.

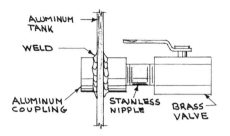

selection of fittings and valves manufactured of suitable stainless steel is limited. Copper-bearing fittings can be used provided a galvanic barrier, such as a 300-series stainless steel nipple, is used to isolate the fitting from the aluminum, as illustrated in Figure 11-1. Other methods of isolating copper-bearing fittings from the fuel tank are the use of a stainless steel bushing or the installation of a short piece of stainless steel pipe between the aluminum and the brass or copper. These prevent direct contact between the aluminum and the copper-bearing alloy, reducing corrosion potential.

Flare-type tube fittings are a much better choice for fuel-system use than compression-type of fittings.

Gasoline Fuel System Installation and Test

The fuel tank is never used as part of the hull's structural support. It is securely mounted to the boat's structure and electrically bonded to the hull. On an aluminim boat, separate electrical bonding of the fill neck and vent fittings normally is not required since the hull acts as a conductor to ground.

After installation, pressure test the entire fuel system to a minimum of 3 PSI or to a head of fuel equal to 1½ times the maxium distance from the lowest point (the top of the fill neck or vent, whichever is lower), making sure there are no leaks.

To perform a head test to 1½ times the maximum head, plug all but one fuel system opening and add a standpipe to the remaining opening. The standpipe must have a vertical rise equal to 1½ times the vertical distance from the bottom of the tank to the top of the fill neck or vent. For example, if the distance from the bottom of the tank to the top of the vent or fill is 36 inches, then a total head of 54 inches (1.5 x 36") is used. The standpipe in this example can be located anywhere on the fuel system as long as the top is at least 54 inches above the lowest point of the fuel tank.

Finally, fill the standpipe to the top with water and inspect the system for signs of leaking. If there are no apparent leaks and the water level in the standpipe does not drop, then the system is tight and it can be drained, dried, and readied for fuel.

You will need a method of determining the quantity of fuel in the tank. Automotive-type electrical fuel-gauge units are not recommended because they are commonly single-wire installations, using the auto frame as the other conductor. Two wire units should always be used on an aluminum boat.

All hose connections in the fuel system (e.g., where the fill hose attaches to the fill neck) should be secured by two stainless steel hose clamps of the type that tighten with a screw; USCG regulations do not allow the use of spring clamps.

Ventilation

Both powered and natural ventilation systems are required in gasoline-powered boats with enclosed engine compartments. The USCG ventilation-system standard is somewhat unique in that it *requires* the boat operator to keep the powered and natural ventilation systems in working order (USCG *33 CFR*, Subpart K, "Ventilation").

Power ventilation system. A forced-air explosion-proof ventilation blower

FIGURE 11-2. Ventilation blower CFM requirements.

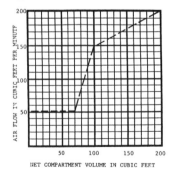

AIR FLOW IN CUBIC FEET PER MINUTE

NET COMPARTMENT VOLUME IN CUBIC FEET

FIGURE 11-3. Engine-compartment ventilation warning label.

WARNING
GASOLINE VAPORS CAN EXPLODE
BEFORE STARTING ENGINE
OPERATE BLOWER FOR 4 MINUTES
CHECK ENGINE COMP'T FOR GAS OR VAPORS
RUN BLOWER WHEN BELOW
CRUISING SPEED

is required in an enclosed engine compartment—to be activated prior to starting the engine to extract any explosive fumes from the boat. The intake duct must extend to the lower third of the compartment but be above the normal level of bilge water. The size of the blower needed depends on the size of the compartment and may be determined from Figure 11-2.

Regulations also require the posting of a warning label in plain view of the operator and near the ignition switch for the engine to remind the boat operator to run the blower for four minutes prior to starting the engine. The warning label must also direct the operator to check that the bilge is free of gas fumes before starting the engine. An appropriate warning label (Figure 11-3) is often included in the package with a new marine bilge blower.

Natural ventilation system. The intake opening on the exterior of the boat must face forward. A duct must extend from the exterior exhaust opening to the lower third of the engine compartment, but be above the normal level of bilge water. The orientation of the exhaust opening is usually aft, but must be such that a natural flow of air will enter and exit the engine compartment when the boat is underway. The required size of natural ventilation openings may be obtained from Figure 11-4.

Diesel Fuel System

Since diesel fuel is considered nonexplosive, standards that pertain to fire hazard are considerably relaxed. The fuel system for diesel fuel is similar to the one used for gasoline—with the following exceptions.

Diesel-fuel Tank

Diesel-fuel tanks are constructed like gasoline tanks, except that a drain valve is permitted at the bottom of the tank, and an additional fuel inlet to the tank, often located alongside the fuel outlet port, is required for the fuel return line. Although diesel tanks may be constructed integral with the hull, it isn't a good idea for aluminum boats. Because of the nature of the fuel, diesel tanks are very difficult to maintain fuel-tight: diesel fuels will penetrate where water will not. For a diesel tank to be fuel-tight, it must be welded under ideal conditions, which—because of limited access, out-of-position welding, and cleanliness problems—are much more difficult to achieve when building integral tanks. Minor weeping from integral tanks is almost impossible to repair and can be very annoying and potentially hazardous. The best option is to install diesel-fuel tanks purchased from an established fuel-tank manufacturer.

FIGURE 11-4. Cross-section requirements for engine-room ventilation openings.

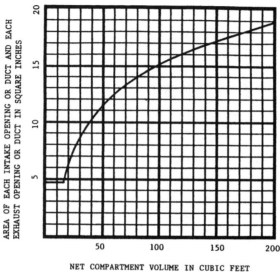

NET COMPARTMENT VOLUME IN CUBIC FEET

On larger diesel boats, it is wise to incorporate clean-out ports in the tops of the fuel tanks for periodic inspection and tank cleaning. Normally circular, clean-out ports should be at least 16 inches in diameter to allow full arm and shoulder access. Cover plates should be attached by welded studs or some other method that doesn't allow fuel to escape around attachment bolts; drilling and tapping into the fuel tank isn't satisfactory, since fuel can escape around the threads. (Fuel can stand in the fill neck, causing a head on the tank at the clean-out opening.) Use a neoprene gasket under the lid to ensure a tight seal.

Diesel-fuel Lines

Black steel pipe, at least schedule 40, may be used for diesel-fuel lines in place of copper or copper-bearing alloys. (The USCG authorizes [*46 CFR* Part 182.20-40, "Diesel Fuel Supply Piping"] seamless steel pipe or tubing providing equivalent safety to copper, nickel-copper, or copper-nickel tubing with .035-inch-minimum wall thickness for use in small passenger-carrying vessels.)

Ventilation

There are no ABYC or U.S. Coast Guard requirements for natural or forced-air engine-compartment ventilation for diesel fuel systems for small boats, as pertains to any explosion hazard of diesel fuel fumes.

References

Safety Standards for Backyard Boatbuilders, COMPTPUB P16761.3. Washington DC: U. S. Department of Transportation (U.S. Coast Guard), 1988.

33 CFR, Part 183, Subpart J, "Fuel Systems." Washington DC: U. S. Department of Transportation (U. S. Coast Guard), 1987.

33 CFR, Part 183, Subpart K, "Ventilation." Washington DC: U. S. Department of Transportation (U. S. Coast Guard), 1987.

Boating Safety Circular 71. Washington DC: U. S. Department of Transportation (U. S. Coast Guard), 1991.

46 CFR, Parts 166-199, Shipping, Subchapter T, 182.20-40, "Machinery Using Diesel Fuel." Washington DC: U. S. Department of Transportation (U. S. Coast Guard), 1988.

Standards and Recommended Practices for Small Craft. Millersville, MD: American Boat and Yacht Council, Inc., 1991.

12

The Electrical System

Since stray electrical currents can cause extensive damage to an aluminum hull, aluminum boats are particularly sensitive to poor wiring practices. It is imperative that the hull *never* be used as an electrical conductor for the boat's electrical system. All electrical equipment must be connected to *both* terminals of the battery by a full two-wire system; the hull must *never* be used as a common ground.

Some automotive equipment—windshield wipers and fuel gauge sending units, for example—are constructed with a single wire arrangement; the metal frame of the automobile is expected to serve as the second conductor. Such items may be used on an aluminum boat only if they are carefully electrically isolated from the hull and provided with an electrical ground wire back to the battery's negative terminal.

To minimize stray-voltage problems, electrically isolate (from the hull) *all* of the vessel's machinery using electrical power, including the controls and exhaust system.

Only the boat's bonding system can use the hull as a conductor. Connect a single-point negative ground from the main-engine negative terminal to one of the engine girders to ground the electrical-power distribution system to the aluminum hull. This ground is a means of maintaining the negative side of the circuit at ground potential and is not to carry current under normal conditions.

DC Electrical System

Most small boats are fitted with a 12-volt DC electrical system. The only USCG regulations that pertain to the electrical systems of small pleasure boats are those concerning the risk of igniting gasoline vapor. Other industry standards and practices are strictly voluntary. Recommended guidelines are provided by the ABYC.

A representative 12-volt DC electrical distribution system for an aluminum boat is provided in Figure 12-1. You will note from this drawing that the positive

FIGURE 12-1. Twelve-volt DC electrical distribution system schematic.

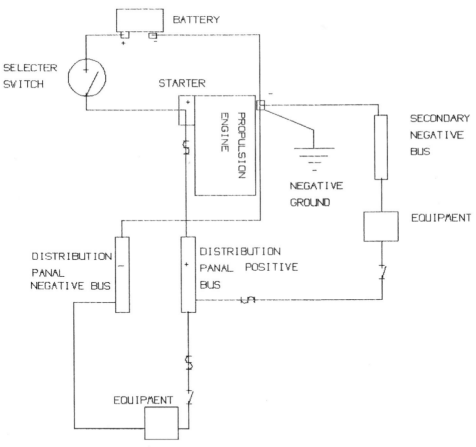

terminal of the battery is connected to the positive terminal of the battery selector switch, then to the positive terminal on the propulsion engine starter (the starter switch and solenoid have been omitted from the schematic for clarity). The negative battery terminal is grounded to the engine. At this point, the circuit is completed to the propulsion engine starter. A short jumper cable from the engine negative ground to the aluminum hull engine girder provides the single point negative ground connection.

The electrical power to energize the DC distribution system is taken from the positive terminal of the battery-selector switch. A circuit breaker, sized to protect the DC system, is placed in the main positive feeder cable near (ABYC E-9.10a) the selector switch, and the cable is connected to the positive busbar of the main power distribution panel. From the distribution panel, branch circuits, individually protected by circuit breakers (or fuses), lead to the boat's various electrical items.

Circuits for electrical equipment mounted forward of the distribution panel are completed by a connection to the negative bus of the power distribution panel, which in turn is connected to the negative battery terminal. For equipment mounted aft—closer to the engine than to the distribution panel—wire runs may be shortened by using a secondary negative busbar located aft and connected to the negative battery terminal.

DC Electrical Load Calculations

To determine the size of the main power-distribution panel, the main-circuit-breaker capacity, and main-cable size, you'll need to calculate the anticipated electrical load. One method is to develop two lists—let's call them list A and list B—similar to those shown in Figure 12-2. List A will include those items that must be available on a continuous basis and are considered necessary for safety at sea. List B will include those items that get intermittent use and aren't normally required for safety at sea.

To properly calculate the total amperage (amps) required for lists A and B, you'll need the actual operating amperage of each item. While some items will be rated in amps, many will indicate only wattage. Convert watts to amps using the following formula:

$$\text{AMPS} = \text{WATTS/VOLTS} \quad \text{or} \quad \text{WATTS} = \text{AMPS} \times \text{VOLTS}$$

A representative list of amperage for some marine items is provided in Figure 12-3.

FIGURE 12-2. Calculating the potential electrical load.

Column A (3% voltage drop)		Column B (10% voltage drop)	
Navigation Lights	_____	Cigarette Lighter	_____
Bilge Blower	_____	Cabin Lighting	_____
Bilge Pump	_____	Horn	_____
Windshield Wiper	_____	Additional Electronics	_____
Radio (Transmitter)	_____	Trim Tabs	_____
Depth Sounder	_____	Power Trim	_____
Radar	_____	Toilets	_____
Searchlight	_____	Anchor Windlass	_____
Instruments	_____	Winches	_____
Alarm System (standby)	_____	Fresh Water Pump	_____
_____	_____	Wash Down Pump	_____
_____	_____	Halon	_____
_____	_____	_____	_____
Total Column A	_____	Total Column B	_____
		10% Column B	_____
		Largest Item in Column B	_____

Total Load Required

Total Column A   _____

The larger of 10% or the largest item in column B   _____

FIGURE 12-3. Typical amperage ratings for selected 12-volt DC equipment.

Navigation Lights (each)	2.0 amps
Bilge Pump	12.0 amps
Bilge Blower	4.0 amps
Windshield wiper (each)	5.0 amps
Radio (VHF)	5.0 amps
Radar	3.3 amps
Loran (fish finder)	17.0 amps
Cabin Lights (each)	1.0 amps
Horn	5.0 amps
Trim Tabs	18.0 amps
Wash-Down Pump	6.3 amps
Heater (engine hot water)	11.0 amps

Circuit Protection and Conductors

Install fuses or trip-free, manual-reset circuit breakers in all the DC circuits to provide overload protection. The current-carrying requirements of each application will determine the conductor (wire) size and type. Bundle conductors when possible and rout them where they will be safe from damage and clear of bilge water. Plastic *snap ties* work well for both bundling wires and securing the bundles to structure attachment points. Where wiring passes through metal bulkheads or other structure, install rubber grommets to protect the wires from damage.

Color codes specified by ABYC for DC electrical systems under 50 volts are provided in Figure 12-4, and adherence to these color codes is highly recommended. Color-coding may be accomplished on systems wired from a single spool of wire (i.e., with one color of wire) by using appropriate-colored sleeves or

FIGURE 12-4. Required and recommended marine-wiring color codes for DC systems under 50 volts.

Required Marine Wiring Color Code	
Green	Bonding
White (W) or Black (B)	Return, Negative Main
Red (R)	Positive Mains, Particularly Unfused
Recommended Marine Wiring Color Code	
Yellow w/ Red Stripe (YR)	Starting Circuit
Yellow (Y)	Alternator Field, Bilge Blower
Dark Gray (Gy)	Navigation Lights, Tachometer
Brown (Br)	Generator Armature, Alternator Charge Light, Pumps
Orange (O)	Accessory Feed, Accessory Common Feed
Purple (Pu)	Ignition, Instrument Feed
Dark Blue	Cabin and Instrument Lights
Light Blue (Lt Bl)	Oil Pressure
Tan	Water Temperature
Pink (Pk)	Fuel Gauge

tape at the ends. If tape is used for color-coding, use at least two full turns of tape at least ³⁄₁₆ inch wide.

Determining Conductor Wire Size

Select wire large enough to ensure that adequate voltage reaches your equipment. Knowing the length of the conductor and the amperage requirement of the device being serviced will allow you to determine the required cross-sectional wire size in circular mills. This is accomplished by plugging these values into the formula for calculating voltage drop. That formula is:

$$E= \frac{(10.75)\ (L)\ (I)}{C}$$

Where: 10.75 is a constant and:

E= voltage drop in volts

L= length of the conductor in feet (to *and* from the device)

I= current in amps (from the device rating)

C= conductor size circular mills.

By rewriting this equation as

$$C= \frac{(10.75)\ (L)\ (I)}{E}$$

you can easily calculate conductor size in circular mills. Convert this into gauge size by consulting Table 12-1.

Example: The total length of the wire run from the positive power source to a bilge pump and back to the negative terminal (the nearest negative busbar) is 20 feet. The pump is rated at 12.0 amps.

Determine the voltage drop (E) by multiplying 12 volts times the allowable 3-percent drop—12 x .03 = 0.36 volts. Plug this number and the two values above into the formula to determine the minimum wire size in circular mills:

$$C = \frac{(10.75)(20)(12)}{0.36} \quad \text{or} \quad C = 7166.7$$

Consult the wire size table (Table 12-1). Since 7166.7 circular mills is the *minimum* wire size, look up the next larger standard size, which is 10,000 circular mills. This corresponds to a gauge size of 10, so use 10-gauge wire to connect the bilge pump.

Wire Gauge Tables. A much faster method of determining the needed wire gauge is to consult standard wire-gauge tables (Table 12-2) for either a 3-percent or 10-percent voltage drop. From the length of conductor and the

TABLE 12-1. Mill to gauge conversion.

Wire Size	
Gauge	Mills*
18	1600
16	2400
14	3800
12	6000
10	10000
8	15000
6	26000
4	38000
2	63000
1	78000
0	100000
00	126000
000	160000

*Circular Mills

amperage requirement of the device, the tables will provide you with the correct wire gauge. To look up the wire size in the table for the previous example, find the 20-feet column in the table designated *12 volt DC, 3-percent voltage drop* and follow it down to where it intersects the 15-amp row—the closest value *exceeding* the 12-amp pump rating. This gives you a wire size of 10 gauge. ABYC recommends that no boat wiring be less than 16 gauge.

Figure 12-5 is a sample wiring diagram for a 23-foot sportfishing boat equipped with two batteries. The wire size and color-coding is shown on each run, along with the amperage rating of each fuse. Note that the automatic bilge-pump switch bypasses the master battery switch so it can still operate with the

TABLE 12-2. Wire gauge per percentage drop.

	Length of Conductor, Feet						
	10	15	20	25	30	40	50
Amps	Wire Gauge (12 V DC, 3% Voltage Drop)						
5	18	16	14	12	12	10	10
10	14	12	10	10	10	8	6
15	12	10	10	8	8	6	6
20	10	10	8	6	6	6	4
25	10	8	6	6	6	4	4
30	10	8	6	6	4	4	2
40	8	6	6	4	4	2	2
50	6	6	4	4	2	2	1
60	6	4	4	2	2	1	0
Amps	Wire Gauge (12 V DC, 10% Voltage Drop)						
5	18	18	18	18	18	16	16
10	18	18	16	16	14	14	12
15	18	16	14	14	12	12	10
20	16	14	14	12	12	10	10
25	16	14	12	12	10	10	8
30	14	12	12	10	10	8	8
40	14	12	10	10	8	8	6
50	12	10	10	8	8	6	6
60	12	10	8	8	6	6	4

FIGURE 12-5. Twelve-volt electrical distribution system for a 23-foot aluminum sportfishing boat.

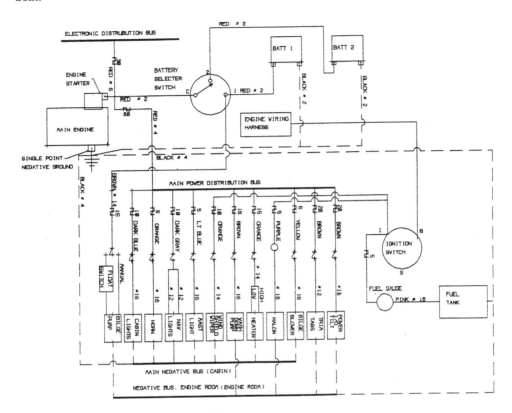

battery selector switch in the *off* position. Equipment items located in the stern of the boat are wired to a negative busbar located in the engine room to reduce the length of wire runs.

Battery Capacity

Most small boats have a single 12-volt battery, but it's a better practice to have two batteries aboard connected through a battery selector switch with four positions: battery 1, battery 2, both, and off. The cranking battery(s) must have at least the *cold-cranking amperage* required by the engine manufacturer. In addition, the accessory (house) battery's rated reserve capacity should be sufficient to power the load in column A (Figure 12-2) for a minimum of 1½ hours.

Battery Charging

If the propulsion-engine alternator is the only battery-charging device aboard, then its rated output must be at least equal to the total calculated load (Figure 12-2).

Bonding of DC Systems

Boats should be fitted with an electrical bonding system that provides a low-resistance electrical path between otherwise isolated metallic items. The bonding conductor provides protection against electrolytic corrosion caused by stray voltage, prevents possible electrical shock from metallic enclosures of electrical equipment, provides a path to ground in the event of a lightning strike, and minimizes radio interference. A common bonding conductor on boats with non-conducting hulls—such as fiberglass—usually runs fore and aft and is connected to the negative ground of the DC electrical system. Individual bonding conductors connect the items being grounded to the common bonding conductor. Bonding conductors are color-coded green.

On a boat with an aluminum hull, the hull itself can act as the bonding conductor. Items that are electrically isolated from the hull may be bonded by a separate conductor between the item and the hull. In the event of a short-circuit, the hull will act as the bonding conductor from the short-circuit item back to the single-point negative ground.

Cathodic Protection

Corrosion of the hull and underwater components can be caused by dissimilar metals in electrical contact or in a current-conducting solution such as sea water. To reduce this potential for corrosion, do not use dissimilar metals below the waterline or in wet spaces. Aluminum is very reactive with most common marine metals and requires electrical isolation from dissimilar metals by the use of insulators. Sacrificial zinc anodes can be used below the water to protect an aluminum hull from electrolysis.

Aluminum—high on the electrolytic scale (Figure 12-6)—is sacrificial to materials lower on the scale. When it is in electrical contact with such materials, electrolytic corrosion to the aluminum results. If dissimilar metals lower on the electrolytic scale (more noble) than aluminum cannot be avoided, install sacrificial anodes higher on the scale—such as zinc; the anodes will sacrifice to the more noble metal, protecting the aluminum hull. A good barrier coat of paint will provide additional protection to an aluminum hull.

Figure 12-6. Galvanic series of metals in seawater.

From least noble to most noble

Magnesium
Zinc
Berylium
Aluminum Alloys
Cadmium
Mild Steel, Cast Iron
Low Alloy Steel
Austenitic Cast Iron
Aluminum Bronze
Naval Brass, Yellow Brass, Red Brass
Tin
Copper
Pb-Sn Solder (50/50)
Admiralty Brass, Aluminum Brass
Manganese Bronze
Silicon Bronze
Tin Bronze (G&M)
Stainless Steel - Types 410,416*
Nickel Silver
90-10 Copper-Nickel
80-20 Copper-Nickel
Stainless Steel - Type 430*
Lead
70-30 Copper-Nickel
Nickel-Aluminum Bronze
Nickel-Chromium Alloy 600*
Silver Braze Alloys
Nickel 200
Silver
Stainless Steel - Types 302, 304, 321, 347*
Nickel-Copper Alloys 400, K-500
Stainless Steel - Types 316, 317*
Alloy "20" Stainless Steels
Nickel-Iron-Chromium Alloy 825
Ni-Cr-Mo-Cu-Si Alloy B
Titanium
Ni-Cr-Mo Alloy C
Platinum
Graphite

Sacrificial hull anodes are unnecessary on small boats that spend the vast majority of their life out of the water. If an aluminum boat without permanently installed sacrificial anodes is to spend a prolonged period in salt water, temporary sacrificial anodes can be attached to the metallic hull structure with a conductor and lowered over the side to provide some protection at the moorage.

Lightning Protection

An aluminum hull is an electrical conductor. If external components such as a mast are all electrically connected to the hull through direct metal-to-metal contact or proper bonding procedures, no further protection is necessary for lightning since current will flow through the hull to ground without resistance.

AC Electrical System

Alternating current—50 to 60 Hertz (Hz)—isn't normally found aboard small boats. When it is used, it's normally supplied by a shore-power connection. If you plan to have 60 Hz AC power on your aluminum boat, you should engage the services of a professional electrician familiar with marine installations. Electrical requirements, as established by the U.S. Coast Guard for small passenger-carrying vessels, can be found in the USCG *46 CFR* Subchapter T. This is an excellent guideline to use when designing marine electrical systems. Corrosion caused by a faulty shore-power connection can cause *extreme* hull damage in a very short time. You must electrically isolate any shore-power system, including the ground wire, from the hull. Stray voltage in a marina often finds a circuit through the shore-power ground. Electrical isolation of the shore power is easily accomplished by installing a marine-type isolation transformer on board and running all shore electrical power through this transformer.

References

Marine Corrosion. Fond du Lac, WI: Mercury Marine (Brunswick Corporation), 1985.

Smead, David, and Ishihara, Ruth. *Wiring 12 Volts for Ample Power*. Seattle, WA: Rides Publishing Company, 1990.

Standards and Recommended Practices for Small Craft. Millersville, MD: American Boat and Yacht Council, Inc., 1991.

Aluminum Boats, 2nd ed. Oakland, CA: Kaiser Aluminum and Chemical Sales, Inc., 1978.

46 CFR, Subchapter T, "Small Passenger-carrying Vessels." Washington DC: U. S. Department of Transportation (U. S. Coast Guard), 1988.

13

Woodwork and Insulation

Small production aluminum boats don't usually have wood aboard, with the exception of the floorboards, and even those are usually covered with some type of all-weather material. On boats up to about 20 feet, decks may also be wood—normally ¾-inch plywood over aluminum-angle subframing—secured with self-tapping stainless steel screws and well painted. Such decks are usually covered with some type of nonskid material, and they aren't watertight. Wood is used on small production-built aluminum boats strictly for reasons of economy and convenience, and not for aesthetics or physical comfort.

For boats over 20 feet, wood decks, when used, are bolted to aluminum margin plates welded to the side shell at the gunnel. Subframing may be wood or aluminum, depending upon the type of deck and the structural requirements. Although wood decks have been used successfully on steel hulls, aluminum expands and contracts much more than steel, causing the attachment bolts to egg out the bolt holes and resulting in leaks. For an aluminum hull, a deck that is to be watertight should be constructed of aluminum.

Special-purpose boats and yachts requiring a very high quality interior often incorporate generous quantities of wood into the interior. Wood is used on the exterior as well, primarily for decorative purposes. The boat shown in Figures 13-1 and 13-2 was constructed as a showpiece to demonstrate special aluminum-coating systems and special equipment. Its decks are aluminum, covered with teak that was glued in place (held in position during the curing of the glue with

FIGURE 13-1. **Wood-trimmed 28-foot aluminum workboat M-28 by Maritime Outfitters, Newport Beach, California.**

FIGURE 13-2. **Mahogany-topped operator's console.**

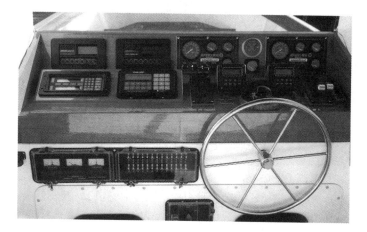

a vacuum blanket). It also features a bright mahogany console top and is trimmed with a bright mahogany coaming around the perimeter of the working deck.

One advantage of wood is its light weight, even compared with aluminum. Wood is about 25 percent the weight of aluminum of equivalent thickness, a significant factor for interior decks. Wood interior decks are also easier to work with, water doesn't easily condense on them, and the wood has better thermal and acoustic insulating properties than aluminum.

Furring Out

The required preparation of the hull for the installation of wood components like interior decks, finish bulkheads, and joiner work is known as *furring out*. Following an established sequence of tasks in furring out the inside of an aluminum boat will save time and labor. Because of the nature of this preparation, thermal and acoustic insulation are included in this section.

Attachments

Attach woodwork to an aluminum hull by first bolting or screwing pieces of wood—*furring strips* or *furring blocks*—to structural members (Figure 13-3). In

FIGURE 13-3. Furring strips attached to furring clips.

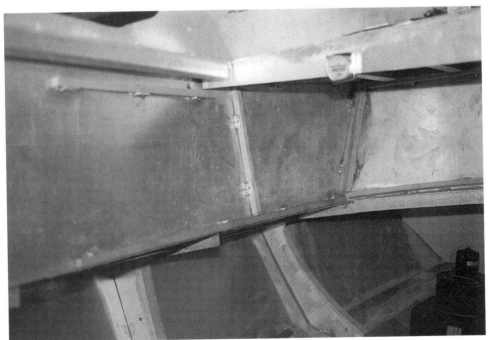

some cases, small pieces of metal called *furring clips* will have to be welded to the boat's aluminum structure to provide attachment points for the furring.

Use stainless steel fasteners to attach the furring. Quarter-inch stainless steel hex-head bolts with flat washers are commonly used to attach wood to furring clips. For attachment to sheet metal, self-tapping screws may be used provided the pilot holes are the right size, which may require a little experimenting. One word of caution about self-tapping screws in aluminum: because aluminum has a tendency to be very sticky, trying to install a self-tapping screw in an undersize hole will result in the head of the fastener twisting off 99 percent of the time. The same goes for trying to cut threads in aluminum with a stainless steel bolt.

Instead of welding, furring clips can be glued in place with a glue designed for metal-to-metal joints. Gluing is especially useful on a light structure that will show objectionable weld shrink marks or in an area that might be subject to fire or explosion because of weld heat. One effective adhesive for this use is Versilok U-404, an acrylic structural adhesive manufactured by the Lord Corporation, Industrial Adhesives Division, Erie, Pennsylvania.

One major advantage aluminum construction has over steel is that no paint barrier coat is required over aluminum-to-aluminum joints to protect against corrosion. Unlike with steel, furring clips can be tack-welded to an aluminum boat as needed during the furring-out process without regard to an interior coating system. But furring out an aluminum boat is not totally without hazards: woods treated with copper compounds, or wet or unseasoned woods of any kind, should not be placed in contact with the aluminum, or the aluminum will corrode. Protect aluminum in contact with wood and subject to moisture by coating the aluminum with zinc-chromate primer and painting the wood with zinc-chromate, aluminum pigmented, or bituminous paint. In normally dry areas, coating of the aluminum-to-wood adjoining surfaces is not required where dry, untreated wood is used.

Furring Strips

Since furring strips or blocks will be used to attach most interior woodwork, they should be fashioned from dry wood of a type suitable for the intended purpose, such as pine or Douglas fir. Attach furring strips or blocks to the structure or to clips as needed to fully secure the interior (Figure 13-4).

FIGURE 13-4. Furring blocks for attaching teak ceiling.

Polyurethane Insulation

The best hull insulation and flotation for an aluminum boat is polyurethane foam. It's available in a number of densities, but 4-pound (per cubic foot) is about the best density for withstanding the minor scrapes and impacts associated with the marine environment. Polyurethane foam comes in precut 4 x 8 sheets (in almost any thickness), in a liquid two-part pour, or as a spray that can be shot directly onto the area requiring insulation or flotation.

Polyurethane foam provides both acoustic and thermal insulation. Where it covers the aluminum it prevents moist air from contacting the cold metal, eliminating condensation problems. It also provides excellent emergency flotation in the event of swamping.

Polyurethane foam does emit hydrocarbons during the foaming process and may be subject to environmental restrictions in the future.

Sprayed-in-place Polyurethane Foam

Spraying is the most common method of installing polyurethane foam in boats. It is usually done by a subcontractor who has the special equipment required. Sprayed-in-place foam insulation is commonly applied to a thickness of about 2 inches or to the height of the hull structural members, whichever is less. The foam rises during the rapid curing cycle, and the surface of the foam takes on a shiny appearance. The uniformity of the foam's thickness and the smoothness of its surface are directly related to the skill of the spray-gun operator. The shiny exterior skin is harder than the material lying just under the surface, and it acts as a seal against water entry. The foam below the surface exhibits very good water resistance as well, but if it's exposed, it will take on small amounts of water, so don't break the surface of the foam unless absolutely necessary.

In areas not subject to moisture, it may be desirable to smooth off the foamed-in-place insulation for a uniform surface. This can be done with a knife or saw, but suprisingly it is much more difficult than it appears. To facilitate rapid foam removal, some foaming contractors can plane the surface with a special foam plane with eggbeater-like blades to provide a uniform foam surface.

Install insulation foam from about the first longitudinal stringer *below* the design waterline up (Figure 13-5), leaving all bilge areas clear. Because sprayed-

FIGURE 13-5. Sprayed-in-place polyurethane foam on the inside of the hull.

in-place foam is very sticky and extremely difficult to remove after it sets, install all hull furring clips and furring strips before the foam is sprayed on the hull. Wiring raceways and below-deck piping will also be easier to install prior to spraying foam. Install machinery and complete the finish work after the foam is in place.

Pouring Polyurethane Foam

Polyurethane foam is also available from most marine hardware stores in a liquid two-part system that when mixed expands into foam with about a 2-pound density. It is used to fill voids and provide flotation material in nonaccessible areas. The rapid expansion of the liquid into foam can exert enough pressure to bulge out or even rupture any confining structure. The liquid unit expands approximately 30 times when it rises into foam and has been known to rupture bulkheads. Avoid this risk by paying very close attention to the amount of foam you pour into an enclosed cavity. Properly applied, a 1-quart unit will yield 1 to 1¼ cubic feet of foam.

The chemical reaction causing the liquid to expand into foam also emits gases that can be corrosive to aluminum. Be sure the area being insulated is well ventilated immediately after pouring the foam to allow these corrosive gases to escape.

Polyurethane Sheet

Sheet polyurethane foam is available in a number of densities, but 4-pound is the recommended density for boat insulation. Cut the foam to size with a knife and attach it directly to the aluminum plate with an insulation adhesive such as Miracle Insulation Adhesive MS 120 (Miracle Adhesives Corp., Bellmore, New York 11710). Both the sheet foam and the adhesive should be available from any large insulation and refractories distributor (such as E. J. Bartells Co., Portland, Oregon).

Use sheet foam on flat areas of the superstructure where a very uniform and smooth insulation is required. Eliminate any air gaps at the joints between panels by using yet another form of polyurethane foam—the aerosol cans of foam that can be purchased at any hardware store. Route any wiring after the panels have been installed by simply cutting channels into the surface of the foam.

A significant amount of structural strength can be added to a flat panel by installing a structurally strong interior panel over a foam core. Gluing plywood directly to the insulation on the inside face of the insulation board will result in a strong sandwich panel.

Engine-compartment Insulation

Engine-noise levels in a metal boat can be quite high. The metal hull and structural components are excellent sound conductors and tend to transmit the noise throughout the boat. To quiet an aluminum boat requires sound deadening insulation that is in direct contact with the metal to reduce the vibration and break up the sound waves.

The insulation around an engine and in engine spaces is usually subject to rougher treatment than that in other areas, partly due to periodic engine maintenance. In addition, engine-compartment insulation can be subject to elevated temperatures and contact with oils, suggesting special insulation requirements.

Hot areas, such as dry exhaust stacks, are usually insulated with high-temperature fiberglass insulation (which has replaced the asbestos insulations used in the past). The insulation material is often covered with fiberglass cloth to protect the surface from damage. This type of insulation is available to fit over pipe and fittings and can be obtained from insulation and refractories dealers.

On small inboard-powered boats with the engine(s) covered by a box, a rubber-like material can be used to insulate the engine box itself. This is an expanded closed-cell material that is flexible and has a low flame spread rate. One such product is Armstrong Armorflex 6408 sheet, available in black in thicknesses of ½, ¾, and 1 inch. Glue it in place with Armstrong #520 adhesive. If a very quiet boat is required, a number of effective sound-deadening fire-resistant special insulations are available, including lead-lined fiberglass.

Cabin Sole (Deck)

Interior decks are usually ¾-inch plywood laid over aluminum structural supports. Attach the plywood to the structure either by direct bolting, drilling and tapping for screws, or by screws driven into furring strips. This method is usually much faster and easier than installing wood support framing since attaching the wood framing to the hull will almost always take more effort than aluminum framing. Plywood decks are lighter than metal and provide for easier through-cutting of hatches and attachment of joiner work.

Cabin soles, or decks, can be finished in any manner desired. A very nice teak and holly plywood is available from marine hardwood dealers that looks like a real teak deck (see Figure 13-8), but since the teak veneer is very thin, you should protect areas subject to heavy wear.

Headliner and Bulkhead Paneling

The choice of headliner material depends upon the owner's preference, but in all cases, headliners and paneling should be washable. One very nice headliner is an FRP textured sheet used in commercial food-processing facilities. Common trade names for FRP paneling are Duratuf, Glasteel, and Lasco. (One source of FRP panels is Paragon Pacific, 5716 NW Hassallo, Portland, Oregon 97213.) Glue FRP paneling over the insulation with insulation adhesive, or install it with thin wood battens screwed to pre-placed furring strips. For a professional look, use stainless steel oval-head screws with finish washers to hold the headliner-securing battens in place.

FIGURE 13-6. **Special corner molding to join composite panels.**

FIGURE 13-7. **Teak ceiling installed and ready for teak plugs.**

Bulkhead paneling can be any rugged material. Teak plywood is always popular. Other paneling, including polyester-impregnated paper overlay on exterior medium-density fiberboard, is available from marine-wood suppliers. Join the panels with pieces of wood, preferably teak or mahogany, shaped into special corner or edge moldings with recessed grooves to take the paneling (Figure 13-6), and no fasteners will show. A source of overlay fiberboard as well as teak and other marine woods is East Teak of Washington, 8510 212th SW, Woodenville, WA 98072. Special moldings, prefabricated wood handrail, louvre doors, cabinet doors, and specialty marine wood items can be obtained from H & L Cabinets and Millwork, 2965 E. Harcourt St. Compton, CA 90221.

Areas that have compound curvature, such as the hull sides toward the bow, are most easily paneled with wood strips installed with a small gap between them (Figure 13-7). The wood strips can be oiled, varnished bright, or painted. Attach them to pre-placed furring strips, and either plug the screw holes or use oval-head stainless steel screws and finish washers. The strips shown in the photo have been installed with countersunk screws and are ready for wood plugs.

FIGURE 13-8. Teak and laminate interior of 23-foot sportfishing boat.

FIGURE 13-9. Prefabricated galley unit.

FIGURE 13-10. Galley unit installed and trimmed. Note hinged helmsman's seat.

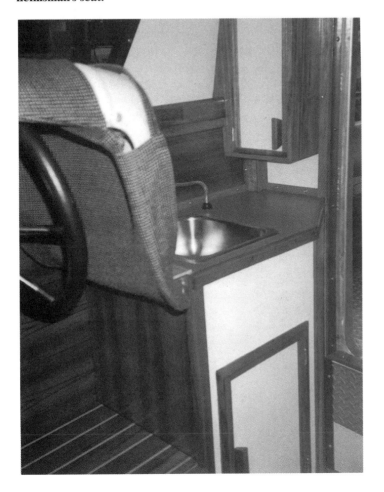

The various types of paneling and methods of installing and joining them mentioned above were used by Specialty Marine of Scappoose, Oregon, to construct the interior of the 23-foot sportfishing boat shown in Figure 13-8. Note the use of oval-head screws and finish washers on the trim strip between the windshield windows.

Construct built-in furniture—berths, galley units, etc.—from paneling and shaped wood moldings. Prefabricating these units in the shop (Figure 13-9) can improve quality and reduce production time. Glued joints are a must. Fit all cabinet doors and drawers with some suitable device to prevent accidental opening in a seaway. Drawers are often fitted with a lift-and-pull stop. Securely fasten the furniture units to the hull structure, then install the final trim (Figure 13-10) to complete the interior woodwork. Be sure you provide some means of access to get behind all units for inspection.

Windows

Rubber *snap-in-place* automotive window retainer moldings can be effectively used on metal boats. Where the superstructure or hull is thin, this type of window retainer is very economical.

Opening windows and high-quality marine windows require a rigid frame. Most marine-hardware stores can provide both off-the-shelf and custom windows—with aluminum or plastic frames. You'll need to pay some attention to the thickness of the house side at the window opening to order the proper frame.

Superstructure side panels requiring windows are not always free of twist, and glass twists very little. If you need a window in a twisted panel, construct a special recess of aluminum to make a flat area for the window installation.

14

Aluminum Painting Systems

A properly constructed and maintained aluminum boat doesn't need paint to protect the hull from corrosion. On boats that will spend prolonged periods in salt water, where marine growth on the hull can be a problem, antifouling paints may be used. Other than antifouling bottom paint, most commercial aluminum boats do not have paint on hull surfaces, neither inside nor out. This is one of the biggest cost savings of an aluminum hull when compared with other hull materials.

On yachts and small pleasure boats, paints are often desired for cosmetic purposes. The combination of a properly prepared aluminum surface and a properly applied paint system can assure a very satisfactory paint bond. The key here is proper *preparation* of the surface and proper *application* of the paint system. All too often paint is applied to aluminum hulls that have not been properly prepared. If the paint system isn't compatible with the marine environment, premature paint system failure—blistering and peeling—is a virtual certainty.

Welded-aluminum boats that are constructed with nondevelopable surfaces, such as round-bilge sailboats, are constructed of a series of small developable surfaces with abrupt surface changes at plate seams. In addition, boats constructed of developable surfaces may not be as fair as desired due to distortion from weld heat. In both cases, the desired fair surface can only be obtained by the application of fairing compounds to fill depressions and by manual longboard sanding. The labor required to fair an aluminum hull in preparation for a high-gloss finish can easily exceed the man-hours to construct the hull.

In the early 1970s, during a time of intensive building of large aluminum sailboats, polyester body putty was the standard hull-fairing compound. Filler was used extensively on those round-bilge boats—constructed of a number of small, rolled plates—to achieve the smooth, high-gloss finish required. The filler was applied to the hull surface, sanded flush, then painted. Unfortunately the polyester putties used were later discovered to slowly absorb water, resulting in premature paint system failure. Epoxies using inert fillers, such as *microballoons*, have replaced polyester body putty, and this seems to have a much better rate of success.

Various trade-name paint systems (which include fairing cements) are on the market that are advertised as excellent for aluminum boats. Not only is an excellent product needed, but excellent technical assistance from the product manufacturer is needed when problems are encountered. This has been a shortfall of at least one large paint manufacturer, to the chagrin of a number of yacht builders and owners. For this reason, not only should you carefully research the product itself before you select it, but you should find out what technical assistance is offered. If the paint system fails, the paint manufacturer always blames the applicator, but having a technician from the paint manufacturer on site during the painting of a large yacht should confirm proper adherence to established application procedures and techniques.

Painting Small Welded Production Boats

Small-aluminum-boat manufacturers in the Pacific Northwest commonly use automotive paints, which aren't formulated for underwater application. The rationalization here is that the boat will spend the vast majority of its life out of the water. In addition, most of the paint schemes are such that the painted surfaces are above the waterline.

For an excellent-looking exterior finish, manufacturers commonly apply automotive-type body putty to specific areas of the boat. The process of filling, then sanding and painting is the same as that used on automobiles. As a matter of fact, a number of small-boat manufactures subcontract out the hull painting to automotive body shops since they have expertise and special equipment not normally available at the boatbuilder's facility.

Automotive paints do provide a very attractive finish and will last for a reasonable period of time. However, it is interesting that the boat-manufacturer's warranty in most cases does not cover the paint system.

The use of automotive body fillers and paints is *not* the proper way to finish an aluminum boat that will be left in the water. Boats normally left afloat must be painted in accordance with the marine-coatings manufacturers' recommended materials and procedures, or the paint system will prematurely fail.

Marine Coatings

Increased awareness of the potential environmental impact of the chemicals in fairing and painting systems have resulted in a number of national and local restrictions. These can be a major problem for the occasional aluminum-hull painter. Paint systems that will do an excellent job on a hull but, because of extreme health hazards and EPA regulations require special equipment to apply, aren't practical for the home builder. Even hull preparation—the use of an etching solution that ultimately flows into a drain or storm sewer, for example—can violate EPA regulations. If the paint system you want to use poses a risk to the environment, let a professional boatshop, equipped to meet EPA requirements, do the work. (Make sure the shop you select is familiar with fairing and painting aluminum.)

If you want to do your own painting, you'll need a paint system you can practically apply. Keep in mind that the application of a marine paint system can be both time consuming and expensive compared with an automotive-type finish. Some paint systems, rather than calling for the use of etching solutions, are designed to be applied over a surface that has been *mechanically prepared*. Sandblasting is *not* recommended as a method of mechanical surface preparation because of the need to carefully monitor both air quality (EPA) and the abrasive being used for contaminants that will damage the aluminum.

Hull Preparation

Each paint-system manufacturer with an aluminum-hull painting system has developed their own hull preparation procedure, but as a general rule the procedures all call for roughing the surface, chemical preparation of the surface, a prime coat, barrier coats, and finish coats—with filling compounds used to improve surface fairness. Specifically, abrade the exterior of an aluminum hull—by sanding or by using abrasive pads—to roughen and clean the surface. Follow this by etching, usually with a phosphoric acid solution to change the chemical properties of the aluminum surface for better paint adhesion. Etching is accomplished using either a special etching primer or a wash system, and it is followed by a primer coat. After the primer, apply high-build barrier coats both above

FIGURE 14-1. Awlgrip Aluminum System 1 application sequence.

Aluminum
SYSTEM 1:

> ### Bare/New
> **Above Waterline Only** where ALUMIPREP™ 33 and ALODINE® 1201 *are not* to be used.

1. Thoroughly clean and degrease the surface. Use commercial non-alkaline detergents, steam cleaners or pressure washers. Be sure *all* detergent residue is rinsed from the surface. Use AWL-PREP-PLUS™ Wax and Grease Remover (T0115) or AWL-PREP™ Surface Cleaner (T0008) for a final wipe down of the surface.

   Steps 2 through 5 need to be completed as quickly as possible so the surface is primed before the aluminum can re-oxidize.

2. Brush blast or grind surface with 60 grit hard disc pads to clean, bright metal.

3. If surface profile is above 4 mils, lightly grind surface to remove "spikes" and achieve 3-4 mil profile. *Thoroughly* remove all blasting/grinding dust or residue by blowing off with clean, dry, compressed air.

4. Immediately apply AWLGRIP® 545 Gray Primer* (D1001 Base, D3001 Converter, T0006 Reducer) to wet film of 5 to 6.5 mils, dry film of 2 to 3 mils. Allow 545 to cure to tack free (minimum of 2 hours at 77°F/50% R.H.) before proceeding to next step. If 545 is allowed to cure more than 24 hours (77°F/50% R.H.), it will have to be lightly sanded before proceeding. If sanding is required *do not* sand through to bare metal. If you do break through to bare metal, re-prime these areas with 545. Remove sanding dust or residue.

5. Apply yellow High Build Epoxy Primer (D9002 Base, D3002 Converter, T0006 Reducer) to completely fill and then cover any remaining surface profile. This usually requires 2 to 3 coats. Apply each coat to 6 to 9 mils WFT, 3 mils DFT. Allow minimum of one hour (77°F/50% R.H.) between coats. Allow High Build Epoxy Primer to cure hard before proceeding.

6. Power sand the High Build Epoxy Primer with 80 grit paper. *Do not sand through.* Should you accidentally sand through to bare aluminum, spot prime with 545. (See step 4)

   Blow off sanding dust and residue with clean dry compressed air while dry wiping with clean cloths. Then solvent clean with AWL-PREP™ (T0008) or AWL-PREP™ PLUS using Two Cloth Method.

   (If fairing is required refer to Section on fairing. If no fairing is required proceed to step 7).

7. Apply AWLGRIP® 545 Primer (either white or gray) to fill sand scratches. This may require 2 to 3 coats at 5 to 6.5 mils WFT, 2 to 3 mils DFT. Allow minimum one hour between coats (77°F/50% R.H.). Allow 545 to cure hard.

8. Sand 545 with 220-400 grit paper to a smooth flat finish. Blow off all sanding residue while dry wiping with clean cloths. Solvent wipe with T0008 or T0115 using Two Cloth Method. Repeat process as necessary until surface is completely clean. Allow surface to dry.

9. Tack off surface with AWLGRIP® Tack Rags.

10. Apply AWLGRIP® Urethane Topcoat to total DFT of 2.5 to 3 mils.

ALODINE® — Registered trademark of Amchem.

*Do Not use roller to apply this first coat. The sharp metal profile can snag the roller, leaving roller fibers or hairs in the paint film. These fibers or hairs can act as wicks, allowing contamination or moisture to enter the paint film. This could lead to premature coating failure.

and below the waterline. Complete the job above the waterline by applying the hull finish paint. A typical above-the-waterline aluminum-hull painting system is shown in Figure 14-1.

Anti-fouling paint below the waterline is required to finish the job for boats that will be based in salt water. Copper-based paints must never be used on an aluminum hull because of galvanic corrosion problems; use tin-based anti-fouling paints on an aluminum hull.

Applying tin-based antifouling paints requires a special license, usually obtainable from state or federal authorities. Major marine-paint retailers can provide data on regulatory restrictions and direct potential boat painters to the proper authorities for required permits.

Reference

Awlgrip Marine Application Guide. Edition X. St. Louis, MO: U. S. Paint, Rev. 3/90.

Laying Out a Camber Curve

The deck of a boat normally has a slight curvature to assist with drainage and to impart some stiffness to the weather decks and house top. This curvature is called *camber*, or *crown*. Camber is always an arc of a circle unless specified otherwise. Decks can have a constant camber, meaning one camber curve will fit all areas of the deck, or they can have camber curves that vary over the deck area.

The simplest deck camber is the constant-camber curve. When a boat designer specifies a 6-inch camber curve, he means that the crown of the camber at the deck centerline is 6 inches higher than the sheer (deck edge) at the maximum beam of the deck. This same camber curve is used for the entire deck area. This type of curve works well for decks that have a fairly uniform width, such as a house top or a section of deck midships.

In the area of the bow, where the beam of the deck will progress from near zero at the tip of the bow and grow progressively wider the farther aft you travel, a variation from a fixed-camber curve is necessary to prevent a reverse curve in

FIGURE I-1. The sheerline effect of a fixed-camber deck.

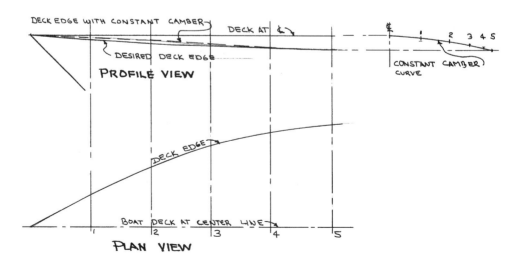

the sheer near the bow, as shown in Figure I-1. To prevent this reverse curve in the sheer, a constantly changing camber over the length of the deck must be developed.

The use of a variable camber in boat decks is not uncommon. Often a boat designer doesn't specify a camber curve, but indicates the amount of deck camber by drawing the boat's centerline and sheer heights in the profile view of the lines drawing. Heights and half-breadths for the sheer and centerline heights for the deck at the station lines will be called out on the table of offsets. From these offsets, individual camber curves for each station must be developed.

It is often impractical to actually draw the arc of the camber curve because its radius is too large for loft-floor space. The camber curve is usually drawn in half-breadth. Later, if needed, the camber is duplicated for the other half of the curve so that a full-size, full-width template can be constructed.

One common method of camber curve development is to draw a quarter-circle segment with a radius equal to the specified camber height, as shown on the left side of Figure I-2. A close approximation of a camber arc is obtained by holding the camber height (ad) constant and stretching line ab and arc db like a rubber band to become line ac and arc dc, effectively stretching the circle segment into a long curve (dc). This new curve is a close approximation of the true camber curve.

The mechanics of doing this stretching starts by dividing the quarter-circle arc (db) and the baseline (ab) into four equal parts (Figure I-2). Join the segment division points, and use the lengths of each of these lines as heights when

FIGURE I-2. **Developing a camber from a quarter circle.**

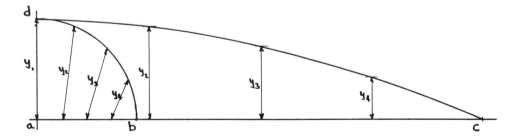

drawing the camber curve. These heights are shown as y_1, y_2, y_3, and y_4 in Figure I-2.

Lay out the half-breadth camber curve with the base (line ac in Figure I-2) equal in length to the maximum half-breadth of the boat's deck. Divide line ac into four equal intervals and lay out the heights (y_1, y_2, etc.) to locate heights of the camber curve above line ac and draw in the curve (dc) using a flexible batten. Curve dc is not a true arc of a circle, but a very close approximation that has proven through experience to be sufficiently accurate for most boatbuilding circular cambers.

It's possible to have a camber with other than an arc of a circle—a parabolic arc, for instance—as the basis of the camber. Each special camber requirement must be developed individually.

FIGURE I-3. Calculating the radius from the camber arc.

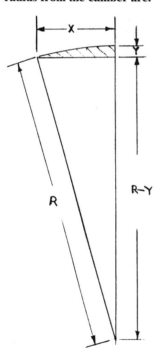

Finding the Radius of a Camber Arc

In some cases, it can be helpful to determine the actual radius of the camber arc when given only the camber height and the half-breadth of the camber curve. This is easy to calculate.

Using Figure I-3 as a reference, x equals the half-breadth of the camber curve, y equals the camber curve height, and R is the unknown radius. The formula for calculating the radius is derived from the Pythagorean theorem for a right triangle, $a^2 + b^2 = c^2$, as follows:

$$x^2 + (R - y)^2 = R^2$$

$$x^2 + R^2 - 2yR + y^2 = R^2$$

$$x^2 - 2yR + y^2 = 0$$

$$x^2 + y^2 = 2yR$$

$$R = \frac{x^2 + y^2}{2y}$$

Appendix II

Calculating Material Stretch-Out for Brake Bending

Bending aluminum with a press brake is one of the most economical construction techniques in aluminum-boat building. You need to determine the actual flat-pattern size of the sheet of aluminum prior to bending so the dimensions of the finished part, after bending, will be correct. You also need to correctly locate the bends and mark them on the flat pattern.

Simple layout of a bent flange requires locating the centerline of bend in relation to at least one side of the material to be formed. This centerline of bend is a straight line that will make contact with the male die of the press brake during the bending operation.

In addition to locating the center of bend, make sure the bend radius is sufficiently large to prevent fracturing during forming. Minimum bend radii for various aluminum alloys are shown in Table II-1. Before calculating the distance

TABLE II-1. Minimum bend radii for 90-degree cold bends in various aluminum alloys, shown as a ratio of material thickness, "t"

Alloy/Temper	Thickness				
	$\frac{1}{8}$	$\frac{3}{16}$	$\frac{1}{4}$	$\frac{3}{8}$	$\frac{1}{2}$
5052	0–1t	0–1t	0–1t	$\frac{1}{2}$–$\frac{3}{2}$t	$\frac{5}{2}$–4t
5052-H32	$\frac{1}{2}$–$\frac{3}{2}$t	$\frac{1}{2}$–$\frac{3}{2}$t	$\frac{1}{2}$–$\frac{3}{2}$t	1–2t	3–4t
5086-0	0–1t	0–1t	$\frac{1}{2}$–1t	1–$\frac{3}{2}$t	1–2t
5086-H32	1–2t	$\frac{3}{2}$–$\frac{5}{2}$t	$\frac{3}{2}$–$\frac{5}{2}$t	2–$\frac{5}{2}$t	$\frac{5}{2}$–3t
5086-H34	$\frac{3}{2}$–$\frac{5}{2}$t	2–3t	2–3t	$\frac{5}{2}$–$\frac{7}{2}$t	3–4t
6061-0	0–1t	0–1t	0–1t	$\frac{1}{2}$–2t	1–$\frac{5}{2}$t
6061-T6	$\frac{3}{2}$–3t	2–4t	3–4t	$\frac{7}{2}$–$1\frac{1}{2}$t	4–6t

around the arc to be formed, or *stretch-out*, consult this table to make sure the bend radius selected will not fracture the alloy.

As a general rule, the thicker the material, the larger the bend radius required to prevent material fracture. The minimum bend radius is expressed as a direct relationship to the thickness of the material being formed, abbreviated as *t*. A minimum bend radius of ½ t for ¼-inch aluminum, for example, is ⅛ inch. Aluminum typically has a grain—usually parallel with the long dimension of the

TABLE II-2. Stretch-out for 90-degree cold bends.

Radii	Material Thickness (inches)						
	⅛	5/32	3/16	¼	5/16	3/8	½
¼	.456						
3/8	.655	.672	.688	.719			
½	.851	.868	.884	.785			
5/8	1.047	1.064	1.080	1.112			
¾	1.243	1.261	1.276	1.308	1.342	1.374	
1	1.636	1.653	1.669	1.700	1.735	1.766	
1¼	2.028	2.046	2.061	2.093	2.127	2.159	
1½	2.421	2.438	2.454	2.485	2.520	2.551	2.617
2	3.206	3.223	3.239	3.270	3.305	3.336	3.402
3	4.776	4.793	4.809	4.840	4.875	4.906	4.972
4	6.346	6.363	6.379	6.410	6.445	6.476	6.542
5	7.916	7.933	7.949	7.980	8.015	8.046	8.112
6	9.486	9.503	9.519	9.550	9.584	9.616	9.682

Stretch out calculated from formula S = 1.57 (r + t/3)

full sheet—and best resists fractures when formed at 90 degrees to the grain. Table II-1 indicates minimum bend radii both with and across the grain.

To calculate the stretch-out of a bend, the distance around the male forming die of the press brake must be considered. For a 90-degree bend, this distance represents ¼ of the circumference of the male die and must be included in the layout of the material to be bent.

Experience has shown that aluminum will stretch more than it will compress when bending on a press brake. Since material being formed has some thickness, some plane within the material must be established as the layout plane. This plane is the neutral axis and is ⅓ of the material thickness being formed, measured from the inside of the bend.

Use a radius equal to the inside radius of the bend plus ⅓ the material thickness to calculate the stretch-out for a flat pattern. To expedite determining stretch-out, Table II-2 has been developed for 90-degree bends, using a modification of the formula to calculate the circumference of a circle, as follows:

$$S = 1.57 \ (r + t/3)$$

Where:

S = Stretch-out (inches)

r = Radius of bend (inches)

t = Thickness of material (inches)

FIGURE II-1. Laying out a 90-degree bend for a fuel-tank bottom.

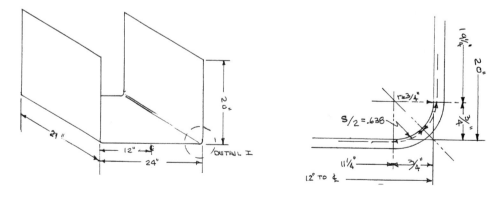

Problem 1—Fuel-tank Layout

Lay out a fuel-tank bottom and side flat pattern for press-brake forming that will result in 24- x 21- x 20-inch inside dimensions, as shown in Figure II-1. Use ³⁄₁₆-inch (.190) aluminum alloy 5052-H32 and a ¾-inch bend radius.

Solution:

- First check the minimum safe bend radius. From Table II-1, the minimum safe bend radius is ½ to ³⁄₂t for ³⁄₁₆-inch 5052-H32 aluminum—½t (.093) if formed across the grain or 1½t (.281) if formed parallel to the grain. The selected ¾-inch (.750) radius is safe.
- Make a sketch showing the detail of the corner (see Figure II-1) with a ¾-inch inside radius and layout dimensions to the inside of the plate. Consult Table II-2 to determine that the stretch-out for a ¾-inch-radius 90-degree bend in .190 material is 1.276 inches. To find the center of the bend, divide 1.276 by 2 to obtain .638.
- Start the process of the flat-pattern layout at the upper right corner of the sketch in Figure II-1. Determine the location of the *start* of the first bend by subtracting the inside radius of the bend from the finished dimension—20 minus ¾ in this case—or 19¼ inches (see Detail I in Figure II-1). To find the *center* of the first bend, add .638 (as determined above) to 19¼ to obtain 19.888—rounded

FIGURE II-2. Flat pattern with stretch-out.

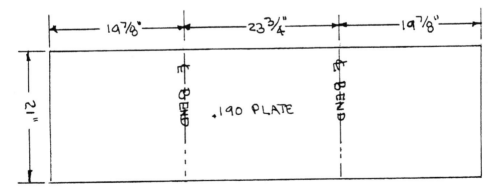

off to 19⅞ inches. Draw a line 19⅞ inches from the far left side
of a 21-inch-wide blank piece of material, as shown in Figure II-2.
This will be the centerline of bend for the first bend.

- To lay out for the next bend, it's easier to work to the center of the symmetrical plate. Starting at the first bend centerline, add the
stretch-out from centerline to the end of the bend plus ½ the distance of the center flat portion. This is .638 + (12 - ¾), or 11⅞
inches to center of the plate. This puts the layout line for the second bend at 2 x 11⅞, or 23¾ inches from the first centerline
(Figure II-2). The end of the plate is then another 19⅞ inches,
for a total material length (stretch-out) of 63½ inches.

Problem 2—Layout for Other Than 90-degree Bends

Lay out the flat pattern for a cockpit floor with the cross section shown in
Figure II-3. Lay out for finished dimensions to the outside of the material using
¼-inch 5086-H32 formed with inside bend radii of ¾ inch.

Solution:

- Sketch the shape to be developed (Figure II-3) on the loft floor. Draw
in the rounded corners, as shown in Figure II-4. Scale the dimensions of the flat areas from the loft floor, and measure angles A and
B—45 and 71¼ degrees, respectively. Modify the formula $S = 1.57$
$(r + t/3)$ by dividing by 1.57 by 90 to obtain stretch per degree of
bend. The new formula is:

$$S = A(.01745)(r+t/3)$$

Where:

S = Stretch-out in inches

A = angle of bend in degrees

r = radius of bend (inches)

t = thickness of material (inches)

From Figure II-4, angle A = 45 degrees, angle B = 71¼ degrees, r = .750, and
t = .250.

$$S_A = (45)(.01745)(.750 + .25/3) = .65$$
$$S_B = (71.5)(.01745)(.750 + .25/3) = 1.04$$

Now simply use these calculated stretch-outs for the arcs of angles A and B
to complete the layout of the flat pattern in a manner similar to Problem 1.

FIGURE II-3. Cross section of formed cockpit well.

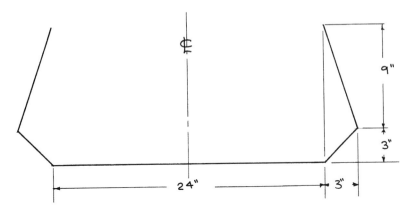

FIGURE II-4. Laying out bends other than 90 degrees.

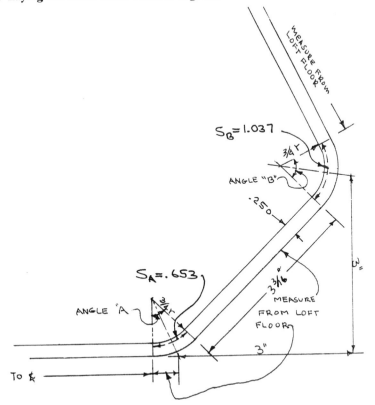

Appendix III

Modifying the Lines for a Developable Surface

A developable surface is often made up of flat areas, sections of cylinders, and sections of cones. Each of these surfaces individually can be developed from a flat sheet of material. When they abut each other on a hull surface, a smooth transition from one form to another allows the composite surface to be formed from a single flat sheet.

All developable surfaces consist of an infinite number of straight-line elements normal to the direction of curvature. In addition, where each different developable surface abuts on a hull, there exists a common straight-line element to both surfaces. Figure III-1 is an example of one such surface with cones, cylinders, and flats sharing straight-line elements. The location of straight-line elements on a hull surface is the key to determining that the surface is developable.

FIGURE III-1. **Developable surface combining flat, cylindrical, and conical surfaces.**

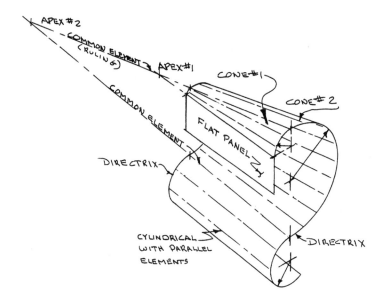

FIGURE III-2. Elements of the generatrix of a conical surface.

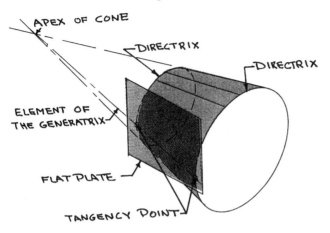

The edges of a developable surface are defined by two lines in space. These lines can be straight or curved, and they're called *directrixes* of the developable surface. When a straight line, called a *generatrix*, is placed in contact with both directrix curves, it will generate a developable surface, as illustrated in Figure III-2.

An *element* is the straight-line generatrix at any one position on a developable surface. For a hard-chine-hull bottom, the keel (or stem) at the centerline is one directrix and the chine can be the other directrix. Elements of the generatrix are located by finding the location of the straight lines that will be in continuous contact with the shell plate between the sheer and chine. These elements are called *rulings* in the boatbuilding industry. The rulings of a developable surface cannot be located at random, but must be located as if they were a straight-line portion of a flat plane touching both directrix curves (Figure III-2).

Designer's Method of Conical Development

In order to understand the logic used to determine if a hull surface is developable, you should first understand the procedures the designer follows. One method to design a developable surface for the bottom plate is to hold either the directrix at the chine or stem fixed and pick some point as an apex of a cone, making the bottom contour a portion of a cone. A straight line from the apex point passing through both directrixes becomes one element on the cone's surface. Continuing this process will develop a sufficient number of elements to construct the bottom contour. If one directrix location is known and an apex point is selected, the other directrix can be developed to fit the elements.

To design a hull bottom that will develop out of a flat plate, the designer can first draw a line for the chine in both profile and plan views. The location of the chine line is based on the desired boat performance and designer's experience. This line becomes one directrix of the bottom developable surface. The stem bar in the plan view is a straight line and is the second directrix curve defining the bottom developable surface. The stem bar has yet to be defined in the profile view to conform with a developable surface.

To actually accomplish a design for developable bottom plate, the designer can, after the chine line has been established, proceed as follows:

- Based on the designer's experience (and some trial and error), an apex point is selected from which to draw rulings in both the plan and profile views.
- In the example (Figure III-3), the first rulings (in lower case letters) were drawn from the apex point in profile—marked *Apex of a cone, Elev.*—to meet the chine line in the profile view at each station.
- The elements were then drawn in the plan view between the second apex point (marked *Apex of a cone, Plan*) and the chine line at each station and were designated by capital letters.
- The stem is located on the centerline in the plan view. The intersections of the elements with the centerline in the plan locate the stem outline when projected to the profile view. A vertical line was then drawn between the intersection of the ruling D and the boat centerline (stem) in the plan view to intersect with ruling d in the profile view and marked *Stem/Element* (Figure III-3). This process was repeated to obtain sufficient points to draw in the stem in the profile view.

A similar process is used to locate buttock lines and waterlines. The resulting lines drawing will conform to a conical bottom development with the apex of the cone used for development as noted above and the stem and chine conforming to the cone geometry.

Development of lines defining a cylindrical surface requires the rulings to be parallel in both plan and profile. Multi-cone development involves a series of cones that share at least one common portion of a straight-line element.

FIGURE III-3. Designer's method of laying out a developable hull bottom using single-cone development.

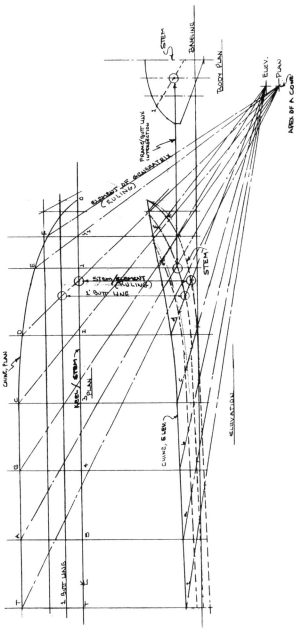

FIGURE III-4. Locating rulings on a completed hull.

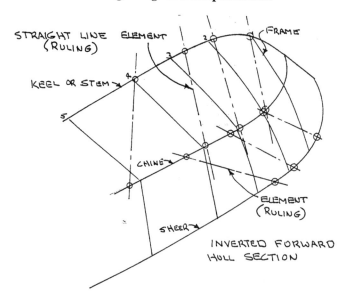

STRAIGHT LINE ELEMENT
(RULING)

KEEL OR STEM

CHINE

FRAME

ELEMENT
(RULING)

SHEER

INVERTED FORWARD
HULL SECTION

FIGURE III-5. Stem and chine model framework.

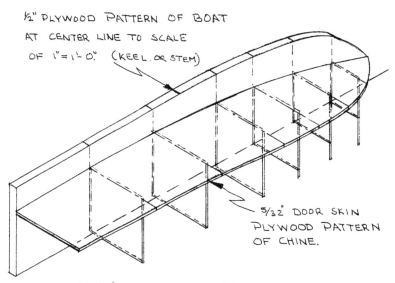

½" PLYWOOD PATTERN OF BOAT
AT CENTER LINE TO SCALE
OF 1"=1'-0". (KEEL OR STEM)

5/32" DOOR SKIN
PLYWOOD PATTERN
OF CHINE.

STEM & CHINE MODEL FRAME WORK
READY FOR SHELL PLATE.

FIGURE III-6. Model to locate rulings.

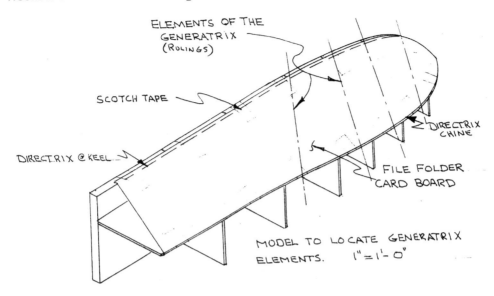

ELEMENTS OF THE
GENERATRIX
(RULINGS)

SCOTCH TAPE

DIRECTRIX @ KEEL

DIRECTRIX
CHINE

FILE FOLDER
CARD BOARD

MODEL TO LOCATE GENERATRIX
ELEMENTS.   1"= 1'- 0"

Checking an Existing Design for a Developable Surface

It's not always practical to find a completed hull and lay a straightedge on the plate to find the location of the rulings (Figure III-4). In almost all cases, the loftsman has only the lines drawing, but from that he should be able to determine if the shell plate is developable.

A fast and sufficiently accurate method to locate rulings is to construct a simple scale model that will allow positioning a straightedge on the model's simulated shell plate. Once a number of rulings are located and drawn on the model's shell plate, they can be located on the existing lines drawing and used to confirm that the hull plate is developable. If the buttock lines and waterlines of the existing lines drawing conform to these straight-line rulings, then the surface is developable. If they don't, the hull form must be modified to be developable.

Construct the model without framing that could interfere with the model's shell plate conforming naturally to a developable surface. Lay out the model to allow some stiff material, such as file-folder cardboard, to be wrapped around the two directrix curves, as shown in Figures III-5 and III-6.

The simulated shell plate may require some pulling to fit snugly to the stem and chine—the directrixes for the developed bottom shell plate. After the shell

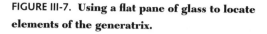

FIGURE III-7. Using a flat pane of glass to locate elements of the generatrix.

plate is attached (usually with scotch tape), a flat plane, simulated by a piece of plate glass, is laid on the bottom in contact with one point on each directrix (stem and chine). These are the tangent points between the plane and the directrix curves, and a straight line connecting these two tangent points is the location of one ruling. Locate a number of these rulings to fair in the bottom (one ruling crossing each station line is usually sufficient).

A simple method to locate the end points of each ruling on the model is to slide a thin piece of paper under the glass as shown in Figure III-7. The edge of the paper will assist in locating the rulings.

The procedure to fair the lines is similar to the conical development described above except you're working backward with known ruling, and the directrix locations are required. The procedure is as follows:

- Carefully pick the locations from the model of the ruling end points at the chine and stem and locate them on the lines drawing in the profile view. Draw in the straight-line rulings as shown in Figure III-8.
- Project the ruling end points at chine and stem to the plan view. Draw the straight-line rulings in the plan view.
- Fair in the buttock lines and waterlines to conform with the straight ruling lines.

FIGURE III-8. Correcting the boat lines to conform to elements of the generatrix.

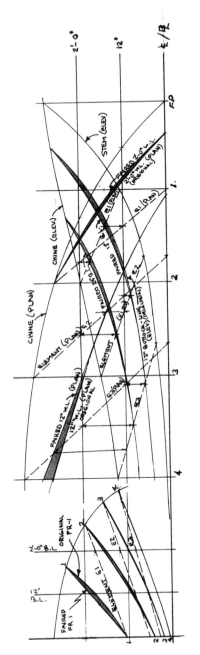

• Check the new developable-surface buttock lines and waterlines to the existing lines for conformance.

If the original lines do not conform to the rulings of the developable surface, then a decision must be made either to modify the original lines to conform or to construct the boat without the benefit of a fully developable surface. The new locations of the waterlines and buttock lines for a developable surface are shown in Figure III-8.

The developable surface defined by the faired lines in Figure III-8 is probably multi-conic as evidenced by the apparent lack of a single apex point when projecting the elements. This is more likely to be the case when working backward from two known directrix curves as multi-conic development allows more latitude in hull design.

References

Charles P. Burgess, "Developable Surfaces for Plywood Boats," *Rudder* (February, 1940).

Clarence E. Werback, "More About Developable Hull Surfaces," *Rudder* (1944).

Ullmann Kilgore, *Developable Hull Surfaces*.

Appendix IV

Line Fairing with a Flexible Batten

A thin wood strip, called a batten, can be used to smooth a curved line between points using a process called *fairing*. Battens can be of different sizes and lengths, and should be sized to best fit the intended application: use short, limber battens for tight curves, and long, stiff battens for long and gentle curves. A number of wood battens are normally found on a working loft floor, from $\frac{1}{16}$ inch x $\frac{1}{4}$ inch x 3 feet for short, tight-radius curves to $\frac{1}{2}$ inch x 2 inch x 20 feet for long curves. A flexible draftsman's spline or a French curve (Figure IV-1) is helpful in some situations.

A good size batten that will fit most applications is $\frac{1}{4}$ inch x $1\frac{1}{2}$ inch x 16 feet made from tight-grained spruce. This batten can be used on edge for fairly tight curves or laid flat for long curves.

Using a Batten

To draw a long curved line (such as the chine) using a batten, first locate points on the curve on the loft floor from the table of offsets or by other means. To provide a guide for the batten, drive finish nails into the loft floor at each known point. Place the 16-foot batten against these nails, and secure it in position

FIGURE IV-1. A draftsman's spline and a French curve.

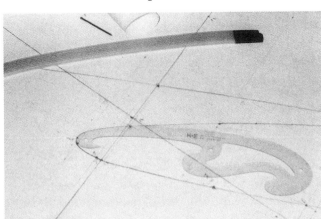

FIGURE IV-2. Using a flexible batten.

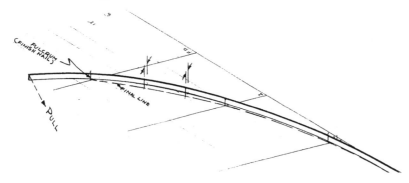

with additional nails driven alongside it at each end. Grip one end of the batten and gently pull it to increase the curve—using the nail driven at the end of the batten as the fulcrum—until the batten just lifts off of the nails in the loft floor immediately behind the fulcrum point (Figure IV-2).

Now slowly release the pressure on the batten until it once again just touches the nails, and secure it in this new position by driving nails alongside. This better approximates the true curve of the line and eliminates a flat spot in the curve near the end of the batten. You will use this process repeatedly during the lofting process. When satisfied that the batten forms a fair line passing through the points, use it as a guide to draw a line with a sharp pencil.

It will be unusual if all points fall exactly on the line. Realize that the naval architect was working to a scale of 1 inch = 1 foot (or even smaller) when he developed the lines drawings; the offsets can be off a little bit at each point because of the difficulty of absolute accuracy when reading a scale rule. Be alert for errors that are an even 1 inch. This is caused by the architect miscounting tick marks on the inches scale. Part of the fairing process is smoothing out the lines from the table of offsets by using a flexible batten and good judgment. Small errors in lifting scale dimensions from the lines drawing will usually be found during fairing of the lines full size on the loft floor.

Straight Line to Curve Transition

Often a curve requires a smooth transition from a straight line. Hold your batten straight for at least 2 feet prior to the start of curvature, and secure it by using finish nails on each side of it. Now use the technique described above to complete the curve.

Conventional Drive-train Installation

A conventional drive train—defined as an inboard engine with transmission gear, a propeller shaft, and a propeller—requires considerably more attention to install than other drive train systems, such as I/Os or water jets. Because aluminum hulls shrink when welded, strut alignment should follow a set routine to minimize error caused by weld heat.

Propeller-strut Alignment

The alignment of the propeller strut with the main engine gear output flange can be a problem if the high rate of weld shrinkage associated with the aluminum structure is not taken into consideration. By following a careful procedure, you can minimize the effects of weld shrinkage, and the strut can be installed without the use of line-boring equipment.

To install the strut, obtain a reasonably straight piece of round stock or pipe of a similar diameter as the required shaft—to be used as a dummy shaft. Machine temporary bushings to fit within the strut-bearing housing to make the dummy shaft fit snugly into the housing. Position the dummy shaft, with the strut bearing housing on it, in the proper location in the boat (determined from the loft floor). Fit the strut legs to the hull and to the bearing housing, and tack-weld them to the hull. After the strut legs are tack-welded to the hull, tack-weld the bearing housing to the strut legs to establish the correct angular relationship between housing and strut legs. At this point, the strut should be very close to the final alignment position.

Break loose the tack-welds holding the strut legs to the hull, and remove the strut assembly from the boat. Apply the final weld between the strut legs and the strut-bearing housing. The weld heat will cause some shrinkage and minor warping of the strut assembly.

The assembled strut is likely to be too large to be fit into a machinist's lathe for machine boring for the press-fit bearing. If it won't fit into the lathe, cut the strut legs approximately 6 inches up each leg from the bearing housing. Take the bearing housing assembly with the stubs of the strut legs attached to your machine shop for final boring for the light press fit of the shaft bearing, and have the housing drilled and tapped for the bearing retainer set screws.

When the machined strut-bearing housing is available, you are ready for the final location of the strut. All weld shrinkage in near proximity to the shaft bearing has been corrected by machine boring the strut after welding. Again locate the strut legs on the hull, put the strut-bearing housing on the dummy shaft, and position the dummy shaft and strut-bearing housing on the boat. Securely tack-weld the strut legs to the stubs on the bearing housing, then tack-weld the strut legs to the hull. Remove the dummy shaft and final weld the strut legs into the hull. Wait on the final weld to join the strut legs together until after fitting and final alignment of the actual propeller shaft.

This procedure of welding, then machining, then welding again compensates for weld shrinkage so that only the final strut-leg welding shrinkage affects the final alignment, and this shrinkage is usually insignificant and disregarded.

Inboard Engine Installation

Once the propeller strut and shaft log are finish-welded to the boat, the location of the propeller shaft is fixed and cannot be changed, so it is the engine that must be moved to align with the propeller shaft. Engine alignment with the propeller shaft is accomplished by placing the engine and shaft coupling flanges in contact and using a feeler gauge to precisely check the gap between the flanges.

Put the propeller shaft into position in the boat and fit it with half the gear

FIGURE V-1. Alignment of the propeller-shaft coupling.

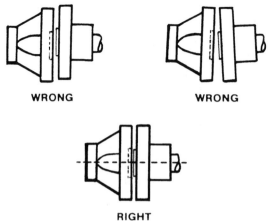

WRONG   WRONG

RIGHT

coupling; the other half of the coupling is attached to the transmission. Check the mating faces on the flanges to be sure they're clean and flat. With both halves of the coupling in contact, adjust the engine mounts to obtain the proper height alignment. Shift the engine laterally for alignment. All four mounts must be positioned properly. Verify the coupling centerline alignment by butting the propeller-shaft coupler against the transmission output flange: the shoulder on the propeller flange should engage the recess on the transmission output flange with no resistance. Keep adjusting the engine position until the coupling faces are parallel and the boss is seated, as shown in Figure V-1. (This applies to both solid and flexible couplings.)

Install the mounting bolts between the adjustable mounts and the engine girders. (For full engine electrical isolation, these bolts must be fitted with isolation sleeves and washers of a nonconducting material.)

Check angular alignment by holding the coupling faces together tightly by hand and inserting a .003-inch feeler gauge between the coupling faces at 90-degree intervals (Figure V-2). Hand-rotate the propeller shaft a few times during the alignment, and adjust the engine mounts as necessary to obtain alignment within .003 inch. (Both front mounts or both rear mounts must be adjusted equally to keep the engine level from side to side.)

FIGURE V-2. Using a feeler gauge to align the shaft coupling.

Check for angular misalignment, by hand holding coupling faces tightly together and checking for a gap between coupling faces with a .003 in. (.07mm) feeler gauge at 90° intervals.

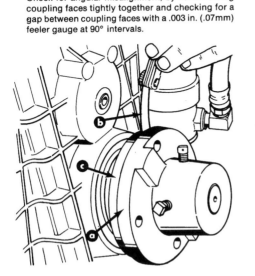

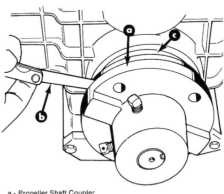

a - Propeller Shaft Coupler
b - Feeler Gauge
c - Transmission Output Flange

FIGURE V-3. **Using the epoxy-pour method to align the engine.**

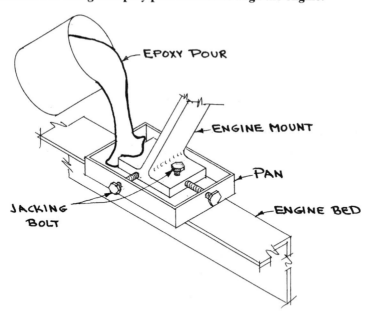

To adjust alignment left and right, loosen the mounting bolts and shift the engine as needed, then retighten the bolts.

Larger engines located on rigid mounts can be aligned with shims or by using jacking bolts and an epoxy pour. The epoxy-pour method is much easier and faster than metal shims.

Install a stout metal pan constructed of ¼-inch aluminum plate around the base of each engine mount (Figure V-3) to contain the liquid epoxy. Drill and tap the outboard side of each pan for a jacking bolt for lateral engine alignment. Drill the engine beds and push stainless steel engine-mount bolts through from below, held in place with a thin nut on the topside of the girder. Now place an additional nut on the bolt to hold the weight of the engine and to serve as the jacking "bolt" to set engine elevation during alignment. When the engine is in proper alignment, suspended on the jacking bolts, pour a special nonshrinking epoxy compound (one source of the epoxy material is Philadelphia Resins, which makes Chock Fast) into the pan up to the level of the base of the engine mounts. The hardened epoxy will take the place of shims. When the epoxy hardens, add nuts to the top of the mounting bolts and tighten them to secure the engine in the desired position. Remove the lateral jacking bolts, if possible, or simply cut them off.

Appendix VI

Leveling a Structure Using a Water Level

A *water level* is nothing more than a water-filled, clear plastic tube. To determine the variation from level of two points of a structure, measure the difference in the water level inside the tube at each end.

To make a water level, find a piece of clear ¼-inch ID flexible tubing about 1½ times the length of the structure being leveled. Fill the tube with water to within about 3 feet of one end and work the air bubbles out. Plug the ends of the tube with a ¼-inch bolt (about 1 inch long) wrapped with electrical tape until you are ready to use the level.

To use the water level, hold up one end and have a helper hold up the other. String the level between the two points that require leveling, and place the helper's end slightly above the starting point. Hold the other end about level with the helper's end and remove the plugs from both ends of the tube. Hold the tube steady until the water in it has stopped moving. If the water in the tube is below

FIGURE VI-1. Leveling a structure with a water level.

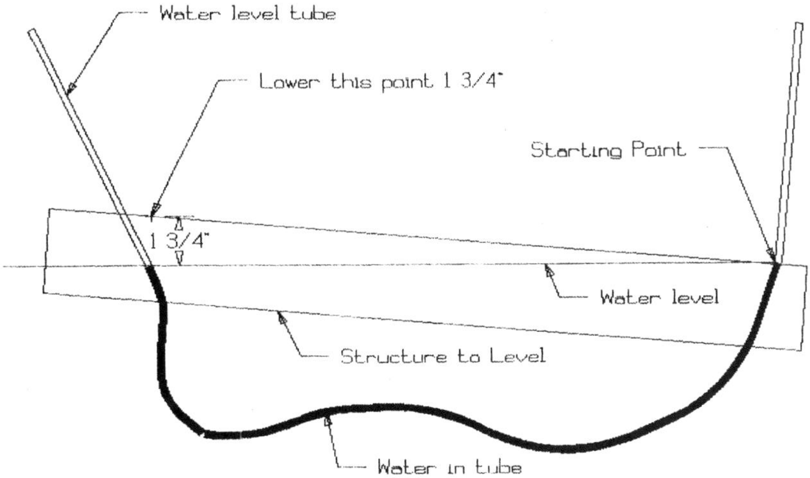

the starting point at the helper's end, slowly elevate the other end of tube, causing the water to rise in the tube, until the helper indicates the water is level with the starting point. When the water stops moving in the tube and is level with the starting point, the water level in the other end of the tube is also level with the starting point.

Move the structure up or down as needed to be level. Repeat these steps as necessary until the water level is the same at all check points.

Glossary

This glossary is provided to clarify boatbuilding terms used in this book, which are based on the author's everyday experience in boatyards on the Pacific Northwest coast of the United States between 1960 and 1990. Other areas and times may have other terms for the same application.

Abaft—behind or toward the rear.

Abeam—some point alongside a ship; used to define a position relative to the ship.

ABL—common abbreviation for *above base line*.

ABYC—abbreviation for American Boat and Yacht Council.

Above baseline—designated dimension above the baseline of the vessel.

American Boat and Yacht Council—an organization that writes and maintains voluntary standards for small craft.

Arc radius—the radius used to draw an arc of a circle.

Back-chipping—removing unwanted weld metal between welding-bead passes. Back-chipping is accomplished by a chisel or other mechanical means; a power saw is often used on aluminum welds.

Baseline—the common reference line for all elevations; parallel with the design waterline (DWL) and generally the lowest point of the keel.

BL—common abbreviation for *baseline*.

BLKD—abbreviation for bulkhead.

Batten—a long, slender, straight-grained wood stick; used to fair lines on the loft floor.

Batten holder—a cut piece of material, usually wood, used to hold a flexible batten in place during the pickup of loft-floor lines for template making.

Beam—width of a vessel at a specific point; generally used to describe the maximum width of the vessel.

Body plan—lines-drawing view of stations at 90 degrees to the centerline; commonly located at center of lines drawing with stations forward of midships on the starboard side and those aft of midships on the port side.

Boot top—a narrow painted band at or slightly above the DWL to some distance (up to about 6 inches) above the DWL; a clearly defined parting between the bottom and topside paints.

Breakwater—a vertical bulkhead located forward on the main deck to deflect the force of water that may wash onto the deck.

Bulkhead—a solid vertical dividing structural member that may be watertight; nautical term for *wall*.

Bulwark—section of the hull side extending above the main deck.

Butt line—short for buttock line.

Buttock line—an edge-on view of a plane parallel with the vertical plane at the boat's centerline. Buttock lines are straight lines in the plan and body plan views, normally equally spaced port and starboard of centerline.

Butt weld—weld joining two pieces of plate edge to edge.

CAD—abbreviation for Computer Assisted Drafting.

Camber—the arch of a surface, usually a deck; a 3-inch camber means the center of the deck is 3 inches higher than the edges at its maximum beam.

Ceiling—longitudinal planking placed on the inboard face of the frames.

Centerline—an imaginary line running down the center of the vessel in the plan and body plan views.

Chine—the intersection of the bottom and side of a hull; a hard chine (normally associated with powerboats) has an abrupt change of direction; a soft chine displays a rounded transition from bottom to side plate.

Chord—the straight line used to join the end points of an arc.

CL—abbreviation for centerline.

Collar—a filler at a bulkhead penetration around an angle or a T-bar that makes the bulkhead watertight or is used for structural purposes.

Compound curvature—description of a surface that is curved in more than one axis, such as the surface of a ball.

Conical developed surface—a surface that consists of a section of a cone or sections of a number of cones; straight-line rulings will point to the apex of the cone.

Construction drawing—drawing prepared by the boatbuilder or naval architect to define details of construction.

Cumulative measurement—laying out a series of dimensions by adding all dimensions together to obtain a total measurement, then laying out only one dimension.

Curve of areas (also *curve of sectional areas*)—developed by the naval architect for hydrostatic calculations; a curve plotted from a straight baseline representing the length of the ship, the ordinates of which represent the areas of the vessel's immersed cross sections; found on lines drawings (not used during the lofting process).

Cylindrical developed surface—surface that consists of a portion of a cylinder; ruling lines are parallel on a cylindrical developed surface.

Deadrise—change in elevation in relation to a horizontal plane, similar to slope; the difference in height between the keel of a boat and the chine is an example of deadrise; a boat's cambered deck has a deadrise at centerline as compared to the deck edge.

Deck—floor or walking surface; commonly parallel with the waterline, but decks may be sloped fore and aft and have camber.

Deck plan—drawing looking down on the deck of a boat.

Declivity—slope of a deck or vertical surface; used in conjunction with *tumblehome* found in a deck house side; normally described in rise over run or in degrees.

Design waterline—the plane defined by the hull at the surface of the water; located by the naval architect during the design phase.

Developable surface—any surface that can be constructed from a flat plate. Hull surfaces can be defined as *developable* and *undevelopable*. A cylinder, which can be rolled from a flat sheet of material, is a developable surface; cones and flat planes are also developable. Surfaces such as spheres and ovoids are not developable; any attempt to construct these or other undevelopable surfaces from a flat sheet will result in wrinkles or stretching.

Diagonal—when used in lofting, a

diagonal is similar to a waterline or buttock line, but is located in a plane other than flat or vertical; commonly found in sailboat lines to assist in defining round-bilge geometry.

Directrix—a line or plane that guides the generatrix of a surface.

Displacement—actual weight of a vessel; defined by the weight of water displaced by the vessel.

Doubler—*see* hull doubler.

Ductile—easily bent or formed; lead is more ductile than steel.

DWL—abbreviation for design waterline.

Element—term used to describe a specific location of the generatrix at any one position; in lofting, often called a ruling.

Elevation view—view on a engineering drawing looking from the side, or in elevation.

Engine bed—girders, generally parallel with a boat's centerline, upon which the main propulsion engines are attached.

Fair line—a continuous natural curve, free of bumps or kinks; a fair line can be a straight line but is usually used in conjunction with a chine, stem, or gunnel line; developed by spanning at least three reference points with a thin strip of straight-grained wood.

Fairing—smoothing a curved line or surface; *fairing a line* is smoothing out the high and low points on a curve and averaging out the bumps—more art than science.

Faying surface—mating surfaces of two adjoining materials.

FDN—abbreviation for foundation.

Fillet weld—a weld joint where the edge of one piece of metal butts the flat surface of another piece of metal.

FL—abbreviation for folding line.

Flair—sloping outboard; opposite of tumblehome.

Flat-plate development—the process used to make a flat pattern of the surface of a three-dimensional object.

Folding line—a 90-degree change of direction of a line of sight; as associated with views of drawings. If a drawing of a boat were to be folded with a sharp crease so that the plan view was 90 degrees to the profile view, the crease would represent the folding line.

Foundation—structure attached to hull or house for mounting items or machinery, such as generators, stoves, liferafts, etc.

FR—abbreviation for frame.

Frame—a structural member, usually in the same plane as a station (they generally do not line up with the stations); in some cases, longitudinal frames run fore and aft.

Freeboard—height of the hull side above the DWL at midships or some other designated position.

Freeing port—a hull opening on a weather deck to allow deck water to escape overboard.

Generatrix—line guided by the directrix to generate a surface; for a developable surface, the generatrix must be a straight line; various locations of the generatrix are called elements.

Girth—the measurement around a curved surface or arc; used in expanding views into flat patterns.

Good shipbuilding practice—standard of quality commonly accepted by boatbuilders and boat owners based on experience and tradition.

Grid—in boat lofting, the basic straight layout lines representing the baseline, waterlines, buttock lines, and station lines.

Half-breadth—horizontal measurement from centerline to some point port or starboard; half the distance from gunnel to gunnel is a half-breadth.

Hard corner—the theoretical corner between two surfaces that actually meet in a rounded corner.

Heights—vertical measurements above the baseline.

House—a ship's cabin or deckhouse.

Hull doubler—a plate welded to the surface of another plate to provide additional thickness in that area; often used to strengthen specific areas of a deck, such as attachment points for deck machinery.

Inboard profile—elevation drawing showing ship cut along the longitudinal axis, looking outboard.

Jig—tooling used to hold parts in position during fabrication.

Keel—backbone of ship at base of hull; usually sits on the baseline; also called the stem when located forward.

KNU—abbreviation for knuckle.

Knuckle—a change in direction between two abutting surfaces.

Ladder—nautical term for stairway; often quite steep.

Ladder riser—vertical portion of a ladder, as compared with the step or rung, which is the horizontal portion.

Laying out—the act of measuring and locating a line or point.

Level—as used on large ships, a specific distance above the baseline; levels are commonly associated with decks, such as the *01* level on a large ship being the first deck above the main deck.

Lightening hole—a hole, commonly circular, where material has been removed to reduce weight.

Limber hole—drainage hole cut through a structural member to allow fluid to drain by gravity.

Lines—abbreviation for lines drawing.

Lines drawing—drawing showing hull geometry of a ship or boat; normally includes plan, elevation (or profile), and body plan views defining the hull form by use of waterlines, buttock lines, and stations.

Loft floor—the actual drawing surface where the lines are drawn full size.

Lofting—drawing of the boat hull full size; drawing full-size bulkheads, frames, and girders, and the layout and construction of templates from the lofted lines.

Loftsman—individual who draws boat lines full size and makes templates.

Long—abbreviation for longitudinal.

Longitudinal—in the fore-and-aft axis; used to describe a long structural member, such as a T-bar hull stiffener.

Lvl—abbreviation for level.

Margin plate—strip of metal, typically about 10 inches wide, welded continuously to the inside edge of the shell plate and used as the attachment surface for a wood deck.

Midships—toward the center of a ship in the fore-and-aft axis.

Mold loft—the area where lines are laid down on the floor; usually a designated area of a shipyard.

MIG process—standard abbreviation for *Metal Inert Gas* welding process, which uses a consumable electrode and an inert shielding gas.

Molded line—The line to which all lay-out dimensions are given. Since the thickness of the material affects dimensions, the molded line is used to determine which side of the surface to lay out. On metal boats, the molded line is the inside of the boat's shell plate, the underside of decks, and the inboard face of longitudinal bulkheads. The molded line on transverse members can vary but is usually the forward face in the forward portion of the boat. Notes on the molded line should be found on the construction drawings.

Molded surface—similar to molded line, but referring to a surface; normally the underside of decks, the inboard surface of longitudinal surfaces, and either the forward or aft face of bulkheads, as specified.

Mullion—slender bar or post that separates windows.

Non-tight—structural members not required to be watertight.

Offsets—dimensions from centerline or above baseline.

Outboard profile—elevation drawing showing the boat from the side view.

P—abbreviation for the port, or left side.

Pad eye—any small metal plate with a hole in it attached to a structure and used as an attachment point for lifting or lashing; also a lifting eye welded to a base.

Panel breaker—similar to *stiffener*; commonly used to break up a vibration in a panel or to provide additional stiffness.

Passageway—a hallway or access route.

Plug welding—process of welding two plates, one on top of the other, by welding through holes in one plate to fuse the two together in a number of spots.

Port—left in nautical terminology; also a hull opening above the waterline.

Portlight—nautical term for window.

Profile—view from the side; elevation view.

Pulse-arc welding—a refinement of the MIG welding process involving rapid on and off of the welding current.

Radial—one of a number of layout lines starting at a common point and radiating outward like the spokes of a wheel.

Rake—forward or aft slope.

Rat hole—a cutout in a structural member for access to a welded seam.

Ray—a radial.

Ruled surface—a plane that may be generated by a straight line; a straightedge may be laid on the plane so that it will touch the surface for its entire length.

Ruling—an element of the generatrix.

Scale—ratio of size in relation to actual size; a drawing showing a scale of ½ inch = 1 foot means ½ inch on the drawing equals 1 foot on the actual vessel.

Scantlings—thickness of plates and sizes of structural members used to construct the hull.

Scribing in—drawing a line using an adjacent surface as a guide; marking a cutting line to fit a surface.

Shaft horsepower—output horsepower at the propeller shaft.

Sheer—a line in the profile view defined by the top of the ships side and the main-deck intersection.

Shell—a boat's exterior skin or hull plate.

Shroud—a wire laterally supporting a mast.

Stanchion—a vertical column or post used for structural support.

STBD—abbreviation for starboard.

Starboard—Right in nautical terminology.

STA—abbreviation for station.

Station—a vertical plane perpendicular to the baseline in the profile view and to the centerline in the plan view; commonly the DWL is divided into 10 equal spaces separated by station lines.

Stem—forward portion of keel; sometimes term used for the entire keel.

Stiffener—structural member used to stiffen a specific panel.

Strake—an exterior hull stiffener running in the longitudinal axis; also one width of plate or planking running the length of the hull.

Stretch—bundle of electrical wires transmitting current and electronic information between the power source to the weld feeder. An inert-gas supply tube is sometimes included.

Stretch-out—the dimension of a piece of material that is laid out flat (similar to flat pattern). Also used to define the flat-pattern layout distance around a circular shape.

Strongback—a temporary structural member used to hold parts in alignment during fabrication; usually removed after welding on the part is complete.

Stuffing box—a packing gland used at the penetration of a shaft, wire or other item through the hull or other watertight surface to keep it watertight; specifically the packing gland where the prop shaft penetrates the hull.

T—abbreviation for transom.

Table of offsets—a table of numeric data included in the lines drawings giving dimensions for heights and half-breadths; usually provided by the naval architect and scaled from the drawings; dimensions commonly shown in feet, inches, and eighths.

Temper—heat treatment to increase the mechanical characteristics of heat-treatable aluminum alloys; also the work-hardened condition of non-heat-treatable aluminum.

Template—a flat pattern defining the geometric shape of a frame or other part; usually "lifted" directly from the loft floor or the structure for fabricating parts; previously called molds.

TIG process—Tungsten Inert Gas welding process using a nonconsumable electrode and an inert shielding gas.

Transom—aft most transverse member of the hull forming a watertight bulkhead.

Transverse—at 90 degrees to the centerline, running across the boat (port to starboard).

Triangulation—method of layout using arcs of circles to locate the corner points of a triangle.

True length—a component shown on a drawing or loft floor in its actual length.

True size—a component shown on a drawing or loft floor in its actual size, such as a flat pattern for a curved surface.

Tumblehome—slope of a surface in relation to a vertical surface; commonly used in conjunction with *declivity*.

Undevelopable surface—*see* Developable surface.

Waterline—a plane parallel with the plane at which the vessel floats; waterlines define hull geometry at specific heights above the baseline.

Watertight—describes any structure that will not allow water to pass under flooding conditions; all hull and deck shell plate should be watertight.

Weather-tight—describes any structure that can withstand a hose test without excessive leakage, such as a cabin door or window.

Wheel—the propeller.

Whip—bundle of conduit, tubes, and electrical cables that provide filler wire, shielding gas, electric power, and electronic information to the welding gun from the welding-wire feeder.

WL—abbreviation for waterline.

W.T.—abbreviation for watertight.

Index